Case Study Research in the Digital Age

Case Study Research in the Digital Age is an in-depth exploration of the case study method as applied to social media, algorithms, digital networks, artificial intelligence, and online life.

By applying and adapting case study theory to digital phenomena, *Case Study Research in the Digital Age* argues for a fundamental change to the unit of analysis in case study research: the entity. It uses this change as a jumping off point for an overview of case study work as applied to a variety of digital phenomena, including online discussions, social media communities, and artificial intelligence. Written in an accessible way, this book presents a rigorous theoretical discussion of the very definitions of a case study while providing guidance on case study definitions, research design, data collection, analysis, ethics, and case reporting.

Case Study Research in the Digital Age can be used by a wide array of scholars, from novice to seasoned case study researchers, as well as a variety of disciplines, including but not limited to anthropology, communication, education, history, information science, psychology, and sociology.

John R. Gallagher is Associate Professor of Writing and Rhetoric in the English department at The University of Illinois, Urbana-Champaign. He is also a faculty affiliate at the School of Information Sciences. His work focuses on social science related to practices of writing in digital spaces.

Case Study Research in the Digital Age

John R. Gallagher

LONDON AND NEW YORK

Designed cover image: Jose Vazquez , ITG, Beckman Institute, UIUC

First published 2024
by Routledge
4 Park Square, Milton Park, Abingdon, Oxon OX14 4RN

and by Routledge
605 Third Avenue, New York, NY 10158

Routledge is an imprint of the Taylor & Francis Group, an informa business

© 2024 John R. Gallagher

The right of John R. Gallagher to be identified as author of this work has been asserted in accordance with sections 77 and 78 of the Copyright, Designs and Patents Act 1988.

All rights reserved. No part of this book may be reprinted or reproduced or utilised in any form or by any electronic, mechanical, or other means, now known or hereafter invented, including photocopying and recording, or in any information storage or retrieval system, without permission in writing from the publishers.

Trademark notice: Product or corporate names may be trademarks or registered trademarks, and are used only for identification and explanation without intent to infringe.

British Library Cataloguing-in-Publication Data
A catalogue record for this book is available from the British Library

ISBN: 978-1-032-51424-6 (hbk)
ISBN: 978-1-032-51425-3 (pbk)
ISBN: 978-1-003-40216-9 (ebk)

DOI: 10.4324/9781003402169

Typeset in Optima
by Taylor & Francis Books

Contents

	List of illustrations	vi
	Acknowledgments	vii
	Introduction: The need for digital case study research	1
1	Definitions, descriptions, and entities	10
2	Iterative design and digital considerations	37
3	Collection practices for digital case studies	66
4	Analysis for digital cases	93
5	Ethical habits in a digital world	121
6	Writing and visualizing the digital case	143
	Conclusion: Case study work in an era of artificial intelligence	166
	Index	168

Illustrations

Figures

2.1 The interconnectedness of boundaries with spheres of influence 47
3.1 A hierarchical matrix of the front- and backstage of many (but not all) social networks and websites 73

Tables

1.1 Definitions, types, and disciplinary approaches to case study research according to well-cited case study theorists and their works 16
2.1 Methodological concepts of overload for case study research 50
3.1 Elements of digital observation and fieldwork 75
3.2 Benefits and drawbacks to unstructured, semi-structured, or structured interviewing 81
3.3 Strengths and weaknesses of synchronous interview modalities 83
3.4 Types of web scraping with their respective levels of automation 86
4.1 Benefits and drawbacks of terms for data pre-processing 105
4.2 Sample template of coding emojis and their ambiguity (answers provided are for illustration only). Coding meanings from both participants and their audiences provides analytical structure when trying to understand emotions, attitudes, and social cues in multimodal, semiotic meaning. This step can be particularly important in cross-cultural, cross-device, and cross-identity digital studies in which the same emoji may be interpreted in divergent ways 110

Acknowledgments

I have had the privilege of drawing on the extensive knowledge and experience from countless case study researchers. Their insights, theories, and cases have not only informed my understanding of case study theory but also the case studies I have conducted. I am indebted to these scholars, past and present, for their contributions to an interdisciplinary academic community at large.

This book is a long time in the making, but it has a distinct start point: Dr. Anne Herrington's graduate course on qualitative research methods at UMass in 2006. I was a first-year graduate student, and I kept wondering what a case study *was*. Anne encouraged me to pursue this query. This book is the result of that driving question for the past (nearly) two decades. Thank you, Anne.

Thank you to Mike Gormley and Aaron Beveridge for listening to me discuss a book not at all relevant to their research. You are both caring and supportive while critical and incisive. I appreciate that. I am grateful and appreciative to Emma Bloomfield and James Wynn for a book writing group during the fall of 2022. Paul Prior's influence on my thinking is immeasurable, even though I don't agree with him on every part of cultural-historical activity theory. I am indebted to his scholarship, research, and compassion. I am grateful to John Duffy for reading a draft of the chapter on virtue ethics and offering generous feedback. I am also grateful to Jeffrey Turner, at Bucknell University, who introduced me to virtue ethics in the spring of 2003 as an undergraduate. That course profoundly changed my thinking on ethics. Richard Fleming, also at Bucknell, introduced me to Wittgenstein's theories and I am grateful for that introduction.

The students in my Fall 2020 seminar about case study research provided me with the opportunity to answer challenging questions about case study theory. I am grateful to Rebecca, Antonio, Yvaine, Neal, Kimber, and Emily for their patience, both with the seminar and the good spirits they provided during an international pandemic.

I'd like to thank Dr. Shelby Hutchens for her support while I wrote this book. Her belief in my ability to write and complete this book, and feedback on how to structure my writing time, is deeply appreciated.

Hutchens is the person I most respect in this world. Quentin and Landry were very patient with me writing this book. I appreciate and love you both. My mom and sister, Karen and Michelle, supported and cheered me along the way. I thank Sandra Gallagher for supporting my writing, something I forgot in my 20s but remember now in my 40s. My dog, Triton, is a faithful companion and friend. He often sits outside my office while I type and reminds me that work can always wait for a walk.

I wrote this book while in pain, specifically nerve damage in my arms, legs, and back. Sometimes I could barely focus on this book or sit comfortably. Outside of my direct family (spouse, children, mother, sister, and a few friends), most people in my life are unaware of my issues. I write this not to complain but to make legible that there are many people suffering in illegible ways. I am sure there are people in your life suffering but who drag their bodies and minds through the grind of life. Have patience with them.

I dedicate this book to my father, John E. Gallagher, who passed away while I wrote it. His enduring love, values, and guidance were a source of stability throughout my life. I miss him dearly and wish he could have been here to see the finished product. It is in his honor and memory that I offer this work, with the hope that it might inspire others as he has inspired me to develop a set of values to live by. I miss you, pops.

Very small segments of Chapters 1 and 2 appeared as the following journal article:

> Gallagher, J. R. (2019). A framework for internet case study methodology in writing studies. *Computers and Composition: An International Journal, 54*, 1–14.

My discussion of web scraping in Chapter 4 is a modified version of what appeared in the following article:

> Gallagher, J. R., & Beveridge, A. (2022). Project-oriented web scraping in technical communication research. *Journal of Business and Technical Communication, 36*(2), 231–250.

Introduction
The need for digital case study research

Three case studies of the digital age to make us ponder. First, imagine researching Reddit, the massive discussion-based website. You want to analyze one community forum, called a "subreddit," in its totality. How do you go about researching this case study? What do you do to ensure analysis of the subreddit? What falls into the "slice of life" of this subreddit? What boundaries are necessary for you to keep the case coherent and organized yet comprehensive and rigorous?

Keeping in mind guiding goals and research questions, one could start this case study by web-scraping (data extraction using computational tools) the entire forum and then analyzing it. But the forum alone does not tell the entire story. Reddit has moderators who prevent certain posts and comments from being displayed and which, therefore, are not scrapable. Researchers likely need to identify, if possible, filtered content as well as the *processes* moderators have for filtering content. They'd need to interview users who participate frequently as well as the lurkers, thereby providing an effective range of perspectives about the forum. But what about these interviewees' activity on *other* forums? Do researchers need to examine this activity? What about links on the target forum, especially when those links direct users to other subreddits? What do they do? The answer depends.

The second example. Near you, a local community of activists has taken to digitally "tagging" buildings around you. No one knows about this electronic graffiti unless you have a specific geolocation application on a smartphone. What conceptual and practical frameworks do you draw upon to research this case study? How do you analyze this group's activity?

Keeping in mind my guiding goals and research questions, I should first perhaps investigate the group, getting to know them and obtain informed consent. I'd likely interview their members and leadership. A survey of their activities would help provide a lay of the land study—a needs analysis. We'd also need to investigate the infrastructure of the application, including its code, interface, and design. Interviewing the designers and programmers would supply added context. Evaluating the application's

DOI: 10.4324/9781003402169-1

geographical capability would describe an alternative perspective to the group's geographical distribution. But again, the aspects we emphasize depend on our research goals and questions. It depends.

Third, one of the most prolific online commenters (a "power user") on *The New York Times* is responsible for several thousand comments across dozens, if not hundreds, of articles. How can a researcher account for the case of this commenter as they move from article to article? We could collect *all* comments from the commenter and interview the commenter. But we likely need to interview other commenters with whom this power user has interacted. Recording and analyzing the articles to which the power user has responded would be helpful. Especially important here is recording and analyzing not only the content of the article but the layout, design, and interface of the article and comments. It wouldn't hurt to get the perspective of the articles' authors, if possible. But the perspective of the articles' authors will depend on the researcher's goals and purposes.

Each of these three examples has a different conception of a case. In the first case, the *unit of analysis* is a forum. The second case has an organization as its unit of analysis. The third case has a person as its case. I have used the word *depend* in describing these cases because case studies—especially digital case studies—can look radically different from one another and across domains. These differences require digital researchers to think *across* physical and electronic contexts, disciplinary boundaries, and temporal/spatial boundaries.

Case study research for digital phenomena

This book is meant to assist digitally oriented researchers with theorizing and developing their case studies. Its purpose is to help digital researchers consider if case studies are suited for their purposes and, if a case study approach is suitable, theorize a case, design a case, collect data, and write up the study. The philosophical goal of this book is to provide *epistemic* underpinnings to the case study as a method, thereby making it into a full methodology for research in a digital era of ubiquitous screens, information networks, and emergent artificial intelligence. I use the term "digital" as shorthand for these contexts and apply that term to case study research.

Like John Gerring (2017) and many others' approaches to case study research, I take a *pluralistic* approach to digital case study research because digital inquiry is itself a transdisciplinary or even sansdisciplinary approach: it necessitates seeing knowledge domains as deeply related and interconnected rather than discrete. By adopting a transdisciplinary approach, I frame the qualifier *digital* as an "ambient condition" (Boyle et al., 2018, p. 252) that is a "common feature of modern existence" (Hess, 2017, p. 6). Such an approach avoids technological determinism and essentialism in that technology and human sociality are inextricably linked and that technology is part of contextual frameworks.

Turning to the case study approach for digital research may seem, at the outset, a methodological mismatch. Case studies are bounded systems created by the researcher or researchers. As Katherine Jocher wrote in 1928, "Case study... presumes a well-defined problem. That is, an intensive study is made of a certain person, a particular community, a definite situation or episode, an economic or a social institution" (p. 206). Case studies are often defined by researchers via particularities and boundaries, whether a person, community, organization, or another central unit of analysis.

Digital phenomena challenge Jocher's notion of a "well-defined problem" in that bounded systems don't seem particularly effective for the spreadable (Jenkins, 2013), participatory, and blurry boundaries of digital research because networked and emergent technologies allow information to permeate spatial and temporal boundaries. Websites, for example, are constantly linked to other sites. Websites are leaky, open to link rot, and consistently updated. Boundaries are messy. Why would digital researchers then turn to a case study framework? There are, as I see it, three distinct advantages in turning to a case study approach for digital research.

First, a case study approach attempts to represent *complexity* and *messiness* (e.g., Flyvbjerg, 2006, p. 237; Gerring, 2017, pp. 28–30; Miles, 2015, p. 309; Yin, 2009, p. 18), often with a focus on context (Merriam, 1998, p. 19; Yin, 2009; p. 18). Some types of research approaches, such as fully- or quasi-experimental research, flatten out such messiness to make determinations about variables. Conversely, case studies examine large swaths of context and do not distill a research project into a single variable—they are holistic in this sense. Social science research approaches that seek to isolate variables are not suitable to case study frameworks. Rather, as a type of qualitative research, case studies attend to "combinations of causes" (Goertz & Mahoney, 2012, p. 57). Digital research, such as studying users across networked spaces and times, benefits from the complexity of a case study approach because this framework emphasizes the importance of contexts and multiple elements at play in holistic, rather than atomistic, situations. Moreover, online information circulates at rapid rates and iteratively, thus necessitating methods that can describe this messiness with a narrative. A case study approach supplies such a narrative because narratives are a "substantial element" of good case studies (Flyvbjerg, 2006, p. 237).

Second, because the boundaries of case studies are reflexively, iteratively, and recursively produced by the case researcher and developed over time (Gallagher, 2019), they provide the flexibility to account for the diffuse, updatable nature of digital inquiry. Boundaries in case studies are not rigid or impermeable; boundaries do not emerge *ex nihilo*, nor are they autotelic. Instead, boundaries are created by researchers and dynamically account for the phenomena under study. Case study boundaries are epistemic schemas designed to investigate phenomena across a variety of contexts. Given the complexity and diffuseness of digital networks, this type of boundary thinking is beneficial and useful to digital research. The reflexivity of case study boundaries, too, assists researchers with accounting for the rapid, emergent, and varied scales of social media and other digital investigations.

Third, case studies of digital research are already being conducted but no books seek to explicitly theorize digital case studies directly. For example, some of the most-cited books on case study do not account for social media, networked technologies, and other digital issues (e.g., Gerring, 2017; Merriam, 1998; Stake, 1995; Yin, 2009, 2018). The approaches of these books can be *applied to* social media and other digital contexts but their frameworks are not explicitly *designed for* such contexts. Case study frameworks strengthen digital work by bringing digital researchers' choices into explicit discussion. As a paradigm that focuses on cases *themselves* as well as the *process* of producing cases, a case study approach directs our attention to the creation of the case. In this latter sense, the case study framework, as a process-oriented paradigm, is practically beneficial to diffuse and spreadable digital research in that it helps to decide what to include and exclude.

Considering these three reasons, case study frameworks oppose reductionism and, therefore, enhance digital research. Case studies are known for their richness of detail (Yin, 2009, pp. 146–147), irreducibility of complexity (Burawoy, 1998, p. 12), and representation of ambiguity and uniqueness for readers (Stake, 1995, p. 126; Stake, 2006). Most case study researchers and frameworks advocate for the case study paradigm as a form of research that opens up inquiry and complexity. The careful treatment of participants' experiences in case study approaches documents and contextualizes multiple subjectivities, viewpoints, and realities. Rich, thick, nuanced descriptions are recorded and written in the case researcher's report(s). Good case studies represent cases with triangulated sources of data that recognize the multiple realities of cases. Case study research, then, emphasizes highly contextualized subjects (Dyson & Genishi, 2005, p. 11) and the "multiple realities" of subjects by constructing interpretations of other people's interpretations (Dyson & Genishi, 2005, p. 18; Stake, 1995, p. 43; Yin, 2009, p. 18).

Case studies, then, show the *multiplicity of experiences* and heterogeneity of the *objects of inquiry* within a case. Think here of a simple square. In terms of a poorly researched case, a square might be the representation of "the" case. However, high-quality case studies seek to represent the case with complexity. We can draw the square in n-dimensions. We might try to represent the square as a cube. Let's push this step further: we might try to represent that the cube contains multiple cubes and permutations of various cubes (and other shapes too) exist simultaneously. Case study researchers attempt to represent this chaotic complexity in a coherent narrative-driven way. The conceptual flexibility of the case study method makes it ripe for digital research.

Digital intensity

While digital research benefits from a case study framework, case study theory needs to respond and be adapted to the ways in which digital phenomenon intensify (1) distribution, (2) frequency, (3) scale, (4) speed, and (5) access. First, digital networks have reduced the cost of information distribution, essentially removing the limit on circulation. One might think here of shared websites being read all over the world, on millions of electronic devices. While companies may put their content behind paywalls, endless circulation of information is hypothetically possible. Texts, images, and videos move about on different sites repeatedly. Discourse is remixed and manipulated to move in and out of a variety of contexts. Digital objects of inquiry thus have an intensity not bound by print or face-to-face notions of distribution and/or circulation. Such issues prompt thinking through the nature of a unit of analysis in digital networks, which I will take up in the next chapter.

Frequency and scale, as the second and third elements of digital intensity, prompt considerations about the irreducibility and uniqueness of case study frameworks. Frequency here means repeatability and occurring multiple times. Scale here means the ability to expand and grow without altering fundamental elements of a phenomenon. The key issue here: what is a case, if it becomes scaled up and frequent across websites or even physical spaces? How do the boundaries of a case need to be considered in these contexts? Chapter 2 addresses these boundary questions.

Digital cases, due to scale and frequency, may not be unique in themselves; instead, their uniqueness may exist in terms of *how* they are repeated, shared, circulated, and spread throughout many spaces and times. Some social media accounts may share the same types of information but at different times. This savvy timing may generate wider distribution and circulations for that account. In this sense, the frequency and scale of the account are unique, even if that account shares information shared by millions of other accounts. The sheer size of a case study can be enormous, even if the bounded system is relatively small, such as a case study of a particular user on a specific social media site. A user may post hundreds or thousands of times during a collection period, making an individual case massive in terms of data collection. Similarly, posted information may take on a life of its own. Automated collection methods, such as web-scraping, can help case study researchers collect large amounts of data that fall within their case's boundaries. Chapter 3 addresses automated and manual collection methods for digital case study research.

Fourth, the rapid movement of information—or the speed—challenges some of the long-standing epistemologies of case study research. If cases are a unit that "…connotes a spatially and temporally delimited phenomenon of theoretical significance" (Gerring, 2017, p. 27), then electronic speeds challenge this delimitation by speeding up circulation of information and discourse. David Harvey (1989) has described this concept as *time-space compression*, locating the origin of such speeds not necessarily in digital technologies *per se* but in the capitalistic drive to delimit distribution costs. In Harvey's formulation, digital technologies that compress time-space are the outgrowth of capitalist ideology seeking such compression. Due to this economic incentive of freeing up the circulation of capital, digital information moves at rapid speeds *while* data is being collected; the goal of these technologies in many cases is to produce as much data as possible that is not limited by temporal or spatial boundaries. Time-space compression overloads researchers with data collection possibilities, thereby rendering older pertinent information invisible. Due to the speed of information exchange, methodological boundaries therefore could be retheorized for digital worlds, which I address throughout this book.

In addition to time-space compression, speed can be invisible for digital researchers because it is occluded in digital infrastructures as backstage processes and routines. The role of speed must then become an explicit aspect of digital case study research. Galloway and Thacker (2007) have noted, by way of Paul Virilio (2006), that the importance of speed may not be perceptible to human beings.

> …disappearance is the unforeseen by-product of speed. Technology has gone beyond defining reality in the quantized frames-per-second of the cinema. Newer technologies still do that, but they also transpose and create quantized data through time stretching, morphing, detailed surface rendering, and motion capture, all with a level of resolution beyond the capacity of the human eye…
>
> (p. 137)

Implicit in Galloway and Thacker's argument is that technologies contain entire worlds below the visible world—and digital researchers necessarily must account for these worlds. Code, HTML and CSS, JavaScript, packets in packet-switching, and tacit software "daemons" (McKelvey, 2018) all move at speeds imperceptible in comparison to typical strategies of case studies. Through the chapters in this book, I advocate for thinking about the ways that these digital concerns make legible and explicit the many realities within case studies.

Fifth, access to digital objects of inquiry or cases may be much broader than researchers anticipate, resulting in a wide range of narrative possibilities. In terms of empirical storytelling, record-keeping can be precise, such as with timestamps. Because case studies are multi-sourced, detailed, and holistic research projects, case study researchers need to contend with such issues. Ethically, the pervasiveness of networked surveillance becomes an issue in terms of how, when, and where researchers collect data. This book will address ethics (Chapter 5) and writing up narratives (Chapter 6).

Description of chapters

Chapter 1, "Definitions, descriptions, and entities," provides background on the scholarly conversation of case study research, providing discussions of the terms "digital" and "case study." By doing so, I identify key descriptions to expand the case study approach into a methodological paradigm based on the concept of an *entity*. Doing so allows digital case study researchers to have more theoretical purchase for evaluating a wide range of networked phenomena.

Chapter 2, "Iterative design and digital considerations," explores designing case studies for digital contexts via iteration. Rather than establishing boundaries ahead of a research investigation, a case study with an entity at its center seeks to represent the phenomena on its own terms without a predetermined framework. In the second half of the chapter, I discuss eight considerations for iterative design: (1) users, (2) interfaces (3–4), websites development and computer code, (5) software/applications, (6) databases, (7) computational models/algorithms, and (8) infrastructure.

In Chapter 3, "Collection practices for digital case studies," I describe digital data collection theory and practice. The chapter explores theoretical stances on data collection and then explores practical qualitative methods, such as digital observations and fieldwork, fieldnotes, interviews, questionnaires, and surveys. It also lays out the basics of web scraping, which is a way to automate data collection for case study work. I conclude with remarks about the conundrum of when to stop collecting data.

Chapter 4, "Analysis for digital cases" provides analytical frameworks for digital case study analysis. It begins with concepts for beginning data analysis, such as atomization, structures, and attention, before moving on to workflow usage. After laying out workflow habits, it describes a variety of analytical techniques, including qualitative techniques such as interface analysis and the integration of texts, images, and emojis. It then discusses quantitative, computational techniques for generative thematizing, including topic modeling, named entity recognition, and sentiment analysis. I touch on generative machine learning and analysis as a type of ethics.

Chapter 5, "Ethical habits in a digital world," presents four ethical paradigms for digital research: deontology (obligation or rule-based ethics), consequentialism (outcome-based ethics), postmodernism (critique-based ethics), and virtue ethics (virtue or character-based ethics). I describe the strengths and weaknesses of each before advocating for the paradigm of virtue ethics to address the intractable problems of pluralism and emotivism in our networked world. I address how habits, rather than strict rules or outcomes, are a contingent yet normative way to build ethics for digital case study research.

Chapter 6, "Writing and visualizing the digital case," provides advice on writing up case study research, as well as visualization suggestions and dissemination practices. I provide general strategies about audience, genre, writing habits, planning, and revision. I discuss writing up case study methods, including positionality statements. I lay out strategies for visualizing case studies. I end this chapter with suggestions for dissemination practices on social media.

In the brief conclusion, "Case study work in an era of artificial intelligence," I remark on (1) the importance of case study in an era of AI, specifically the granularity that case study research provides, (2) the concepts of a "study" and "macro" cases, and (3) future directions of case study research.

How to read this book

This book has attempted to balance nuanced, complex theoretical concerns with practical applications. As a result, parts of this book will be more or less relevant depending on the purpose a reader brings to it. For audiences more theoretically inclined, I recommend Chapters 1 and 2, as well as the first half of each chapter. For those practically inclined, Chapters 3 through 6 are likely to be more relevant, notably in the second half of each chapter. Because print books are necessarily linear, some relationships between chapters are left unexplored, notably the back-and-forth nature of data collection and data analysis. I have attempted to gesture to this non-linearity; however, I stress here that moving across and between chapters is encouraged.

References

Boyle, C., Brown, J. J., & Ceraso, S. (2018). The digital: Rhetoric behind and beyond the screen. *Rhetoric Society Quarterly*, 48(3), 251–259. https://doi.org/10.1080/02773945.2018.1454187.

Burawoy, M. (1998). The extended case method. *Sociological Theory*, 16(1), 4–33. https://doi.org/10.1111/0735-2751.00040.

Dyson, A. H., & Genishi, C. (2005). *On the case: Approaches to language and literacy research*. Teachers College Press.

Flyvbjerg, B. (2006). Five misunderstandings about case-study research. *Qualitative Inquiry*, 12(2), 219–245. https://doi.org/10.1177/1077800405284363.

Gallagher, J. R. (2019). A framework for internet case study methodology in writing studies. *Computers and Composition*, 54, 1–14. https://doi.org/10.1016/j.compcom.2019.102509.

Galloway, A. R., & Thacker, E. (2007). *The exploit: A theory of networks*. University of Minnesota Press.

Gerring, J. (2017). *Case study research: Principles and practices*. Cambridge University Press.
Goertz, G., & Mahoney, J. (2012). *A tale of two cultures: Qualitative and quantitative research in the social sciences*. Princeton University Press.
Harvey, D. (1989). *The condition of postmodernity: An enquiry into the origins of cultural change*. Blackwell Publishing.
Hess, A. (2017). Introduction. In *Theorizing digital rhetoric* (pp. 1–16). Routledge.
Jenkins, H. (2013). *Spreadable media: Creating value and meaning in a networked culture*. New York University Press.
Jocher, K. (1928). The case method in social research. *Social Forces*, 7(2), 203–211. https://doi.org/10.2307/2570141.
McKelvey, F. (2018). *Internet daemons: Digital communications possessed*. University of Minnesota Press.
Merriam, S. B. (1998). *Qualitative research and case study applications in education*. Jossey-Bass.
Miles, R. (2015). Complexity, representation and practice: Case study as method and methodology. *Issues in Educational Research*, 25(2), 309–319.
Stake, R. E. (1995). *The art of case study research*. Sage Publications.
Stake, R. E. (2006). *Multiple case study analysis*. The Gilford Press.
Virilio, P. (2006). *Speed and politics*. Semiotext(e).
Yin, R. K. (2009). *Case study research: Design and methods*. Sage Publications.

1 Definitions, descriptions, and entities

What exactly is a *digital case study*? What *isn't* digital in the twenty-first century? In the introduction, I loosely referred to case study research and case studies as involving bounded systems of inquiry conducted for research purposes. A case study is a type of *study*, which distinguishes it from an example, exemplar, or anecdote. While case studies absolutely contain examples and granular details, they are neither examples nor stories alone. Certainly, high-quality case studies involve stories and have a narrative. What distinguishes a case study from an example or story is that a case study implies a multi-source collection of data, such as historical archives, surveys, interviews, and observations. Case studies are consequently informed by data and first-hand research. This distinction helps to separate case study research from the more popular and less rigorous version of the term "case study" that tends to accompany digital marketing and online retail wherein a case study is an example of a phenomenon.

The above qualification addresses the term "study" in "digital case study," leaving us with two remaining terms: digital and case. The first half of this chapter examines the term digital, arguing for its relevance. Digital phenomena saturate contemporary life. Digital media, networked devices, and electronic infrastructure enable and encourage inordinate amounts of information to be shared by users and disseminated by organizations. They speed up the flow of information and, as noted in the introduction, create a hyper-availability of it. Our electronic devices and the multiple realities of online and networked culture have made us into cyborgs; one need only watch strangers dodge each other on the street while staring into their multipurpose networked devices (phones) to know this is true. Children climb on playgrounds with one hand because the other holds their phone. We already know that the distinctions between human and non-human, human and animal, and human and machine are epistemologically thin at best and, at worst, myths built to maintain hegemonic conditions. Our cyborg world has made those epistemological conditions materially relevant. Consequently, any case is now fundamentally digital.

DOI: 10.4324/9781003402169-2

Following this discussion of the digital, the second half of this chapter examines the term "case," focusing on the epistemological center of a case. For most case study researchers, a case's center is conceived as a unit or "unit of analysis." This perspective understands cases as people, places, or things but not relationships. I reconceive of the center as an entity, which allows for relationships and processes to be included as cases. By having entities, rather than units, as an epistemological and ontological center, digital phenomena can be more accurately depicted and narrated in case studies and as case studies. In turn, this allows more purchase for a case study approach to be understood as a full methodology, as opposed to a less robust approach or method. Equipping ourselves with entity as a conceptual and theoretical center provides researchers of digital phenomena, such as social media or artificial intelligence (AI), with a broader way to construct a case. Practically, entities, as a term, suggests a flexible theoretical framework for understanding the various complex *relationships* between online and offline relationships necessary for a case study to be created.

The term "digital"

Nearly everything is digital, or at least touched upon by digital elements, in our screen-saturated world. Using the qualifier "digital" thus may seem outmoded in the twenty-first century. As Benjamin Peters (2016) notes,

> the sweeping success of digital techniques has rendered the term a quintessentially twentieth-, not twenty-first-, century keyword. As digital techniques continue to saturate the modern world, we increasingly find the keyword digital, understood in its most conventional sense, slouching past its prime.
>
> (p. 93)

These perspectives are emblematic of a post 2010s perspective: everything is digital, rendering the term so ubiquitous that it is obsolete. However, simply because a term can be applied to a broad array of activities does not mean it is worth abandoning. Or as James Wynn (2017) writes,

> The ubiquity of digital technology and the myriad ways that it has become integrated into the fabric of modern life have changed the quantity of available information, the speed with which it can be accessed, and the distances across which it can be broadcast. Though there is a widely shared recognition that the Internet has transformed the ways we communicate and interact, there is less frequently an understanding of how this technology actually impacts our communications and interactions.
>
> (p. 1)

The ubiquity of digital objects, phenomena, and research requires us to examine our methodologies more closely, including *how* we create digital research studies and the way a case coalesces. The rubric of "digital" is useful precisely because it encompasses so many phenomena.

There are two related but distinct meanings of "digital" research as I use it: research *about* explicitly digital phenomena (such as studying a virtual world) and research that *uses* digital tools (think here of using machine learning techniques to reveal/create latent patterns in data). There are, of course, other connotations of the term: electronic components, computational processes and processing, networked social worlds, media platforms, gaming elements, screen design and user experience, infrastructures, and so on. A flexible approach of "digital" is therefore necessary to account for a broad swath of phenomena.

My primary use of "digital" in digital case study research relates to networked phenomena that use electronic means, partially or entirely. While using digital tools to create a case study also falls within this scope, I foreground the phenomena—rather than tools—in my discussions and examples. From time to time, I will invoke the tool aspect of "digital." As will become clear in my discussion of case-as-entity, however, I do not draw a distinct demarcation between online and offline phenomena when referring to digital research. Rather, digital describes the ways that phenomena are both electronic and embodied in which online and offline lives are imbricated and inseparable.

The labor practices of social media platforms are some of the most compelling examples of the blurriness between online and offline activity. We have seen how content moderators (Gillespie, 2018; Roberts, 2019) experience PTSD (post-traumatic stress disorder) from observing, identifying, and deleting heinous content on social media websites, such as Facebook, Twitter, and YouTube. These jobs often come with other physical consequences, including a lack of bathroom breaks (Roberts, 2019), that are often legalized due to these jobs being outsourced to countries with lax labor laws (Duffy, 2017) or even because "big tech" companies have seized law-making capabilities (Suzor, 2019).

Likewise, the infrastructure of the internet replicates historical precedence and biases, demonstrating that digital lives are part of offline lives. Starosielski (2015) shows that our internet traffic patterns follow material networks, including environmental, political, colonial, and military histories. These histories and infrastructures become baked into social media cultures, creating an algorithmic feedback loop of what is deemed acceptable. For example, we know that the literary publishing industry was (and still is) predominantly white. Using a massive corpus of fiction, So's *Redlining culture* (2020) identifies that people of color are predominantly excluded from publishing fiction. So addresses the reception of literature as crucial to equality because, he finds, that most of the reviewed fiction is written by white authors. White-centric fiction becomes the basis for what is reviewed, discussed, and analyzed on social media platforms such as YouTube, Goodreads, and Amazon. In turn, these websites use algorithms to determine what content is popular. Social media platforms cannot program their way of the problem. Code will not solve the problem because it's a data problem. It's a problem of the empirical world. No model could correct biased data.

As a result, the historical racism of the publishing industry, Hollywood, and mass media conspire to create consequences for digital researchers. This conundrum might be understood as an outgrowth of the *ideology of prediction*, or what Wendy Chun (2021) calls an ideology of correlation (pp. 180–184). That is, social media platforms and other industries use previous data to train models upon which future decisions are made, regardless of whether causality can be determined. All these companies use representations of activity, not the activity itself. Regardless of the model deployed, the *training data* will corrupt models because it contains bias—as all data will, especially when harvested with historical racism, misogyny, and homophobia. The data are representations of activity.

These examples show the ways that "digital" remains highly relevant, if not always hearkening back to the utopian vision of early internet research from the 1980s, 1990s, and early 2000s. Without an explicit focus on digital, we lose focus on the networked and mediated nature of contemporary phenomena. With such a focus, we can better connect contexts, understand offline and online activity as intimately tied together, and find resonance between offline histories and online contemporary experiences.

From a practical standpoint, foregrounding the term "digital" prods us to explore connections within networks and communication technologies. As Mejias (2013) writes, "While the Internet is the most notorious example of a digital network… digital networks can encompass other technologies not based on the Internet, technologies such as mobile phones, radio-frequency identification (RFID) devices, and so on" (xiii). To reframe Mejias with case studies in mind, digitality can refer to a panoply of technologies, relationships, artifacts, and discursive social issues that deserve granular investigations in which the phenomena are understood on their terms, within their contexts, and not reduced to variables.

Within our current era of big data, machine learning, and artificial intelligence, an emphasis on statistical inference without much explanatory power (Lipton & Steinhardt, 2019, p. 2) has emerged to obfuscate— or worse, replace—granular complexity. As multiple scholars have noted, the use of large-scale tools with ideologies based on averages, matrices, and linear regressions are themselves outgrowths of the Eugenics movements of the 1800s and 1900s (e.g., MacKenzie, 1981). The simplification that occurs with these approaches leads to issues of systemic bias from computational, algorithmic approaches (Bender et al., 2020; Eubanks, 2018; Noble, 2018; O'Neil, 2016; Pasquale, 2015) and instances in which no individual fits the average (Rose, 2016).

"Digital" case studies provide a counterweight to these approaches as a major part of their value is to reflect the "multiple realities" of a case (Dyson & Genishi, 2005, p. 18; Stake, 1995, p. 43; Yin, 2009, p. 18). If machine learning and large-scale data analyses are now normalized and accepted, then we need granular narratives to counterbalance these approaches. In an exemplary article about misunderstandings of case study research, Bent Flyvbjerg (2006) crystalizes the importance of narrative and story when he writes,

> The problems in summarizing case studies, however, are due more often to the properties of the reality studied than to the case study as a research method. Often it is not desirable to summarize and generalize case studies. Good studies should be read as narratives in their entirety.
>
> (p. 241)

Narrative, as a case study method, attempts to understand contradictions and paradoxes, issues that can arise in any research project but often with networked digital research. The value of a digital case is thus its ability to tell a coherent story with detailed explanation—something that large-scale data analyses, such as machine learning, often miss: "[machine learning] papers often offer speculation in the guise of explanations, which are then interpreted as authoritative due to the trappings of a scientific paper and the presumed expertise of the authors" (Lipton & Steinhardt, 2019, p. 2). The relevance for "digital" in case study research is the necessary complement that cases provide. Machinic approaches often do not account for narratives, granularity, complexity. Case study approaches do precisely this.

The value of case studies, including digital case studies, is consequently their *irreducibility*. Data do not tell complex contextualized narratives, nor do computational models. That's our job as researchers. The ability to look at a bounded system in a deep, meaningful way creates exceptional contextualized knowledge that could be applicable in spaces where variables are difficult to categorize and recognize. Digital case studies, and case studies more generally, look at specific segments to craft a detailed and particularized narrative about social encounters so that others might learn about a case. But if that's a goal of digital case study research, what marks the beginning? Or perhaps more accurately, we might ask, what is the center or core of a case study?

Wrestling with the term "case study"

At the heart of case study research is a case. A case is a source of confusion for researchers, who typically note that a case has no unifying definition and is responsive to domain knowledge, disciplinary conventions, and practical constraints (e.g., Bartlett & Vavrus, 2017; Bennett & Elman, 2007; Bromley, 1986; Dyson & Genishi, 2005; Gerring, 2017; Jocher, 1928; Spinuzzi, 2023; Tellis, 1997; Yin, 2009). A decided lack of consensus about a "case" creates friction between domains and disciplines. (See Table 1.1 for case study definitions and descriptions of case studies from major case study monographs.) There are no templates or strict rules for what describes a case study or case that transcends disciplines or knowledge domains. Some have simply described case studies as a trans-paradigmatic heuristic.[1] This book wrestles with what it means to be a case.

There are, however, recurring patterns and Wittgensteinian "family resemblances" (Wittgenstein, 1968) regarding case study definitions. To examine a case more closely, I want to describe the case study through four foundational elements: case studies are (1) epistemically open-ended, and (2) do not draw clear demarcations between subject of analysis and its context. Case studies are demarcated through (3) a bounded system aimed at holistic investigations, and (4) are based on multiple types of data to better understand the multiple realities of a case.

First and second, the case study is an open-ended in-depth investigation (Dyson & Genishi, 2005; Merriam, 1998; Morgan, 2012; Stake, 1995; Yin, 2009), where the delineation between the subject of analysis and context is not clear or inseparable (e.g., Duff, 2008, p. 30; Flyvbjerg, 2006, p. 222; Lillis, 2008, pp. 374–377; Morgan, 2012, p. 668). Case studies are epistemically open-ended with a detailed level of *density* and *holism*. Researchers such as Crowe et al. (2011), Dyson and Genishi (2005), Gerring (2017), Kenny and Grotelueschen (1984), Stake (1995), and Swanborn (2010) argue that cases are holistic and intense due to their comprehensive and fully elaborated nature. Colloquially, case studies examine phenomena "up close." For this reason, researchers should come to case study research understanding that their investigations will not "pin down" their inquiries. Maxwell (2009) reflects this epistemic positioning by framing the case study as about the process of research, not the product of a research investigation, writing that case study research questions "involve an open-ended, inductive approach to discover what these meanings and influences are and how they are involved in these events and activities—an inherently processual orientation" (p. 83). The case study approach, as I view it, *necessarily* sees multiple meanings in an investigation, reflecting a multiplicity of contexts, some of which are contradictory, paradoxical, and messy. Case study knowledge is therefore context-dependent rather than "ground truth." The implications here will be discussed in the following chapters but they include: the role of generalizability (either intrinsic or extrinsic) when analyzing and writing up case studies, the extent to which case study research is preliminary (leading to further study and studies in terms of design), and the purpose of a case itself (to learn about phenomena or to transfer knowledge from one context to another).

16 *Definitions, descriptions, and entities*

Table 1.1 Definitions, types, and disciplinary approaches to case study research according to well-cited case study theorists and their works

Author	Year	Title	Definition	Types of case studies or their selection criteria	Discipline from which author emerges
Bartlett and Vavrus	2017	*Rethinking case study research*	Depends on epistemology and methodology of author (p. 27)	• Variance-oriented • Interpretivist • Process-oriented (pp. 27–42)	Education
Bassey	1999	*Case study research in educational settings*	No definition but provides overview of others (pp. 22–36)	Argues that taxonomies of others are overlapping and intersecting (p. 35)	Education
Blatter and Haverland	2012	*Designing case studies: Explanatory approaches in small-N research*	A non-experimental approach that has the following four elements: "1. a small number of cases; a large number of empirical observations per case; a huge diversity of empirical observations for each case; and an intensive reflection on the relationship between concrete empirical observations and abstract theoretical concepts" (p. 19)	• Co-variational Analysis • Causal-Process Tracing • Congruence Analysis (pp. 27–29)	Political science
Bromley	1986	*The case-study method in psychology and related disciplines*	"...a relatively short, self-contained episode or segment of a person's life" or "a close view of important life-event" (p. 1)	Case studies are contrast with life-history (p. 39)	Psychology

Definitions, descriptions, and entities 17

Author	Year	Title	Definition	Types of case studies or their selection criteria	Discipline from which author emerges
Duff	2008	Case study research in applied linguistics	Identifies key recurring principles: • boundedness • singularity • in-depth study • multiple perspectives • triangulation • particularity • contextualization • interpretation (p. 23)	• Single case study (p. 36) • Multiple case studies (p. 36) • Longitudinal (pp. 40–42)	Linguistics
Dyson and Genishi	2005	On the case: Approaches to language and literacy research	A case study is "a small naturalistic social unit" recognized by participants (p. 2). The researcher focuses on others' understanding of the phenomena under study (p. 12)	Only addresses single case study design but seems to imply other frameworks exist. Single case studies do not "determine context-free associations" (p. 11)	Education (literacy)
Orum, Feagin, and Sjoberg	1991	A case for the case study (Introduction)	"A case study is... an in-depth multifaceted investigation using qualitative research methods, of a single social phenomenon." The study is detailed and "... often relies on the use of several data sources" (p. 2)	Single case study approach	Sociology

18 *Definitions, descriptions, and entities*

Author	Year	Title	Definition	Types of case studies or their selection criteria	Discipline from which author emerges
Gerring	2017	*Case study research: Principles and practices*	"A case study is an intensive study of a single case or a small number of cases which draws on observational data and promises to shed light on larger population of cases." It is "highly focused" (p. 28)	Descriptive, causal, or omnibus (p. 41)	Political science / government
George and Bennett	2005	*Case studies and theory development in the social sciences*	A case is "an instance of class events" out of which the research can develop theory regarding the similarities and differences among related instances (pp. 17–18)	n/a (generally appears to be a single case study approach)	Political science / government
Hamel, Dufour, and Fortin	1993 (1991 in French)	*Case study methods*	Case study is a "monographic approach" (p. 1) deploying multiple methods. This approach consolidates various "objects of study" (p. 32) into the approach (for further elaboration, see pp. 41–44)	While a taxonomy is not presented, cases are generally conceived of as a way to view larger social forces and cultures	Sociology
Hamilton and Corbett-Whittier	2013	*Using case study in education research*	Does not define case study. Instead, discusses various researchers' conceptions of case study. Approaches case study research as a genre	Views the case study as an approach "…within a bounded unit, using different forms of data collection and is likely to explore more than one perspective. Case study as a research genre could then be defined as a way of framing a particularity (bounded unit), providing guiding principles for the research design, process, quality and communication" (p. 10)	Education

Definitions, descriptions, and entities   19

Author	Year	Title	Definition	Types of case studies or their selection criteria	Discipline from which author emerges
Merriam	1998	Qualitative research and case study applications in education	The case is "a thing, a single entity, a unit around which there are boundaries." The case needs to be "intrinsically bounded" (p. 27)	Disciplinary, descriptive ("intent"), and multiple	Education
Stake	1995	The art of case study research	"The case is a specific, complex functioning thing" that includes a bounded system that is an integrated system (p. 2)	• Intrinsic: to learn about the phenomenon itself (p. 3) • Instrumental: to learn about the phenomenon for purposes outside the phenomenon (pp. 3–4)	Education
Swanborn	2010	Case study research: What, why, and how?	An in-depth study conducted within its natural setting. Full definition in the notes[2]	Multiple and single	Sociology
Yin	2009	Case study research: Design and methods	"Case study is an empirical inquiry that investigates contemporary phenomena in-depth within its real-life context, wherein this phenomenon and context are not clear" (p. 18)	Exploratory, descriptive, and explanation case studies (pp. 7–8)	Social science

Third and fourth, case studies are holistic, bounded systems (Dyson & Genishi, 2005; Gerring, 2017; Stake, 1995; Yin, 2009) that draw on multiple sources of data, that is *triangulation* (e.g., Baxter & Jack, 2008; Blatter & Haverland, 2012; Gerring, 2017; Miles, 2015; Simons, 2012; Yin, 2009). A bounded system is identified by the researcher through their own research questions, disciplinary background, tools, life histories, and practical constraints. A bounded system, though, is not rigid. Rather, it is a *flexible* approach for demarcating when, where, and how to begin and end conducting research. Merriam (1998) writes that a case can be "an intensive, holistic description and analysis of a bounded phenomenon such as a program, an institution, a person, a process, or a social unit" (xiii). The "case study approach moves us one step closer to being able to study a phenomenon as an integrated whole" (Anderson et al., 2005, p. 681).

Because case studies are in-depth and attempt to understand the system under investigation in rich ways representing complexity, triangulation is necessary. Of triangulation, psychologist Bromley (1986) writes, "The navigational metaphor suggests that if several independent sources of evidence point to a common conclusion, then one's confidence in that conclusion is strengthened" (p. 6). Duff (2008) elaborates on Bromley's claims when she writes:

> Data, methods, perspectives, theories, and even researchers can be triangulated in order to produce either converging or diverging observations and interpretations. Although the notion of triangulation may have originally had positivist undertones (multiple sources of information leading to one "truth" to be discovered by the researcher), it can also be used to ascertain multiple forms of interpretation (or multiple realities) at work in order to clarify meaning by identifying different ways the case is being seen.
>
> (p. 30)

Baxter and Jack (2008), too, write, "Triangulation of data sources, data types or researchers is a primary strategy that can be used and would support the principle in case study research that the phenomena be viewed and explored from multiple perspectives" (p. 556). With these perspectives in mind, researchers can, consequently, develop a case study that combines interviews, surveys, observations, fieldwork, user experiences, and many other data sources. The use of multiple data sources underscores the epistemic open-endedness of the case study as a methodology.

Typically, these data sources are combined to reflect the "multiple-realities" (Dyson & Genishi, 2005, p. 18; Stake 1995, p. 43; Yin, 2009, p. 18) of a case, meaning that case studies do not represent a single unifying reality but rather sets of historically contingent activity. Indeed, Baxter and Jack (2008) note that "researchers should... plan for opportunities to have either a prolonged or intense exposure to the phenomenon under study within its context so that rapport with participants can be established and so that multiple perspectives can be collected and understood" (p. 556). Due to these multiple realities and perspectives, including the blurring of work boundaries (Spinuzzi, 2023, p. 2), the bounded system of a case study can be *iterative* in nature (Gallagher, 2019, p. 5), meaning that bounded systems are recreated over time if the inquiry needs the boundaries to be redesigned or rethought. In fact, because case studies are meant to be detailed in nature, boundary production probably should be iterative in nature (cf., Gerring, 2017; Yin, 2009).

In addition to these four descriptive elements, there are two common themes around the case study as a research approach. First, case studies yield complex results that are often unable to be distilled into summarized bullet points. Philosopher of science Mary S. Morgan (2012), for instance, writes, "The outcome is a complex, often narrated, account that typically contains some of the raw evidence as well as its analysis and that ties together the many different bits of evidence in the study" (p. 668). Likewise, Bent Flyvbjerg argues that the case study should result in a narrative, one that does not close the inquiry but *opens* it to possibility. Flyvbjerg (2006) writes:

> I try to leave scope for readers of different backgrounds to make different interpretations and draw diverse conclusions regarding the question of what the case is a case of. The goal is not to make the case study be all things to all people. The goal is to allow the study to be different things to different people. I try to achieve this by describing the case with so many facets—like life itself—that different readers may be attracted, or repelled, by different things in the case. Readers are not pointed down any one theoretical path or given the impression that truth might lie at the end of such a path. Readers will have to discover their own path and truth inside the case.
>
> (p. 238)

Here, Flyvbjerg echoes the open-endedness of case study research but with an emphasis on writing up the study. The narrative of a case study can be scaled up or down to account for the inquiry and allows the multiple realities to be reflected directly in the writing.

The second theme is to understand the history of the case study as a maligned form of research—generally before the 1990s and especially within the fields of psychology and sociology—and then to argue for the strengths of the case study approach (Gerring, 2004; Stoecker, 1991). However, I have not read many articles published since the 2000s that explicitly malign case study research. Most researchers appear to me to accept the case study as a legitimate approach, although there is considerable debate over its status as an approach, a method, or a methodology. Gerring (2017) and Bartlett and Vavrus (2017) articulate some of these issues, although the discussions tend to be ensconced in disciplinary conversations, such as causal case studies or small-N versus large-N case studies.

Wrestling with the term "case"

Some researchers avoid a *case* (not case study) definition and thereby allow readers to fill in their own approaches/definitions for what a case study is and means. For instance, Yin (2009), whose canonical multi-edition *Case study research* has been cited over 200,000 times, does not define a case by itself.[3] Bassey (1999), Merriam (1998), and Stake (1995) opt not to define a case, instead going with the fuller-fledged term, "case study." Ragin (1992) has addressed this question of a "case" by simply arguing, "it depends" (p. 6). Political scientist John Gerring (2017) notes that a case "connotes a spatially and temporally delimited phenomenon of theoretical significance" (p. 27).

While Gerring's definition is direct and clear, this definition immediately poses two queries, both related to how a case exists or, more precisely, comes into existence. First, if a case is to be investigated and *learned about*, it is unlikely that researchers can immediately delimit a case before investigation. Case study research is not experimental. Researchers do not thus find neatly bounded cases *ex nihilo*. Researchers need to investigate to understand the phenomenon under investigation. Due to the theme of "multiple realities" discussed earlier, I have often been left with questions about the boundary issue: what is included in the case and what is left out of the case?[4] My answer here is the refrain I began this book with: it depends on the case and its context.

The second query: Gerring's use of "theoretical significance" implies that the significance is already manifestly clear before investigation. By extension, then, the researcher—who brings the theory to bear on the research—makes the decision about when, where, how, and why to delimit a case—thus complicating the implied notion that a case exists outside the investigation. From this perspective, a case study is a case with the study of the researcher included as scaffolding. If a case is a temporally and spatially delimited thing, then what is at a case's core?

Typically, case study researchers have labeled this core a "unit of analysis" (Bartlett & Vavrus, 2017; Bassey, 1999; Bromley, 1986; Burowoy, 2009; Dyson & Genishi, 2005; Orum et al., 1991; Flyvbjerg, 2006; Gerring, 2017; Merriam, 1998; Stake, 1995; Swanborn, 2010; Yin, 2009). Others have tried complicating the unit of analysis (Spinuzzi, 2023; Wertsch, 2009). The unit of analysis represents the fundamental building block of a case similar to the concept of a sample in survey research. This causes some confusion between case and unit of analysis, a tension that Bartlett and Vavrus (2017) highlight:

> Case is often defined as place. Researchers may use "case" to mean one setting, place, or institution, or they may use "case" for both the institution (or place or setting) and each person in it. We may also use case interchangeably with "units of analysis," but this can be problematic because it does not sufficiently separate the categories we use to organize our data and the categories we construct based on our theoretical framework.
>
> (p. 27)

Bartlett and Vavrus are leery to conflate the case with a place, setting, or thing because (1) their sociocultural approach understands that context is not a container but rather is the phenomenon, and (2) that a case contains analysis, thereby making a case the unit of analysis and analysis from the researcher(s). The case, on this view, already contains analysis through the construction of the case itself.

The ambiguity between a case and unit of analysis (hereafter referred to as a unit) underscores that a unit is generally understood to be a thing, person, or program that *prefigures* and *presupposes* the researcher. A "unit" of analysis is a thing researchers choose to study outside of themselves. Two frequently cited case study researchers adopt the view that cases exist outside the researcher. First, Stake (1995) asserts that the "case is a specific, a complex functioning thing" (p. 2). Stake goes on to write, "The case is an integrated system. The parts do not have to be working well, the purposes maybe irrational, but it is a system. People and programs are clearly prospective cases. Events and processes fit the definition less well" (Stake, 1995, p. 2). This system is a crucial epistemic understanding of case study research. For Stake, the integrated systems of case studies are identified, not created. People and programs are conceived of as units, systems before the researcher arrives. Events, relationships, and processes, in Stake's view, are not systems because they are too leaky and porous. The spatial component of a unit is determined by the case, not by the researcher's investigation, according to Stake. A case thus cannot be a relationship—and I will argue this view must be disrupted to make case study research more effective for our networked, digital era.

Second, Yin (2009) implicitly asserts that a unit of analysis exists outside the researcher: "Selection of the appropriate unit of analysis will start to occur when you accurately specify your primary research questions" (p. 30). While Bartlett and Vavrus (2017) address Yin's statement, the main point here is that a unit, for Yin, is prefabricated prior to the researcher. Despite his careful avoidance of epistemological commitments (Yazan, 2015, p. 137), Yin goes on to note that the unit can be refined or redefined but the unit remains outside the researcher. The researcher is convinced by the data, the case, or another consideration (such as practicality) to re-evaluate the unit. Yet the unit, or in Yin's approach the case, remains a stable thing. Both Stake and Yin, then, take a flexible approach to the unit in a case study but understand the unit as a stable center that a researcher refines or a stable thing that is uncovered as the research project progresses—colloquially, as the research project unfurls.

Contra Stake (1995) and Yin (2009), Gerring (2017) posits that units are made by the researcher. Units are the building blocks of the case study method. As Gerring writes,

> Occasionally, the temporal boundaries of a case are more obvious than its spatial boundaries. This is true when the phenomena under study are eventful but the unit undergoing the event is amorphous. For example, if one is studying terrorist attacks it may not be clear how the spatial unit of analysis should be understood, but the events themselves may be well bounded.
>
> (p. 20)

Gerring's conception of a unit of analysis relies on implicit understanding that the unit "tells" or "informs" the researchers on how to make demarcations and bounded systems—that same type of systems to which Stake refers. But with Gerring's shift in perspective, the agency, onus, and responsibility falls to the researcher(s) because the researchers need to make cuts not into a unit but into the case itself. It's a slight distinction but crucial as an epistemology of case study research.

Extending Gerring's theoretical formulation of the unit thereby achieves a fuller and transparent version of the case study as a methodology, one especially relevant to digital research. A case study's center is necessarily complex but conceiving of the unit as persons, places, or things does not account for the relationships that form in our digital, networked world. In a world of social media and networked websites, cases are inherently relationships in that cases contain a milieu of connections.

From an epistemic view of digital case study research, the case study and its center are the needed complement—a salve—to big data analyses. Machine learning is not especially useful without case studies to serve as the core to connect correlations. Centers of cases are consequently relationally ideographic; they are the granular level of understanding the things/people/events/relationships that surround us. In our cyborg cultures and networked world, studying phenomena at granular level consequently necessitates a reconceptualization of the unit.

From unit to entity

The term and concept "entity" reframes the center of a case study. "Entity" draws from Albert North Whitehead's *Process and reality* (1979). As a conceptual schema, entities as Whitehead conceives them never exist in isolation—and this is the reason that entities are not solipsistic. Whitehead writes the following:

> For you cannot abstract the university from any entity, actual or non-actual, so as to consider that entity in complete isolation. Whatever we think of some entity, we are asking, What is it fit for here? In a sense, every entity pervades the whole world; for this question has a definite answer for each entity in respect to any actual entity or any nexus of actual entities.
>
> (1979, p. 28)

Two points are relevant here for case study research. First, entities are situated, specific, and grounded ("Fit for *here*," my emphasis). They possess concrete granular details—particularities—that case study researchers seek. Entities exist in a context but only by someone asking the question; they are *hailed* into existence. Whitehead's phrase of "we are asking" is noteworthy: entities require direct thinking. In this sense, entities are created through, in part, the act of conceiving of them. The implication here is that the question-poser is partially responsible for the creation of the entity under study. Researchers, of course, don't create their subjects of inquiry but they do create the inquiry.

Second, entities can be nested inside and adjacent to one another; they cannot be isolated from one another. Through their mere existence, they draw on a host of other relationships. Those relationships are emergent, more than the sum of their parts. A useful supplementary here is Manuel DeLanda's work in *Assemblage theory* (2016). He writes,

> Assemblages have a fully contingent historical identity, and each of them is therefore an *individual entity*: an individual person, an individual community, an individual organisation, an individual city. Because the ontological status of all assemblages is the same, entities operating at different scales can directly interact with one another, individual to individual, a possibility that does not exist in a hierarchical ontology, like that composed of genera, species, and individuals.
>
> (DeLanda, 2016, pp. 19–20, emphasis in original)

The entity to which DeLanda (2006, 2016) is referring is the ontologically flat nature of case inquiry. Even when researchers are confronted with different investigative scales, such as a person, a group of people, a large organization of people, or a collection of organizations, these entities are ontologically—and I add epistemologically too—flat. This position allows for a fundamental blurring between people, places, things, and the relationship among them. By adopting such an emergent perspective, case study research can methodologically collect and analyze data in ways that represent the multiple realities of their entities under study.

Since case study researchers assert that cases are *holistic* representations (e.g., Stake, 1995; Yin, 2009), *entities*—as the unit of analysis of the case—elicit the multiple and possibly contradictory relationships of such perspectives. Indeed, most statistical approaches could not represent the contradictory elements of an entity because such relationships would likely be *dismissed as noise*. Entities, both in nomenclature and philosophy, can better account for the contradictory stories and entanglements that accompany the creation of a case study's center.

Whitehead goes on to elaborate on the depth of connections between entities in "Facts and forms":

> The principle of universal relativity directly traverses Aristotle's dictum, "A substance is not present in a subject." On the contrary, according to this principle an actual entity *is* present in other actual entities. In fact if we allow for degrees of relevance and for negligible relevance, we must say that every actual entity is present in every other actual entity.
>
> (1979, p. 50, emphasis in original)

The connections between entities are not homogenous but rather by degree. For example, the relationship between a social media post and how it is shared possesses connections to a variety of other platforms. But the degree of sharing—how often it is shared—on a platform does matter to the relationship between the post and other platforms.

Isabelle Stengers, in *Thinking with Whitehead* (2014), directly and lucidly explicates the previous passage, reminding us that Whiteheadian metaphysics is perhaps counterintuitive.

> We have, for better or worse, become accustomed to think that two bodies can interact "at a distance," that is, *qua* distant, but we are reassured by the fact that distance makes itself felt (at least in the definition of the gravitational interaction), and that the interaction responds to a regular mathematical function. Here, the conceptual scandal is fully deployed, irreducible to a redefinition of space-time as Einstein proposed it. If I feel something, this thing certainly enters into the definition of my experience: it belongs to my experience, and it is not forged by my experience. I sense it insofar as it testifies to something else. I produce myself *qua* feeling that which is not me.
>
> (p. 295)

Stengers' lengthy explication points to two important aspects that an entity, rather than a unit, brings to case study research generally, and digital research specifically.

First, different entities can "touch" and influence one another even if they are not necessarily in contact. While there is some ontological and imperialist baggage with this perspective, i.e., not everything is equally connected to everything else,[5] we can more readily see the messy edges of an entity and that connections in a case are made by the researcher to draw out the entity's emergent nature. Practically, by conceiving of entity as the unit of analysis, digital case study researchers can show how, for example, real-time social media posts can have an impact on the case study. Watching a speech on a social media platform equipped with real-time reaction emojis—as YouTube is—can influence users' experiences with that video (Riddick, 2019) and their subsequent views of that speech even if those reactions are *no longer present*. Because entities themselves are relationships, uncommon connections are more readily made with entities than with units, the latter of which has an embedded implication: units precede the researcher. Entity, on the other hand, emphasizes the multiplicity of realities—a common reframe from case study researchers—of a case study. This gives new meaning to the BF Skinner passage often quoted by case study researchers: "instead of studying a thousand rats for one hour each or a hundred rats for ten hours each the investigator is more likely to study one rat for a thousand hours" (Skinner, 1966, p. 21). Entities ask us to think about how thousands of rats might affect our one rat and vice-versa.

Second, Stengers argues that Whitehead's approaches go against an Einsteinian version of physics. An example helps to frame such a radical proposition. Within an Einsteinian framework, i.e., principles of relativity, scientists measuring in the same way would find their measurements the same. In a Whiteheadian framework, those scientists have the same measurement principles but due to their experiences, they measure differently and there is variation in what measurement means and in the measuring methods. This difference is more than the result of equipment, approaches, or techniques. *It's a difference of actual experiences.* One caveat: it's easy to render this approach as nonsensical: I did for many years and even still have some reservations of such a perspective. However, as I have grown more experienced, this means that measurement and statistics means different things to different individuals—and the *same individual at different times*. This perspective is key to changing the ontological nature of case studies to make them suitable for the networked nature of digital phenomena.

The center of a case study, as an entity, helpfully shows the instability of a unit for digital case study research. Most "units" of digital phenomena are far too leaky as bounded systems. For example, researching the case of a social media user on one platform typically requires examining their spaces in and across multiple platforms. Entities, both in language and theory, account for leaky phenomena, rife with relationships that *constitute* people, places, and things. Since people, places, and things are often considered the center of cases, I have attempted to show that these centers are themselves processes and relational. Entities, as an alternative term to units, explicitly frames relationships as cases.

Agential cuts: Practical implications of entities

Using entity, rather than unit, enables case study to include relationships and processes as cases. Karen Barad's notion of agential realism (AR; 2007) is important methodologically, and quite practically, to understand how things are relationships. *Entities* allow digital case study researchers to leverage a methodology for seeing *potential* relationships in their cases as part of the case.

AR prompts researchers to see case studies becoming a series of relationships that are necessarily snipped and culled. Digital, networked inquiries become processes. For example, for online research, understanding the ways that users exist materially on screens but have embodied presences off screen requires connecting non-human screens with human effects of the body; some of my participants have recounted experiencing panic attacks from reading threatening or misogynistic social media posts. Likewise, understanding the cultures and languages of a country as intimately connected to its websites, digital realities, and electronic devices (Takhteyev, 2012) thereby demonstrates that a case's center is not a unit but rather *always-already* a relationship.

Barad argues that an indeterminacy exists between people, objects, things, and phenomena. Barad's AR is not a unified theory but rather functions as inquiry by which cultural and natural forces are differentiated (2007, p. 66). AR then does not begin with a point at "this is culture" and "that is nature" but functions to question how "culture" and "nature" come into being and come to be treated as such. I quote Barad at length:

> knowing, thinking, measuring, theorizing, and observing are material practices of intra-acting within and as part of the world. What do we learn by engaging in such practices? We do not uncover preexisting facts about independently existing things as they exist frozen in time like little statues positioned in the world. Rather, we learn about phenomena—about specific material configurations of the world's becoming. The point is not simply to put the observer or knower back in the world (as if the world were a container and we needed merely to acknowledge our situatedness in it) but to understand and take account of the fact that we too are part of the world's differential becoming. And furthermore, the point is not merely that knowledge practices have material consequences but that practices of knowing are specific material entanglements that participate in (re)configuring the world.
>
> (2007, pp. 90–91)

Cases are the construction of a particular reality by the researcher, but the reality depicted is an attempt to highlight variability of the phenomena

Definitions, descriptions, and entities 29

under consideration. By creating a case study, researchers genuinely produce a specific version of reality in relation to a combination of research questions, methodologies/methods, and theories.

One of the most consequential ideas for case study researchers from Barad's AR is agential cuts, or the idea that doing research requires a cutting apart of phenomena that simultaneously puts the phenomena together. Barad (2007) writes:

> the agential cut enacts a resolution *within* the phenomenon of the inherent ontological (and semantic) indeterminacy. In other words, relata do not preexist relations; rather, relata-within-phenomena emerge through specific intra-actions. Crucially, then, intra-actions enact *agential separability*—the condition of *exteriority-within-phenomena*. The notion of agential separability is of fundamental importance, for in the absence of a classical ontological condition of exteriority between observer and observed, it provides an alternative ontological condition for the possibility of objectivity. Moreover, the agential cut enacts a causal structure among components of a phenomenon in the marking of the "measuring agencies" ("effect") by the "measured object" ("cause"). It is in this sense that the measurement can be said to express particular facts about that which is measured; that is, the measurement is a causal intra-action and not "any old playing around." Hence *the notion of intra-action constitutes a reworking of the traditional notion of causality.*
> (p. 140, emphasis added)

To orient this passage for case study researchers, the bounded system is not just slicing entity away or "carving it" from reality. Agential cuts function as different moments of power to create boundaries, distinctions, and disjunctions. They are formed in relation to the researchers and the research project but not solely the result of the researcher's own choices. Those choices are entwined with entities under study, emergent together. The bounded system is a way to "cut" and to put back together, or as Barad argues, *together-apart* (2007).

Agential cuts, when thought about in terms of case study creation, frame researcher subjectivity as necessary to investigations. Most qualitative researchers accept the poststructuralist approach that subjectivity is unavoidable. As linguist Patricia Duff (2008) writes, "[qualitative researchers] see [subjectivity] as an inevitable engagement with the world in which meanings and realities are constructed (not just discovered) and in which the researcher is very much present" (p. 56). Duff goes on to argue that researchers need to be forthright, transparent, and credible with their qualitative schemas and coding procedures. Perspectives such as Duff's are useful for us without wrestling with postmodern theories and their anti-foundational perspective toward truth: digital case studies can *literally* look different to different researchers. For example, the texts, videos, audio clips, and even augmented realities displayed to one researcher can vary with the algorithmic and computational procedures researchers encounter as they make observations, record audio, take fieldnotes, and collect texts, images, and screenshots. These data appear different due to time, place, user, and other factors. Shifting realities are thus not a theoretical poststructuralist element; they are a practical consequence of the scale of digital phenomena interacting with the researcher(s) as they proceed with their investigations.

Let me offer a few emblematic observations I have from my research on social media. I have studied redditors, Amazon reviewers (people who write reviews), and aspirational influencers. The entities at the core of my case studies are typically the people, although some might describe them as "users." I collect data on these users over the course of time. I notice that their habits are different depending on the time of year. Users tend to have different habits around holidays, summertime versus wintertime, and day of the week. The reviewers post more often and with a more critical tone around and during holidays. Redditors have different tones when at work versus the weekends. YouTubers produce different types of content depending on the season. On the one hand, we might simply be describing how users change over time. But on the other hand, as entities, these changes constitute the multiple realities of the cases. By adopting entities that require agential cuts, we can bound users' embodied relationships with their respective online communities and with our own encounters of them, thereby accounting for change within the case study.

Digital entities

Using entities, rather than unit of analysis, is not simply a shift in language. The language shift undeniably prods us, as researchers, to think of cases as lived entities rather than finished units. Part of my motivation for shifting the language is to avoid the implications invoked by the figurative language of "unit of analysis." Even now, when I read or hear the phrase "unit of analysis," the image of a completed house or a block comes to my mind. Entity, alternatively, invokes something much more lived and living and connected with other entities. Entity along with agential cuts elicits living relationships in ways that "unit of analysis" does not, notably through an epistemic apparatus that approaches phenomena as emergent. An entity, within a case, is only ever partial. There are always-already more elements to account for and create. A consequence of this theoretical commitment is that entities contain other entities and are inherently relational. Case study research becomes an outgrowth of such relationality and researchers' attempts to produce a narrative about the research undertaken and ways in which they both present and do not present such information. The cases are consequently a direct result of the researchers' choices, an issue that I discuss at length in the next chapters.

Two final notes here about entities as centers of case study research. The first is that most readers may ask, "Isn't this entity approach applicable to all case study research and not just digital research?" My direct answer is yes. All phenomena are networked. The earth is an ecology, with relationships emerging in unexpected and unforeseen ways. Second, entities are, conceptually, especially useful for digital phenomena because such phenomena are networked at a higher intensity and broader scale. Let's use two examples. First, let's imagine a student in a classroom without any mobile devices. The classroom is certainly networked: students interact with students, teachers, and other living creatures, such as classroom pets and bugs that enter the space. Classrooms are typically nested with other classrooms in larger networks of activity. But once we add elements of mobile devices and electronic technologies that possess internet access, suddenly the scale of networking and its role in networked interactions become significantly more prominent. Second, a social media user engages with their respective platforms, e.g., Twitter, Facebook, and TikTok, at a more frequent pace than mass media. While it's true that listeners of radio and watchers of television are participating to some degree, these mediums do not hail us to participate. Listeners and watchers have no intentionally designed space for participation. On the other hand, social media interfaces and UX templates are overtly designed not only for users to participate but also to entice participation through habituation and attention (see Fogg, 2002). These interfaces use metrics and qualitative affordances, such as "likes," "upvotes," and other descriptions of user-to-user attention, to connect users to content and other users. These spaces are designed to be networked intentionally, often via algorithms and other computational means.

Conclusion: Sansdisciplinarity

My efforts in this chapter have conceived of digital case study research through the lens of *sansdisciplinarity*. *Sansdisciplinarity*, as I understand it, does not deny the existence of disciplines. Rather, *sansdisciplinarity* sees disciplinary knowledge as incomplete when used with respect to any digital—or non-digital—case study research. Case study research, in general, must do away with disciplinary boundaries and silos. As James Wertsch (2009) writes, "the way out of the quandaries associated with disciplinary fragmentation is a fundamentally different type of unit of analysis, one that cuts across, or, better yet, ignores existing disciplinary lines" (p. 121). Digital case study research does not fit into neat, coordinated boxes. This chapter has built on this argument by framing the term *digital* to describe our everyday experiences, actions, and activities. Digital, as a term, is useful precisely because it is ubiquitous.

To underscore *sansdisciplinarity*, it's useful to remember that disciplines are a relatively new endeavor. Disciplines arose in response to, centrally, the historical development of research universities that sought to coordinate, corral, and demarcate knowledge. Walls of disciplinary knowledge, though, are built with the *sansdisciplinary* mortar of problems. These walls serve to keep people inside as much as outside. They limit researchers' practices and, crucially, the very conception of a research problem or project—including my own. The shortcomings of these boundaries are rapidly becoming clear across academic and political life. Groundbreaking engineering work, for example, draws on mechanical engineering, material science, computer science, physics, chemical engineering, and other fields. It's useful here to quote again from Wertsch (2009):

> the key to such an explication is the use of the notion of mediated action as a unit of analysis and the person(s)-acting-with-mediational-means as the relevant description of the agent of this action. From this perspective, any tendency to focus exclusively on the action, the person(s), or the mediational means in isolation is misleading. Yet the tendency to isolate various dimensions of a phenomenon is precisely what is encouraged by the disciplinary fragmentation that characterizes so much of the contemporary scholarship in the social sciences and humanities.
>
> (p. 119)

My use of entity is an attempt to avoid the isolation of various dimensions mentioned above. In fact, the inordinate flexibility of case study research, with its insistence on multiple realities of a case, is what drove me to reconceptualize the traditional term "case" and "unit of analysis" and to receive them into an "entity" in the second half of this chapter. But to study a social media campaign, an influencer, a content moderation policy, artificial intelligence, a set of algorithms, or a platform—just to name a few—requires a panoply of knowledges, a variety of rich methods, and sound case design. It is to these issues, and design specifically, that I now turn.

Notes

1 "We suggest in our proposed definition of case study that it is a transparadigmatic heuristic that enables the circumscription of the unit of analysis. The circumscription of the unit of analysis is accomplished by (a) providing detailed descriptions obtained from immersion in the context of the case, (b) bounding the case temporally and spatially, and (c) frequent engagement between the case itself and the unit of analysis" (VanWynsberghe & Khan, 2016, p. 90). This definition is a fairly similar definition that seeks to avoid labeling the case study as a method, methodology, or research design. This book argues the case study can be a full fledged methodology.

2 Swanborn offers the following lengthy definition:
- a case study is "carried out within the boundaries of one social system (the case), or within the boundaries of a few social systems (the cases), such as people, organisations, groups, individuals, local communities or nation-states, in which the phenomenon to be studied enrols
- in the case's natural context
- by monitoring the phenomenon during a certain period or, alternatively, by collecting information afterwards with respect to the development of the phenomenon during a certain period
- in which the researcher focuses on process-tracing: the description and explanation of social processes that unfold between persons participating in the process, people with their values, expectations, opinions, perceptions, resources, controversies, decisions, mutual relations and behaviour, or the description and explanation of processes within and between social institutions
- where the researcher, guided by an initially broad research question, explores the data and only after some time formulates more precise research questions, keeping an open eye to unexpected aspects of the process by abstaining from pre-arranged procedures and operationalisations using several data sources, the main ones being (in this order) available documents, interviews with informants and (participatory) observation
- in which (optionally), in the final stage of an applied research case study project, the investigator invites the studied persons and stakeholders to a debate on their subjective perspectives, to confront them with preliminary research conclusions, in order not only to attain a more solid base for the final research report, but sometimes also to clear up misunderstandings, ameliorate internal social relations and 'point everyone in the same direction'" (p. 13).
3 The flaws in Yin's (2009) conceptualization of case study research include the following: (1) prioritization of current events over the past, (2) understanding context as a container, (3) seeing a case as a single data point, (4) *a priori* efforts to bound a case before study, (5) positivist claims about a case's validity, and (6) underestimating the importance of case study work in social science (Bartlett & Vavrus, 2017, pp. 29–32). Much of the tensions between Yin's (2009) perspectives and Bartlett and Vavrus's (2017) arguments are due to disciplinary differences: the former is a social scientist who excludes teaching cases from his scope of analysis (pp. 4–5) whereas the latter are educational researchers specializing in multilingual, migration-based literacy practices.
4 See Spinuzzi (2023).
5 Whitehead even recognizes this inequality by referencing degrees of separation (1979, p. 50).

References

Anderson, R. A., Crabtree, B. F., Steele, D. J., & McDaniel, R. R. (2005). Case study research: The view from complexity science. *Qualitative Health Research*, 15(5), 669–685. https://doi.org/10.1177/1049732305275208.

Barad, K. (2007). *Meeting the universe halfway: Quantum physics and the entanglement of matter and meaning* (2nd ed.). Duke University Press.

Bartlett, L., & Vavrus, F. (2017). *Rethinking case study research: A comparative approach*. Routledge.

Bassey, M. (1999). *Case study research in educational settings*. Open University Press.

Baxter, P., & Jack, S. (2008). Qualitative case study methodology: Study design and implementation for novice researchers. *The Qualitative Report*, 13(2), 544–559.

Bender, E. M., Gebru, T., McMillan-Major, A., & Shmitchell, S. (2020). On the dangers of stochastic parrots: Can language models be too big?*Proceedings of the ACM/IEEE Joint Conference on Digital Libraries* (Vol. 1). https://doi.org/10.1145/3442188.3445922.

Bennett, A., & Elman, C. (2007). Case study methods in the international relations subfield. *Comparative Political Studies*, 40(2), 170–195. https://doi.org/10.4135/9781446286425.

Blatter, J., & Haverland, M. (2012). *Designing case studies: Explanatory approaches in small-N research*. Palgrave Macmillan.

Bromley, D. B. (1986). *The case-study method in psychology and related disciplines*. John Wiley & Sons.

Burowoy, M. (2009). *The extended case method: Four countries, four decades, four great transformation, and one theoretical tradition*. University of California Press.

Chun, W. (2021). *Discriminating data: Correlation, neighborhoods, and the new politics of recognition*. MIT Press.

Crowe, S., Cresswell, K., Robertson, A., Huby, G., Avery, A., & Sheikh, A. (2011). The case study approach. *BMC Medical Research Methodology*, 11(100), 1–9. https://doi.org/10.1177/108056999305600409.

DeLanda, M. (2006). *A new philosophy of society: Assemblage theory and social complexity*. Continuum.

DeLanda, M. (2016). *Assemblage theory*. Edinburgh University Press.

Duff, P. (2008). *Case study research in applied linguistics*. Lawrence Erlbaum Associates.

Duffy, B. E. (2017). *(Not) getting paid to do what you love: Gender, social media, and aspirational work*. Yale University Press.

Dyson, A. H., & Genishi, C. (2005). *On the case: Approaches to language and literacy research*. Teachers College Press.

Eubanks, V. (2018). *Automating inequality: How high-tech tools profile, police, and punish the poor*. St. Martin's Press.

Flyvbjerg, B. (2006). Five misunderstandings about case-study research. *Qualitative Inquiry*, 12(2), 219–245. https://doi.org/10.1177/1077800405284363.

Fogg, B. J. (2002). *Persuasive technology: Using computers to change what we think and do*. Morgan Kaufmann. https://doi.org/10.1016/S0749-3797(99)00093-8.

Gallagher, J. R. (2019). A framework for internet case study methodology in writing studies. *Computers and Composition*, 54, 1–14. https://doi.org/10.1016/j.compcom.2019.102509

George, A., & Bennett, A. (2005). *Case studies and theory development in the social sciences*. MIT Press.

Gerring, J. (2004). What is a case study and what is it good for? *American Political Science Review*, 98(2), 341–354. https://doi.org/10.1017/S0003055404001182

Gerring, J. (2017). *Case study research: Principles and practices*. Cambridge University Press.

Gillespie, T. (2018). *Custodians of the internet: Platforms, content moderation, and the hidden decisions that shape social media*. Yale University Press.

Hamel, J., Dufour, S., & Fortin, D. (1993). *Case study methods*. Sage Publications.
Hamilton, L., & Corbett-Whittier, C. (2013). *Using case study in education research*. Sage Publications.
Jocher, K. (1928). The case method in social research. *Social Forces*, 7(2), 203–211. https://doi.org/10.2307/2570141.
Kenny, W. R., & Grotelueschen, A. D. (1984). Making the case for case study. *Journal of Curriculum Studies*, 16(1), 37–51. https://doi.org/10.1080/0022027840160106.
Lillis, T. (2008). Ethnography as method, methodology, and "deep theorizing": Closing the gap between text and context in academic writing research. *Written Communication*, 25(3), 353–388. https://doi.org/10.1177/0741088308319229.
Lipton, Z. C., & Steinhardt, J. (2019). Troubling trends in machine-learning scholarship. *Queue*, 17(1), 1–15. https://doi.org/10.1145/3317287.3328534.
MacKenzie, D. A. (1981). *Statistics in Britain, 1865–1930: The social construction of scientific knowledge*. Edinburgh University Press.
Maxwell, J. A. (2009). Designing a qualitative study. In L. Bickman & D. J. Rog (Eds.), *The SAGE handbook of applied social research methods* (pp. 214–253). Sage Publications.
Mejias, U. A. (2013). *Off the network: Disrupting the digital world*. University of Minnesota Press. https://doi.org/10.5860/CHOICE.51-4485.
Merriam, S. B. (1998). *Qualitative research and case study applications in education*. Jossey-Bass.
Miles, R. (2015). Complexity, representation and practice: Case study as method and methodology. *Issues in Educational Research*, 25(2), 309–319.
Morgan, M. S. (2012). Case studies: One observation or many? Justification or discovery? *Philosophy of Science*, 79(5), 667–677. https://doi.org/10.1086/667848.
Noble, S. U. (2018). *Algorithms of oppression: How search engines reinforce racism*. New York University Press.
O'Neil, C. (2016). *Weapons of math destruction: How big data increases inequality and threatens democracy*. Crown.
Orum, A. M., Feagin, J. R., & Sjoberg, G. (1991). Introduction: The nature of the case study. In *A case for the case study* (pp. 1–26). University of North Carolina Press.
Pasquale, F. (2015). *The black box society: The secret algorithms that control money and information*. Harvard University Press.
Peters, B. (2016). Digital. In B. Peters (Ed.), *Digital keywords* (pp. 93–108). Princeton University Press. https://doi.org/10.2307/j.ctvct0023.
Ragin, C. (1992). Introduction: Cases of "What is a case?" In *What Is a Case? Exploring the Foundations of Social Inquiry* (pp. 1–18). Cambridge University Press.
Riddick, S. A. (2019). Deliberative drifting: A rhetorical field method for audience studies on social media. *Computers and Composition*, 54, 1–27. https://doi.org/10.1016/j.compcom.2019.102520
Roberts, S. (2019). *Behind the screen: Content moderation in the shadows of social media*. Yale University Press.
Rose, T. (2016). *The end of average: How we succeed in a world that values sameness*. HarperOne.
Simons, H. (2012). Case study research in practice. In *Case study research in practice*. Sage Publications. https://doi.org/10.4135/9781446268322.n1.

Skinner, B. (1966). What is the experimental analysis of behavior? *Journal of the Experimental Analysis of Behavior*, 9(3), 213–218.

So, R. J. (2020). *Redlining culture: A data history of racial inequality and postwar fiction*. Columbia University Press.

Spinuzzi, C. (2023). What is a workplace? Principles for bounding case studies of genres, processes, objects, and organizations. *Written Communication*, 40(4), 1027–1069. https://doi.org/10.1177/07410883231185875.

Stake, R. E. (1995). *The art of case study research*. Sage Publications.

Starosielski, N. (2015). *The undersea network*. Duke University Press.

Stengers, I. (2014). *Thinking with Whitehead: A free and wild creation of concepts*. Harvard University Press.

Stoecker, R. (1991). Evaluating and rethinking the case study. *Sociological Review*, 39(1), 88–112. https://doi.org/10.1111/j.1467-954X.1991.tb02970.x.

Suzor, N. P. (2019). *Lawless: The secret rules that govern our digital lives*. Cambridge University Press.

Swanborn, P. (2010). *Case study research: What, why, and how?* Sage Publications. https://doi.org/10.1136/eb-2017-102845.

Takhteyev, Y. (2012). *Coding places: Software practice in a South American city*. MIT Press.

Tellis, W. (1997). Application of a case study methodology. *The Qualitative Report*, 3(3), 1–17.

VanWynsberghe, R., & Khan, S. (2016). Redefining case study. *Internatonal Journal of Qualitative Methods*, 6(2), 80–94. https://doi.org/10.4135/9781473915480.n9.

Wertsch, J. V. (2009). *Voices of the mind: Sociocultural approach to mediated action*. Harvard University Press.

Whitehead, A. N. (1979). *Process and reality (Gifford Lectures Delivered in the University of Edinburgh During the Session 1927–28)*. Free Press.

Wittgenstein, L. (1968). *Philosophical investigations*. Basil Blackwell.

Wynn, J. (2017). *Citizen science in the digital age*. The University of Alabama Press.

Yazan, B. (2015). Three approaches to case study methods in education: Yin, Merriam, and Stake. *The Qualitative Report*, 20(2), 134–152. https://doi.org/10.22347/2175-2753v8i22.1038.

Yin, R. K. (2009). *Case study research: Design and methods*. Sage Publications.

2 Iterative design and digital considerations

A scenario: a researcher aims to study an internet meme and its role in propaganda. The meme is the core of the case study, the entity under study. As the case is scaled up, and the propaganda spreads rapidly, the entity begins to change. The meme is no longer simply a humorous image. It's a set of images and relationships, sometimes not even identifiable as the original meme. Diligently, the researcher continues collecting data from multiple social networks, using manual and automated processes. They've received approval from their institutional review board (IRB) to interview people who share this meme because they need to address processes of replication, amplification, and circulation on social networks related to the meme.

But as the researcher continues working, a realization slowly occurs: the meme has an entire digital life that is not on social media. People are *emailing* the meme to one another and they're editing the image with each iterative exchange of email. The project remains digital but is no longer on social media. The researcher wonders if the study's design needs adjusting. The researcher gets tired, rubs their eyes, and decides to grab a cup of coffee at their local late-night diner. They arrive and quickly use the bathroom. On the bathroom walls is a graffiti picture of the original meme. Several drawings surround the meme. These drawings aren't really about the meme but they do argue about the political significance of the meme, along with a blend of off-color humor and offensive remarks. The researcher snags a cup of coffee. As the researcher is about to leave the diner, a customer walks in wearing the meme as a shirt. The researcher waits, curious. A few minutes later, three more individuals arrive, all wearing the same meme shirt.

The researcher stays and begins observing them. After several minutes, the researcher notices the individuals holding their phones up to the walls and ceilings. Working up courage, the researcher approaches them and asks them about the meme. They laugh and explain the meme is just a giant joke. They don't care about the propaganda. It's just a silly way to waste time. They recommend a mobile app for the researcher to download. The researcher downloads it. It's an augmented reality app. The researcher turns

DOI: 10.4324/9781003402169-3

38 Iterative design and digital considerations

it on and realizes the walls and ceiling are digitally spraypainted with versions of the meme. The researcher gives the group a card, hoping to interview them.

At home that night, the researcher realizes their study's design is too limited. The meme is too diffuse for social media networks. It's too alive. It has many afterlives. Consequently, the investigation needs a more fluid understanding of the research questions, data collection procedures, and the boundaries of the meme. Investigations of networked, connected phenomena demand a non-linear, recursive research design.

Designing a case study for problems such as the one above requires an emergent perspective. With entity as the guiding epicenter of a case study, an *emergent, iterative design* is necessary. This approach sees research questions as fluid and emergent, thereby extending pivotal case study research inquiry as question-driven (e.g., Bartlett & Vavrus, 2017; Burawoy, 1998; Dyson & Genishi, 2005; Gerring, 2017; Stake, 1995; Yin, 2009). Digital contexts challenge—but do not undermine—this question-driven design. Digital contexts change and mutate, not only due to the time-space compression (Harvey, 1989) of websites and social media wherein distribution costs are practically zero, but also due to researcher presence wherein participants change their behavior due to being observed ("Hawthorne effect") or in reaction to being asked questions about their activity (updating websites, etc.). Digital contexts operate, too, at rapid speeds and large scale. Due to the rate of change, speeds, and scales of digital contexts, question-driven research may need adjustments.

Research questions remain highly relevant and become an iterative recursive process. Because relationships, especially those in networked environments, can change rapidly, study design becomes *ongoing*. Agential cuts, discussed in the previous chapter, are possibly infinite; therefore, a case study design needs to emphasize boundaries for *when to stop*, including methods, domain knowledges, contexts, and questions. Thus, rather than establishing boundaries ahead of a research investigation, a case study with an entity at its epicenter represents the phenomena on its own terms with a stance of explicit openness of how, where, and when to study the entity.

I label this process *iterative bounding*. Via iterative bounding, researchers initially set temporal, spatial, and ethical boundaries around their case to write up the research but these boundaries are epistemological and practically flexible. The first half of this chapter consequently explores a more philosophical approach to boundary creation and iterative bounding. Here, I discuss boundary creation and the challenges of a "holistic approach." The second half of the chapter applies iterative bounding, and case study design more generally, to eight key terms related to digital phenomena: (1) users, (2) interfaces (3–4) website development and computer code, (5) software/applications, (6) databases, (7) computational models/algorithms and (8) infrastructure. These key terms could be considered principles of selection for digital case studies. For readers with less patience, the key design takeaway of this chapter is the following: there are no closed systems for case studies. They are emergent and must be negotiated as such.

Boundary creation and the challenges of holism

Where do boundaries come from? Research boundaries are not easy to identify and are not always self-evident, although boundaries are critical to the definition of a case. The truism of "it depends" is an *accurate* response to the question of when, how, and where to create the bounded system of a case study. Drawing the boundaries around the inquiry is up to the researcher, who is simultaneously guided by inquiry. While some view boundaries as selected *a priori* before empirical investigation (Gerring, 2017; Stake, 1995; Yin, 2009), other researchers define—non-linearly and recursively—the parameters and boundaries to account for context (Dyson & Genishi, 2005; Gallagher, 2019; Spinuzzi, 2023). This selection process is often qualitative, although some researchers insightfully argue the selection of the case can be quantitative and algorithmic (Elman et al., 2016). Ultimately, then, boundaries come from a researcher's decisions informed by the ongoing relationship the researcher has with the entity and its contexts, as well as *the application of the data to the case* (Foreman, 1948, p. 413). The researcher must therefore decide what aspects of the contexts to include and exclude (Gallagher, 2019; Spinuzzi, 2023). Ragin (1992) tacitly gets at this question by taking the stance that the case is not fixed due to the lived context surrounding a case (pp. 8–9). If we adopt the view of the case as an entity, then the boundaries probably should change or else researchers likely are not exploring holistically enough. As Piekkari, Welch, and Paavilainen (2009) assert, "Redirecting the case study may involve incorporation of additional theory and redefinitions of the unit of analysis, including its spatial and temporal boundaries" (p. 573).

Here is where the importance of "holistic" investigations cannot be stressed enough and the concept "holistic" must be interrogated, both practically and critically, to understand how boundaries are created when designing a study. A case study is not a study of a lifeworld, meaning it necessarily has limits. The goal of a case study is not to tell, for example, a person's entire life story or present a complete picture of an institution or organization from its origins to its demise. Rather, a case study is meant to be a holistic story about a segment—the bounded system.

This word *holistic* often appears in research on case studies, typically with competing meanings or shaded nuances of meaning (cf., Bassey, 1999; Crowe et al., 2011; Flyvbjerg, 2006; Simons, 2012; Stake, 1995; Swanborn, 2010; Thomas & Myers, 2015; Yin, 2009). An added layer of complexity is that these authors often attribute the use of *holistic* to previous researchers while accepting the term. This tacit approval of "holistic" tends to equate holistic with detailed, granular, or intense. Interpreting holistic in a positive sense is intuitive: every research investigation should ideally be holistic.

Bartlett and Vavrus (2017) have however critiqued this understanding of *holism* as viewing the divide between culture and the inquiry as too stark, one that takes a functionalist theoretical stance. I quote them at length to represent their argument accurately and transparently:

> We find this repeated reference to holism troubling. Holism is a concept linked to a traditional notion of culture and a functionalist theoretical stance. Classical ethnographies aimed to portray a whole way of life, which "implied a coherence of discrete cultures, a timeless 'ethnographic present'" (O'Reilly, 2009, p. 100). In its contemporary form, holism denotes a respect for context (and contextual validity). However, the claim to value holism is an effort to distinguish, but ultimately conflates, case and context (often defined as place), and it is premised upon a bounded view of culture. It also defines out of the realm of study far-flung factors and processes that may be immensely relevant for understanding how a *sense of boundedness* is socially and historically produced. The notion of holism used in interpretive case studies is limited to thick description, to a dedication to "the particular," and to a reduced notion of context that does not attend to how processes, politics, and ideoscapes—the ideologies and other political images that circulate globally (Appadurai, 1996)—at other scales impinge upon the case. Holism is surprisingly limited and rather blind to historical, social, and economic trends. Instead of this *a priori* bounding of the case to the "particular," we propose an iterative and contingent tracing of relevant factors, actors, and features.
>
> (p. 37)

Here, the authors argue that the idea of *holistic* positions the phenomena under study in a timeless present, metaphorically "freezing" the entity under study. Holistic, as a concept, concretizes the inquiry into fixed positions within the specific contexts of the case study. Holism tacitly endorses an ideological position of simultaneity. Cultural, socio-political, geographical, and historical forces unfurl within the case study in a flattened way: boundaries appear to be self-evident, naturally occurring, and/or deterministic.

Holism limits a unit of analysis to a person, place, organization, or thing and not a relationship. If a case study is a person, place, organization, or thing, the term *holistic* gives the misplaced impression that holistic is merely extended or thick description. Holistic becomes a placeholder for more description. Such description epistemologically halts the inquiry. Holism thus does not fully account for the change within a case study, instead framing the phenomena as something to be "filled in and filled out" rather than dynamic. The elements of a case are not additive but emergent, with many fits and starts, disappearances and reappearances.

To reconceptualize the "unit of analysis" into entity foregrounds change and that a case study itself contains a past, present, and future. As such, when I use the term holistic, I mean for it to denote the various processes emergent from entities and that entities themselves are holistic. This sense of holistic, while different from Bartlett and Vavrus's (2017) discussion of the term, reflects their efforts to unfix a case study. In fact, like this book, an important element in their project is to develop a more process-oriented approach to case study research. Both their project and mine take a process-oriented stance on case study research. Bartlett and Vavrus (2017) label their process approach the "comparative case study approach" (CCS):

> The CCS approach does not start with a bounded case. The effort to "bound" a case relies on a problematic notion of culture, place, and community; it also, quite inappropriately, defines out of the realm of study factors that may well be very relevant, such as historical circumstances that date back decades or more.
>
> (pp. 38–39)

They go on to write, "Instead of this *a priori* bounding of the case, the CCS approach features an iterative and contingent tracing of relevant factors, actors, and features" (p. 39). Here, they endorse bounding iteratively and recursively because the boundaries of both the unit and case are not clear from the outset of the investigation. Their stance anticipates a possible miscommunication about this iteration through the mention of "relevance" twice: bounding exists in relation to the entity (the unit in their case), maintaining an openness of what falls within the purview of the case study. The construction of those boundaries is transparent in that the researcher conducts tracing, meaning that the entity can be connected to contingent features.

Boundaries are messy things and need to be wrestled with, a crucial activity that reflects a multidimensional approach to holism. Researchers likely do not know what needs to fall into their purview at the onset of a research design. Bartlett and Vavrus, as an example, mention looking back decades or more, reaching back historically to understand social, political, geographical factors that shape the case study and the unit of analysis in non-linear recursive ways. Such a position is contra to Yin's (2009) claims that the boundaries are demarcated or delineated prior to investigation (*a priori* according to Bartlett and Vavrus). This view is significantly less normative and more haphazard than many textbooks on research wish to portray but it honestly reflects the *messiness* of research (Law, 2004; Pink et al., 2016; Sanscartier, 2020). Being transparent about our messiness should be an explicit goal: a research investigation is unlikely to be demarcated before the investigation is underway. Being open to the unexpected, analyzing it, and then incorporating that into the study design develops a more expansive and dynamic understanding of holism.

An example here helps to illustrate this dynamism. If researchers are attempting to understand the development of a software application (the entity), they might begin their investigation with the application's brainstorming session and end with its deployment to users. Of course, the story is much more complicated, and researchers can complicate to various degrees as warranted by their study and obligations to scholarly theory. They could iteratively tell the story of how users deployed the application, including how this reception reshaped the application's subsequent development stage. They might even tell the stories of the people on the development team, though it is not feasible to tell the team members' entire life stories. Parts of their stories could be—and probably should be—important, but that's not a chief goal. Case studies have boundaries and do end, if only because the researcher concludes the case study.

A researcher might begin this investigation by collecting various pieces of technical documentation of the application and interviewing team members extensively. We might initially think of the boundaries as the development team. Of course, the boundaries may rapidly expand to the executive and management teams. Further documentation may be needed, thereby necessitating visits to the company's archives. Here, researchers may discover seemingly innocuous records of the company that reshape the entire project. What was once a study of a software application shifts to, perhaps, a study of a software application's organization. When boundary creation is understood holistically in the study's design, it enables the entity under study to shift, contract, or expand to accommodate the entity or entities.

To recap, then, boundaries are created through the vibrant interplay between entity and researcher, non-linearly, recursively, and iteratively. Boundaries are not inherently obvious in a given study's design. Boundaries do not appear *ex nihilo* and do not remain static. Boundary creation should be given explicit attention in the study design and throughout the investigation (e.g., Gallagher, 2019; Spinuzzi, 2023). This decision is process-oriented and should be transparent and explicit. The process is aimed at creating a holistic entity, which means that the entity is never "finished." Contradictions and paradoxes are bound to emerge.

Practically, there are three consequences of this holistic approach, aside from detailed method sections. First, boundaries are better conceived as guideposts rather than walls. They assist researchers with determining what to include and exclude in a study. Boundaries are the infrastructure of the case and help to determine principles of selection. Second, researchers need to state their boundaries and the way those boundaries change even if it makes the findings less exciting or disrupts the story of the case study. This perspective provides a transparent commitment about the nature of such research: researchers *oversee* the investigation by conducting it. Researchers can be guided by entities and evidence but the researcher still formulates the research framework. It's ethically responsible to acknowledge this epistemological commitment. Third, researchers need to consider the pathways outside the boundaries they did not take and gesture to those pathways in "limits" or "further research" sections of their investigations (see more in Chapter 6).

Iterative bounding in a digital era

Developing boundary categories stretches across the design phase, including project preparation, posing research questions, and methods deployed. Kendall (2009), responding to Christine Hine's internet ethnographic critique (2009), provides three useful and practical starting points for boundaries: spatial, temporal, and relational. She writes:

> Spatial boundaries refer to questions of where, who, and what to study. Temporal boundaries refer to questions of time spent and the issues of beginning and ending research. Relational boundaries refer primarily to relationships between researchers and the people they study.
> (Kendall, 2009, p. 22)

All three boundaries will blur for digital case studies because digital investigations can compress spatial-temporal relationships (think of online comment threads that unfold over the course of several days but are displayed as a unified thread) as well as accelerate the speed of spatial-temporal boundaries (think of a participant's texts going viral and shared on thousands of different accounts and, possibly, websites).

To create boundaries then is not a rote deployment of spatial, temporal, or relational boundaries ("I am going to study this website for this amount of time with these participants in it") but rather a series of ongoing, interrelated decisions ("I will study this segment of this website or these participants in this particular way and keep reassessing my decisions as the research proceeds"). Reshaping boundaries augments the intense relationship between phenomena and context, which is a strength of the case study as a methodology: "The case method can facilitate shifting foreground and background multiple times during a research study" (Anderson et al., 2005, p. 679). Digital case study researchers can use the notion of boundaries to frame and construct research in a coherent and organized fashion. The very idea of boundaries assists to sort through the sheer amount of potential data available on the internet, from networked objects (the Internet of Things), and mobile devices.

Spatial boundaries

Digital spaces can be literal configurations and disembodied ones; they are both physical and conceptual. Space defines how researchers position themselves to their work through epistemology: "Spatial epistemologies... define a subject's relation to a world, the preconditions for being in that world, and the limits for movement and action within it" (Shepard, 2022, p. 9). On the internet, for instance, spaces involve nested interfaces, that is, sites within browsers within windows. But these internet spaces presuppose physical spaces, such as where users are sitting; for example, in a seat in a vehicle in a country. Spatial *digital* boundaries are thus necessarily multiple and intersecting in nature. Researchers producing case studies must initially identify and choose how they understand space and its relationships to their research questions, guiding goals and other boundaries (temporal and relational). In terms of iteration, they need to be open to that conception of space changing as the investigation unfolds. In a study of a social network, researchers for example might disregard the specific phone that users access the application with, but the phone may in fact become a central concern later in the study. Alternatively, researchers could assume that a physical space is central to the study only to learn that the physical space is less important than initially anticipated. Researchers might try to locate the case across digital spaces, e.g., websites or online group chats, if they are creating a case of a participant's activity. Locating the bounds of one's system spatially means to consider what is included in terms of spatial relations before, during, and after data gathering.

For digital case study research, then, creating honest and transparent articulations of how researchers bounded their entities offers an effective way to navigate multiple online realities, notably to develop self-reflexive awareness, particularly when examining the blurry and various roles that networked digital research entails. If creating a case study of a vlogger, for example, a researcher might choose to limit the scope of the case to the source of videos, such as YouTube or TikTok. On the other hand, if one is studying a user's social networking activity, the researcher might need to take on a different perspective on spatial boundaries, opting to account for the user's full range of social media activity, e.g., Twitter, Facebook, Reddit, Instagram, and Snapchat in addition to YouTube and TikTok. These choices are neither correct nor incorrect; rather, researchers need to have a trust-generating rationale for choices made.

In concrete terms, writing out spatial boundaries provides opportunities for a case study researcher—guided by tools, research questions, and goals—to make choices about how to collect data, to select which data are important, and where to collect data. Having been intentional about these decisions when planning a study, a researcher is then in a better position as the study proceeds to re-examine and, as seems relevant to the study goals, to revise them. In a networked video game, for example, researchers can choose to investigate, contact, and interview a participant (1) outside the game, (2) in the game but out of character, or (3) avatar-to-avatar. In these situations, the participant has remained the same and yet the point of contact is different. The space of the website is the same, but the perspective of the space changes as a researcher makes crucial choices. Consequently, spatial boundaries of a case help digital case study researchers consider situated *ethos* when they are planning, conducting, and reporting on the case study.

Temporal boundaries

Temporal bounding means bounding a case study in terms of time. In broad terms, this might mean choosing to study a case for an established time period, along with having a guiding goal for doing so. Temporal bounding is a process that occurs before an investigation, and, as noted, non-linearly and iteratively over the course of the investigation. As with spatial boundaries, temporal boundaries imply more than quantities, rote measurements, or periods of time. Decisions about temporal bounding are particularly important if a researcher aims to account for power relations in a case because such decisions account for and adjust to the changes in digital avenues of inquiry as well as changes that arise from what a researcher learns over the course of an investigation. Temporality can prompt researchers to consider and question how sites of research are constructed and change over time according to power relations, including asking the following questions:

- Who has the power in such spaces?
- What are these people within their subject positions trying to accomplish?
- How are these positions represented over time?

Temporal bounding emphasizes the social way networked phenomena change according to time, including devices, infrastructure, website "curators" (Kennedy, 2016), front-end managers, back-end developers, cultural expectations, and algorithms.

This last factor, algorithms, complicates our understandings of temporal boundaries for constructing case studies and, more generally, qualitative research. Algorithms are procedures for sorting information. In a literal sense, they often appear as equations. They are input/output solutions with terminating endpoints. They have come to prominence with the advent of massive scales of data due to the prevalence of networked,

46 *Iterative design and digital considerations*

internet-based search and social media use. While I write more on this in the second half of the chapter, the design of a case study should/could account for algorithms when constructing a case study in three ways.

First, researchers need to account for how algorithms categorize digital content in different ways from linear time and other traditional notions of time. Research designs need to determine, when possible, if algorithmically sorted content can affect the case study. For example, online commenting can shape how algorithms deliver content and, therefore, distribute networked content (see Powers, 2017). Second, researchers should investigate if participants see their digital writing and content as being shaped by algorithms. They need to determine if algorithms explicitly and/or implicitly shape a participant's recall of experiences and perceptions. Third, researchers need to explicitly observe the ways that their observations and other data collection methods are shaped over the course of time to determine if their own perceptions and methods are being shaped by algorithms and the way that algorithms display content. This last point necessitates multiple viewings, collections, fieldnotes, and analyses to determine, as best a researcher can, to what extent algorithms shape their efforts to bound a case study.

Relational boundaries

Relational digital boundaries identify relationships to the project under study, our investment in it, and the extent of our personal participation. To develop spatial and temporal boundaries means, additionally, to consider the relationships that enable (or not) those boundaries to be constructed. A relational boundary, therefore, determines who is included (the number of participants and who they are) as well as the rationale for why these people are included. Relational bounding is perhaps the most important boundary but may not be possible to develop initially. Relational bounding is likely a recursive affair that happens during *and* after the selection and construction of spatial and temporal boundaries. In fact, relational boundaries likely reshape and reformulate spatial and temporal boundaries. Researchers interested in relational boundaries could ask themselves the following questions about a digital entity:

- How are the people or users (perhaps even online bots) interacting on this website or across social media platforms?
- How are people interacting with a website's interface?
- In terms of researcher–participant relationships, researchers could ask: what is my relationship to the participants and spaces under study?
- How are these relationships shaping the case's temporal boundaries?

These questions for digital contexts demonstrate the intersecting nature of boundaries. For instance, where (the website) and who (the producers of the website) often slip into each other, presenting challenges and opportunities to spatial and temporal bounding for digital case study research. Because case studies focus so much on particularization, digital researchers must determine which subjects and objects of inquiry they are more interested in and be explicit about these choices.

Spheres of influence

While defining boundaries is useful, researchers make choices while guided by spheres of influence, including boundaries: analytical, ethical, personal, and practical (Kendall, 2009, p. 22). The first sphere of influence refers to theoretical and analytical decisions, the second to ethical decisions, and the third to "various aspects of the researcher's background that might influence the choice of project boundaries" (Kendall, 2009, p. 22). The last references pragmatic decisions made by a researcher; for instance, the equipment a researcher uses to conduct investigations is often based on their institutional circumstances. I have refashioned the relationship between the spheres of influence and boundaries considerations to show their interconnectedness (Figure 2.1). Before continuing, I want to note that while these 12 considerations are not mutually exclusive, it may be helpful to run through each consideration when designing studies. Writing these down in the design phase is a crucial step and may take the form of planning meetings and formal research notes.

Each circle represents the intersecting nature of each sphere of influence with the others. For instance, ethical influences are often practical ones when conducting IRB-approved research. This figure serves to demonstrate that each boundary needs to account for all four spheres of influence as a "mangle of practice" (Pickering, 1995). The non-linear recursive process of considering these spheres and boundaries assists

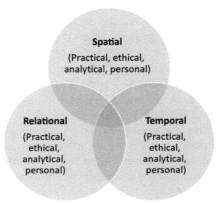

Figure 2.1 The interconnectedness of boundaries with spheres of influence

researchers with crafting a case. While we know case study research is a messy process, spheres of influence and boundaries provide coherent guidance for engaging that messiness to shape and craft case studies.

Boundaries and spheres of influence are ways to build case studies reflexively and iteratively. I prefer to think of them as iteratively connected methodological concerns. Researchers might begin with their analytical spheres of influence, considering the theories, literatures, and methodologies they bring to a case. This analytical concern possesses ethical considerations, both within the researcher's analytical sphere as well as practical and personal ethical concerns. Ethical concerns, as a sphere of influence, are thus deeply interwoven with the other spheres of influence. As an example, I have conducted case studies of digital writers who consider their audiences via online comments. My analytical framework is primarily based on participatory audience theory and digital writing. This framework shares a concern for the identities of the case study participant (the writer). However, this analytical framework does not have an extensive ethical conversation about publicly available online comments because, if comments are available on the internet without a required "log-in," they are allowed to be included in research publications without IRB approval. My personal ethical concerns—yet another way spheres of influence are related—extend to the identity of commenters that fall within my cases. With each case, I deliberate carefully about how and why I will reveal the identity of a commenter as well as ways to obfuscate commenters' identities if I believe they deserve privacy protection.

Within a case study, researchers might find significant relationships between various digital and non-digital spaces of their case, relationships that reflect the multiple realities of a case study. The internet has in many ways become part of our everyday lives. Networked technologies enable objects of inquiry to exist in online and offline capacities synchronously. A researcher creating a case study of a writer might need to consider the spatial boundaries in terms of what the writer publishes online as well as what the writer may publish in print. From this perspective, constructing digital case studies means to construct systematic boundaries without viewing digital boundaries as entirely discrete, separate, or special from offline boundaries. Alternatively, researchers may need to account for the multiple realities that a single text published in different venues would have upon temporal and relational boundaries. For instance, I have had writers publish the same text on a personal blog, a corporate website, and as a long Facebook post. How do these different venues change the case study's boundaries? To what extent might I need to change my temporal boundaries to better account for audience reaction and reception to that text? In terms of relational boundaries, should I observe the text and track the way different users take up the text?

Avoiding overstatement and overload of the digital case study

Because iterative bounding draws out the complexity of study design, researchers will likely encounter the practical concerns of overstatement and overload. Regarding overstatement, we want to make sure that our statements are effectively qualified. When we begin to bound digital case studies, questions and methods require qualifications for many reasons including algorithms making our perceptions partial and incomplete (due to black boxing), rapid updates to application's interface designs, location-based changes that occur with digital technologies, and hardware differences between researchers and their entities.

Overload, which can cause overstatement, is the idea of being overwhelmed by the sheer number of possible queries. I have found myself feeling overwhelmed by the number of possibilities that, for example, studying an online forum can pose: do I study the participants and the layout and observe *all* the interactions? How can I possibly stay up to date all on these interactions? Methodologically, overload is a coalescence of at least five networked factors that have emerged from the internet and digital technologies: speed, searchability, frequency, scale, and record-keeping. The internet has increased the intensity of these aspects of everyday life. Jim Ridolfo and Dànielle Nicole DeVoss (2009) have coined the term "rhetorical velocity" to capture better the speed, searchability, frequency, and scale of digital and internet technologies and affordances. As they write, rhetorical velocity is:

> a term that describes an understanding of how the speed at which information composed to be recomposed travels—that is, it refers to the understanding and rapidity at which information is crafted, delivered, distributed, recomposed, redelivered, redistributed, etc., across physical and virtual networks and spaces.
>
> (2009, n.p.)

Networked research speeds up and flattens some obstacles of previous instantiations of research, such as access to record-keeping, while making the sheer amount of data and information overwhelming. This condition is worsened for researchers who are forced to work individually due to institutional pressures of single-authored manuscripts.

Digital case study researchers need to take advantages of these positive qualities when defining the boundaries of case studies, while guarding against the negative aspects of overload. I have sketched out some of the qualities in the following schematic (Table 2.1). One of the main strengths that cuts across these five factors is that researchers might be able to see the boundedness of their systems more readily. Digital networks may help researchers become reflexive about the cases they construct, helping us to use boundaries iteratively throughout the research

Table 2.1 Methodological concepts of overload for case study research

Subcategory of digital overload	Positive qualities for case study research	Negative qualities for case study research
Speed	• Expedites the data collection process • Allows researchers to better see how the systems of cases interact	• Researchers may miss or overlook information, especially if algorithms control the output of data or information • Temporal boundaries may need to be adjusted to avoid overload
Searchability	• Researchers can search their data and for participants • Participants can find more out about the researcher (build trust) • Digital venues of study can be found readily	• Researchers and participants can become the target of harassment (especially at scale) • Privacy issues may arise due to the ability to search online • Spatial boundaries become problematized due to shared information or duplicate data and spaces
Frequency	• Triangulation is quicker • Repetition and replication are expedited	• Researchers may need to be observing or recording at all times of the day or any day of the week ("always on") • Participants may be overwhelmed and suddenly withdraw from a study
Scale	• Repetition and traceability are expedited • Larger systems and broader cases can be created • Longer term temporal boundaries are possible	• Larger systems require larger teams of researchers and content management • Data may not be standardized or, if standardized, researchers may resort to algorithmic classification (distant reading, thin description)
Record-keeping	• Easy access for creating in-depth case studies • Multiple spaces, in terms of boundaries, for cases are possible • Multiple websites provide data (if unstructured)	• Too much data may prohibit thorough analysis • Categorization can be difficult to create or sustain (on the part of researchers)

process. While vigilance against overstatement and overload is required for all case study research, it is not feasible or realistic to think of ourselves as assumption-free or blank vessels. Researchers, then, should see our experiences not "as a failing needing to be eliminated but as an essential element of understanding" (Yin, 2009, p. 45). All qualitative research, including case study research, relies on valuing the experiences of researchers. But experience and observations should not be taken at face value without hesitation or concern. In fact, there should be "a deliberate effort to disconfirm own interpretations," "assist readers to make their own interpretations," and "assist readers in recognition of subjectivity" (Yin, 2009, p. 48).

Digital considerations

In the second half of this chapter, I apply iterative bounding to eight typical elements for digital case study research: (1) users, (2) interfaces (3–4) websites development and computer code, (5) software/applications, (6) databases, (7) computational models/algorithms, and (8) infrastructure. These terms are possible entities, aspects of entities, and considerations when designing a case study for digital contexts.

Users

User is one of the most deployed terms when conducting digital research. Typically, when researchers adopt the term user, they often mean a manipulator of a particular software or hardware. At the core of the term, user is often a person or at least a persona. *User* can include, and often occludes, numerous roles that people engage or can potentially engage, including writer, speaker, image and video creator, manipulator of images/videos, software customer, and so forth. Typically, these roles are in conjunction with some sort of networked technology or online platform. When considered from an iterative bounding perspective, investigators need to identify the various relationships that become proxied for the term "user." Studying users, via interviews, questionnaires, and surveys, enables digital researchers to look at the *internal states* of users, which helps coordinate *external states*, or what appears on screens, in documents, and in observations.

User, as a term, is complicated by conjoining the term with multiple concepts, such as user experience, user interface, user generated, user generated content, user content, user display, user profile, and user centered. The conjoined terminology reminds researchers that their entities are never singular and always contingent upon socio-historic relationships by which machines, engineers, technological activities, and semiotics "configure" the user (Woolgar, 1990). Practically, hardware and software produce users in specific constellations of procedures. Hardware and software coerce people into specific ways of comporting themselves, going as far as interpellating the users. For example, operating systems provide specific "procedural rhetorics" (see Bogost, 2007) to influence users and establish frameworks for user behaviors to emerge. The behavior is therefore a synthesis of person, hardware, software, and other people involved in socio-historical schemas. This process is dialogic because users influence the way machines are written, expressly through testing and evaluation. Woolgar (1990) writes:

> [R]epresentations (descriptions, determinations of many kinds) of "what the machine is" take their sense from descriptions of "the machine's context"; at the same time, an understanding of "the context" derives from a sense of the machine in its context. The sense of context and machine mutually elaborate each other. For that aspect of context called the user, the reflexive tie is especially marked. The capacity and boundedness of the machine take their sense and meaning from the capacity and boundedness of the user.
>
> (p. 68)

The user, here, is mutually constitutive of the machine, for designers and programmers need to draw on a mental conception of the user as type of audience for their "text," i.e., a machine. Other people are involved in such processes: "Engineers, and other actors involved in the design process, configure the user and the context of use as an integrated part of the entire process of technological development" (Oudshoorn et al., 2004, p. 31).

In my experiences, defining, describing, and delineating how the *user* will be deployed in a study's design explicitly draws out tacit assumptions on the researcher(s) part. When researchers identify and name the activities of a user in the investigation, e.g., writing, speaking, meme creator, etc., this naming convention configures the activity collected and analyzed. For example, by studying a writer, researchers collect writing. By studying a content creator, researchers collect content. Practically, I have found the easiest way to begin here is to ask participants about how they understand their activities as users and to inquire, via survey, interview, or questionnaire, about the mediated activities they engage in digitally. Structurally and experientially, the most common sources of mediation in digital investigations are interfaces.

Interfaces

Users often interact, deploy, and manipulate interfaces in digital research. Interfaces are ongoing chains of semiotic relationships consistently remediated through and by one another (Galloway, 2012, pp. 30–48). They are not singular but ongoing processes. Digital research that involves interfaces, then, is more than screens but clearly involves screens of computers and mobile devices especially. Broadly, interfaces are *mediated moments of discontinuity* through which peoples, users, communities, and societies come into contact and interact. In addition to screens, interfaces are keyboards, writing objects, sitting in a chair, and so forth. Interfaces can be ways of navigation too: doors, locks, windows, vehicles, and so much more. From a less grand perspective, interfaces allow, encourage, and enable interactions to occur. They prestructure, prefigure, and delimit interaction.

In digital research, interfaces most often reference these moments of discontinuity that occur on screens and websites in terms of layout, designed specifically to be sleek, easy to use, and free from the design concept of friction—or *extreme usability* (Dilger, 2006).[1] The science behind friction comes from seeing computers as persuasive technologies, or what B. J. Fogg (2002) has labeled captology. Fogg's work is important both historically and conceptually, perhaps more due to the former. Fogg's work on how interfaces persuade users enticed graduate students at Stanford to work for Silicon Valley technology companies and apply Fogg's principles to social media. As a historical quirk, social media interfaces have a built-in legacy of captology-influenced ideology. As Steve Holmes (2017) writes of the social impact of Fogg's work:

> The idea of persuasive technologies has even generated derivative concepts such as "prescriptive persuasion" across computer science, mobile media, and game design journals. Fogg currently sponsors an international conference on persuasive technologies with published conference proceedings and offers annual designer boot camps. Notable boot camp attendees include founders of popular social media interfaces such as Instagram, LikeALittle, and Friend.ly.
>
> (p. 33)

Interfaces, on Fogg's terms, habituate users to their use and are designed to be easy to use not by happenstance but by a theoretically sophisticated model. Interfaces are not rote empty templates but rich semiotic procedural templates that can influence, mold, and model human behavior in subtle and implicit ways. For these reasons, identifying and describing interfaces, including their evolution inside and outside the investigation should, generally, be part of a digital case study.

Of note, interfaces on social media often come in the form of interactive templates, at least since the advent of Web 2.0, wherein the templates *train* and *habituate* people to learn procedures of the particular ideology of software or platforms (for more, see Gallagher, 2017, 2020). Effective interface design makes interfaces melt away, or the attempt to naturalize interfaces as something that users have always known and encountered. These habits are meant to be routinized and conventionalized:

> Search fields, menu options, and interface design more generally all instantiate habits of routinized, even compliant, use. They are the ground on which behavioral patterns form and give rise to unconscious expectations: we anticipate immediate and functional intelligibility (what does this word mean?) and are perplexed when thwarted.
>
> (Raley, 2016, p. 122)

The interface becomes all that users know or are meant to know. The iPhone's interface, as a canonical example, is meant to habituate users to its iconography, ensuring that users think of the device as the way that all other mobile phones are meant to function. Alternatively, designers can add friction to interfaces, such as Captcha tests or checkmarks for making sure the user is not a "robot." This effect, when used intentionally for the purposes of analysis, is known as denaturalization.

Denaturalizing interfaces, broadly, provides additional schematics for designing case study boundaries because interfaces typically form the underlying structures through which data collection will be done. Interfaces inherently shape spatial and temporal boundaries while shaping relational boundaries by affecting the researcher-to-participant relationship and the research-to-interface relationship. Because interfaces are the interstitial tissue of mediated and interactive networked activity, interfaces structure user-to-user relationships.

Documenting interfaces, including via screen captures, wireframing sketches, and real-time video, enhances case study design in four ways. First, documenting interfaces enables researchers to identify the various procedures that users experience when entering or exiting specific situations, websites, and contexts. Second, because updates are frequent to software, interfaces change rapidly, including the ways that interactions of phenomena occur. Such documentation provides evidence of how these interfaces function and evolve, allowing researchers to see, literally, ways spatial and temporal boundaries evolve. Third, real-time video provides researchers with evidence of user reactions and movement within interfaces early in the process of designing a study. These videos assist researchers with considering their relational boundaries as they iterate on case study design procedures. Fourth, this evidence, coupled with high-quality fieldnotes, prevents interfaces from being naturalized *to the researcher*. Over the course of investigations, researchers may naturalize interfaces wherein they look *through* them rather than *at* them. By having this evidence and our fieldnotes, we can remind ourselves of the initial research identity, a crucial identity to recall when we rethink our study's design during iterative bounding.

In terms of digital case study design, interfaces themselves could be case studies and foregrounded or be part of the case study wherein their emphasis is more backgrounded. Researchers might choose to do a study of TikTok's, Twitter's, or YouTube's interface. Other interfaces could include the underlying structures of websites such as WordPress, Wikipedia, or newspaper sites.

Websites and computer code

Case studies are often augmented and complemented by accounting for websites, HTML/CSS, and/or code, thereby increasing the depth of the study while providing additional sources of data. While these elements may be black boxed during investigatory procedures, researchers create a more holistic approach when they account for aspects. While it's true that users do not often have access to these elements, researchers need to get "under the hood" of those websites to understand how precisely they're functioning and integrate the HTML and other computational elements into their designs.

Practically, a gap exists between the typical user interface and the "under the hood" elements for which researchers need to account. A focus on HTML, JavaScript, and other markup language—as well as code—benefits digital case studies by providing non-user centric aspects of case studies and backstage processes that could tacitly alter users and interfaces. An excellent case study of a browser as case study is Black's (2015) analysis of Mozilla's open-source web-browser Firefox. Black examines 60 iterations of the code to understand changes over time. Part of Black's findings include analyzing the code using topic models to identify

> decisions made in response to the demands of their users, changing Internet standards, and other extra-technical influences on the development process… [T]opic modeling source code exposes software's relationship to its sociocultural context, removing it from the technoscientific narratives that sublimate process in favor of presenting only finished products and proven theories.
>
> (2015, n.p.)

Black goes on to provide granular details of the ways the public comments of the Mozilla corporation do not reflect the more subtle changes in the Mozilla Suite:

> there is a steady rise in JavaScript code beginning early in the Suite period that suddenly increases during the Firefox period at version 40, quickly reaching a point at which over 40% of the source code for the browser is no longer in C++. Mozilla's changing user interface, in other words, was preceded by a substantial material change to the relationship between the browser's user interface and core components. Without topic modeling the JavaScript code, the exact

nature of the relationship between the two sets of source code cannot be determined; however, this trend does help to highlight a narrative present in developer documentation that does not appear in Mozilla's public announcements, blogs, or other avenues used to advertise its software.

(2015, n.p.)

Black deploys a digital method (Latent Dirichlet Allocation or LDA) to identify how substantial changes to underlying HTML and JavaScript are likely driving changes to Firefox's graphical interface. Such an approach underscores the narrative disjunction between public documentation of Mozilla and the browser's technical documentation. Beyond a novel and groundbreaking digital methodology, Black's case study demonstrates that

> A commitment to openness and transparency does not necessarily produce an environment in which users are free to use software or data as they see fit... The textual history of Mozilla highlights the arbitrary nature of the linkages between the interface and the core components of a software system.
>
> (2015, n.p.)

In terms of digital design, a case study such as Black's demonstrates a longitudinal way to account for temporal boundaries, i.e., the 60 iterations of code on Mozilla's Firefox Suite. Case studies of users and interfaces benefit from extensive examination of underlying and black boxed process end procedures.

Software/applications

In the 1990s and 2000s, software was an enormously popular term. Since the 2010s, however, other terms have replaced software, including applications ("apps"), algorithms, and code. All of these terms are important to build into study designs but software and applications are important terminologically because they are the way users experience their devices. Very few people could directly interact with a device at the level of machine code, and therefore we need some sort of application or software. Even programmers generally need some sort of application to help them write their code. In this sense, programs are *packages of procedures* that inform users through interfaces of ways to interact and act with computers.

Building theories of procedures into digital case study design punctuates the inherent connectedness of users, interfaces, web development, and code with software. The most well-known theory for how procedures persuade is Ian Bogost's notion of procedural rhetoric (2007). Bogost writes,

> Procedural rhetoric is a general name for the practice of authoring arguments through processes… [Procedural rhetoric's] arguments are made not through the construction of words or images, but through the authorship of rules of behavior, the construction of dynamic models.
>
> (Bogost, 2007, p. 29)

Others have extended procedural rhetoric to relate structures to their intended interactions. Matheson (2014), for instance, writes that "procedural rhetoric is a theory of the interaction between particular acts of persuasion (contingency) and the conditions that make them possible (structure)" (p. 466). Software persuades users via sets of procedures and their logics. To identify those processes, then, researchers must identify the ways procedures align with behavior, shape decorum and behavior, and influence habits that emerge from the procedures. Histories and ideologies of the software could be investigated to reveal the implicit habits they engender, thereby requiring a lengthy temporal bounding. For example, Facebook was a mashup of college campus face booklets and online rating sites, designed to showcase and rank college women. This misogyny was baked into the website's approach, and analysis of Facebook should consider this historical, ideological element.

Writing software, such as Microsoft Word, Google docs, LaTeX, and Overleaf demonstrate written procedural habits. Each software application teaches users to be document producers through an ideology of white-collar office work. These applications provide users with sets of managerial iconography: ribbons, menu bars, drop-drop item lists, and other interfaces. They make writing documents rapid, easy-to-format, and reformattable. Microsoft Word is part of the company's Office Suite designed for office workers who are generally knowledge workers. As a result, the user and the interface draw on language associated with those professions: folders, files, documents, and so forth. There could be alternative language for these objects, such as container or craft, but the labels ideologically prefigure and configure users to comport themselves in specific ways designed for functioning in a capitalist office. By accounting for the procedures and logics of software, digital case study researchers can better formulate research questions and reflect on the validity of their designs. I have found for research questions that identifying, anticipating, and describing procedures of the software *before* formulating questions will prevent too many false starts or endless iteration.

Databases

Databases, as possible objects of study and/or elements in a case study, are the repositories of data, both physical and digital. Databases are value-laden elements, too, and are more than vessels or sites of storage. As Thomer and Wickett note (2020), databases are often discussed as though their meaning is clear even though the literature on the issue offers differing perspectives, notably between systems engineers and end-users (p. 1). Through a relational approach to databases, they write, "Although computer scientists typically define databases in terms of the information models supporting the system (e.g., Edgar "Ted" Codd's relational model, or the graph databases of Neo4j or NoSQL systems), users tend to more generously define "database" as any sort of system of data in a computer that is organized for storage and retrieval (p. 1). Databases store information alongside the *internal models* of storage, such as logics and technical operations of structured query language. For users, databases invoke the information itself *and* the political implications of such storage. The database may function as a site of cultural and social operations, making it vital to explicitly observe and document (see Hine, 2005). For case study researchers, then, I discuss two important aspects of databases: (1) physical repositories, and (2) socio-political management systems.

Databases are physical, as is the case with libraries and server farms, to the point of having environmental effects. Google searches use electricity. Massive Facebook/Meta server farms use precious water in New Mexico (Edwards, 2020). Digital technologies, too, use batteries that require oceans of lithium from polluting mines, demonstrating that databases are non-neutral repositories of data.

In addition to physical repositories, databases must be understood as socio-political management systems that transform data when stored. The repository is not a neutral container of information. They contain realities but also produce and inscribe realties through organization, management, and structure. While databases could be described as coordinating the *flow* or *journey* of information (Bates et al., 2016, p. 4), they structure information, thereby exerting control over information. Three examples are illustrative. First, we might think of the way that CSV files coerce textual data in vectors (Dourish, 2017, pp. 87–110). Alternatively, structured query language (SQL) operates through Boolean logics, notably trinary logical categories of true, false, and other (Jagadish et al., 2007). Third, databases have a three-part schema architecture, i.e., the internal schema (storage models), the conceptual schema (the structure of the database and its relationship to users), and the external schema (high-level representations to users themselves) (Elmasri & Navathe, 2011, p. 33). In all three examples, databases transform data in specific, operable ways that come infused with values. Metaphorically, databases ferment stored information, meaning in their very storage they change something about the information stored.

Because case studies will contain different types of data that are often compared within a database, the database(s) subsequently must be considered in the design phase of case study research as objects of inquiry *and* for their role in the collection process (see Chapter 3). Good case study researchers, then, anticipate the kind of database choices they will make as well as adjusting to emergent changes as the case develops.

Computational models/algorithms

Users are connected to databases and other digital elements through algorithms and computational models. Computational modeling and algorithms have entered the public imaginary and lexicon to the point that we now have cottage industries around "algorithm studies" in scholarly venues. Algorithms garner wide cultural impact for many reasons, including their pervasive use on social media platforms, their ability to black box complex processes, and for the ways that people can use the language without technical knowledge. The ways users without technical knowledge understand algorithms have become entire areas of study, including knowledge (Cotter & Reisdorf, 2020), gossip (Bishop, 2019, 2020), folklore (e.g., DeVito et al., 2018; Eslami et al., 2015, 2016, 2017; Karizat et al., 2021; Ziewitz, 2015), timing (Gallagher, 2020), and power (Bucher, 2012, 2018). Alongside understandings of users, ethical commentary about the use of algorithms has been offered by cultural critics (Eubanks, 2018; Noble, 2018; O'Neil, 2016; Pasquale, 2015).

Case study researchers need to account for algorithms and computational models in two ways related to study design. First, designing studies that explicitly account for algorithmic and computational processes as inquiry. Nearly all digital research encounters these processes too: whether on social media platforms or in software packages. Making these black boxes more transparent, if possible, delineates what falls into, or is excluded from, the study design. Gradual and sudden changes in algorithms can dramatically reshape a project's scope, as it will rearrange relationships between digital elements. Second, algorithms and computational models automate collection procedures and influence the scale of data that falls within or outside a case study.

Infrastructure

Infrastructures refer to the material-cultural structures that comprise networked technologies. Hardware, wireless stations, wires, pipes, and buildings are infrastructures. Electricity, too, is part of infrastructures. In terms of digital case study research, users, interfaces, software/applications, databases, and computational models/algorithms are nestled inside and alongside infrastructures, leading researchers to account for the material-cultural ways that technologies shape their entities under study. For example, charging our mobile devices is such an important activity that researchers have found that phone users report anxiety when their devices are low on battery (Tang et al., 2020). Infrastructures are often obfuscated through metaphors that make them seem disembodied. For example, "the cloud" refers to the machinery of data centers, thereby obscuring the material, environmental, and socio-political implications of infrastructure.

Under the category of infrastructures falls a remarkably heterogeneous range of objects and activities that shape culture too. Most relevant is the concept of a platform, which could be understood as infrastructure. For digital case study researchers, it's extraordinarily difficult to do a case study of a platform because they are simply too large for an empirical study. Rather, platforms will often function as the undergirding infrastructure of a case study.

Platforms are weaved into case studies, shaping descriptions in often occluded ways. Nieborg and Poell (2018) argue that platforms condense a range of complex activities, including: the multisided market (first and third parties) and grappling with the network effects of interacting and often competing agents; commodification of digital labor and the way it concentrates corporate power; and computational infrastructures. Because platforms penetrate economic, governmental, and infrastructural sectors, they shape digital culture industries (Nielsen & Ganter, 2022). Any digital case study is touched by them.

That said, infrastructures are intertwined recursively inside the other digital concepts presented in this chapter. Benjamin Bratton, in the opus *The Stack: On software and sovereignty* (2016), has gestured toward the complexity of such relations. Bratton conceives of "The Stack" as an "emergent mega-infrastructure" (p. 94) composed of six parts: User, Interface, Address, City, Cloud, and Earth (p. 11).[2] The Stack is an amalgamation of socio-techno-political forces literally forming a stack of layered infrastructures that are the "hungriest thing in the world" and, consequently, "The Stack not only consumes energy; it also mediates it and rationalizes its metabolic distribution" (p. 94). Bratton here is not using metabolism as a metaphor: technology is literally developing a life-sustaining metabolism.

There are four practical takeaways in Bratton's conception of infrastructures for digital case study design. First, infrastructures could very well be entities for inclusion as a digital case study and certainly part of the case study. "The Stack" makes manifest the web of relations that arise with a case study of infrastructure. Second, users typically make use of infrastructures; therefore users' relationships with, and in, infrastructures are crucial components of case studies of users. Third, determining how infrastructures circumscribe a case study design hones researchers' meta-cognition for the types of research questions they can pose. The very tools we have at our disposal afford us the ability to pose certain questions. "The Stack" as a mega-infrastructure influences what types of material-cultural elements inform our question-making and question-posing activities. Fourth, "The Stack" allows infrastructures some sense of non-human agency. This agency, for digital case study researchers engaged in designing a study, means that multiple data collection methods are likely needed. The various parts of infrastructures (devices, buildings, networks of wires) should be examined *before-during-after* collection has begun. While researchers may determine these infrastructural elements to be outside the scope of their inquiries, that determination is made alongside and iteratively during the design phase. But at some point, iteration must stop. How do we know when to stop? We can't build that answer into our designs. Rather, it relies on data collection and analyses, the next two chapters in this book.

Notes

1 For more about this type of transparent design, see Black (2022). Black argues that users are provided with designs that are *meant* to be easy to use, undergirding an ideology of acceptance on behalf of the designers.
2 Bratton's six-part model is extraordinarily complex. But in short, he summarizes the six parts by writing: "Each layer is understood as a unique technology capable of generating its own kinds of integral accidents, which, perhaps counterintuitively, may ultimately bind that larger architecture into a more stable order. These layers are not just computational. As much as it is made from computational forms (multiplexed fiber-optic cables, data centers, databases, systems standards and protocols, urban-scale networks, embedded systems, universal addressing tables), The Stack is also composed of social, human, and concrete forces (energy sources, gestures, effects, self-interested maneuvers, dashboards, cities and streets, rooms and buildings, physical and virtual envelopes, empathies and enemies). These hard and soft systems intermingle and swap roles, some becoming relatively 'harder' or 'softer' according to seemingly arcane conditions" (p. 11).

References

Anderson, R. A., Crabtree, B. F., Steele, D. J., & McDaniel, R. R. (2005). Case study research: The view from complexity science. *Qualitative Health Research*, 15(5), 669–685. https://doi.org/10.1177/1049732305275208.

Bartlett, L., & Vavrus, F. (2017). *Rethinking case study research: A comparative approach*. Routledge.

Bassey, M. (1999). *Case study research in educational settings*. Open University Press.

Bates, J., Lin, Y.-W., & Goodale, P. (2016). Data journeys: Capturing the sociomaterial constitution of data objects and flows. *Big Data & Society*, 3(2), 205395171665450. https://doi.org/10.1177/2053951716654502.

Bishop, S. (2019). Managing visibility on YouTube through algorithmic gossip. *New Media and Society*, 21(11–12), 2589–2606. https://doi.org/10.1177/1461444819854731

Bishop, S. (2020). Algorithmic experts: Selling algorithmic lore on YouTube. *Social Media and Society*, 6(1), 1–11. https://doi.org/10.1177/2056305119897323

Black, M. L. (2015). A textual history of Mozilla: Using topic modeling to trace sociocultural influences on software development. *Digital Humanities Quarterly*, 9(3). https://digitalhumanities.org/dhq/vol/9/3/000224/000224.html.

Black, M. L. (2022). *Transparent designs: Personal computing and the politics of user-friendliness*. Johns Hopkins University Press.

Bogost, I. (2007). *Persuasive games: The expressive power of videogames*. MIT Press.

Bratton, B. H. (2016). *The stack: On software and sovereignty*. MIT Press. https://doi.org/10.3917/cca.121.0045.

Bucher, T. (2012). Want to be on the top? Algorithmic power and the threat of invisibility on Facebook. *New Media and Society*, 14(7), 1164–1180. https://doi.org/10.1177/1461444812440159.

Bucher, T. (2018). *If... then: Algorithmic power and politics*. Oxford University Press.

Burawoy, M. (1998). The extended case method. *Sociological Theory*, 16(1), 4–33. https://doi.org/10.1111/0735-2751.00040.

Cotter, K., & Reisdorf, B. C. (2020). Algorithmic knowledge gaps: A new dimension of (digital) inequality. *International Journal of Communication*, 14(January), 745–765.

Crowe, S., Cresswell, K., Robertson, A., Huby, G., Avery, A., & Sheikh, A. (2011). The case study approach. *BMC Medical Research Methodology*, 11(100), 1–9. https://doi.org/10.1177/108056999305600409.

DeVito, M. A., Birnholtz, J., Hancock, J. T., French, M., & Liu, S. (2018). How people form folk theories of social media feeds and what it means for how we study self-presentation. *Proceedings of the 2018 CHI conference on human factors in computing systems*, 1–12. doi:10.1145/3173574.3173694.

Dilger, B. (2006). Extreme usability and technical communication. In *Critical power tools: Technical communication and cultural studies*. State University of New York Press.

Dourish, P. (2017). Spreadsheets and spreadsheet events in organizational life. In *The stuff of bits*. The MIT Press. https://doi.org/10.7551/mitpress/10999.003.0005.

Dyson, A. H., & Genishi, C. (2005). *On the case: Approaches to language and literacy research*. Teachers College Press.

Edwards, D. W. (2020). Digital rhetoric on a damaged planet: Storying digital damage as inventive response to the anthropocene. *Rhetoric Review*, 39(1), 59–72. https://doi.org/10.1080/07350198.2019.1690372.

Elman, C., Gerring, J., & Mahoney, J. (2016). Case study research: Putting the quant into the qual. *Sociological Methods & Research*, 45(3), 375–391. https://doi.org/10.1177/0049124116644273.

Elmasri, R., & Navathe, S. (2011). *Fundamentals of database systems* (6th ed.). Addison-Wesley.

Eslami, M., Karahalios, K., Sandvig, C., Vaccaro, K., Rickman, A., Hamilton, K., & Kirlik, A. (2016). First I "like" it, then I hide it: Folk theories of social feeds. *Conference on Human Factors in Computing Systems—Proceedings*, 2371–2382. https://doi.org/10.1145/2858036.2858494.

Eslami, M., Rickman, A., Vaccaro, K., Aleyasen, A., Vuong, A., Karahalios, K., Hamilton, K., & Sandvig, C. (2015). "I always assumed that I wasn't really that close to [her]": Reasoning about invisible algorithms in the news feed. *Proceedings of the 33rd Annual ACM Conference on Human Factors in Computing Systems—CHI '15*, 153–162. https://doi.org/10.1145/2702123.2702556.

Eslami, M., Vaccaro, K., Karahalios, K., & Hamilton, K. (2017). "Be careful; things can be worse than they appear": Understanding biased algorithms and users' behavior around them in rating platforms. *Proceedings of the international AAAI conference on web and social media 11*, 62–71. doi:10.1609/icwsm.v11i1.14898.

Eubanks, V. (2018). *Automating inequality: How high-tech tools profile, police, and punish the poor*. St. Martin's Press.
Flyvbjerg, B. (2006). Five misunderstandings about case-study research. *Qualitative Inquiry*, 12(2), 219–245. https://doi.org/10.1177/1077800405284363.
Fogg, B. J. (2002). *Persuasive technology: Using computers to change what we think and do*. Morgan Kaufmann. https://doi.org/10.1016/S0749-3797(99)00093-8.
Foreman, P. B. (1948). The theory of case studies. *Social Forces*, 26(4), 408–419.
Gallagher, J. R. (2017). Writing for algorithmic audiences. *Computers and Composition*, 45, 25–35. https://doi.org/10.1016/j.compcom.2017.06.002.
Gallagher, J. R. (2019). A framework for internet case study methodology in writing studies. *Computers and Composition*, 54, 1–14. https://doi.org/10.1016/j.compcom.2019.102509.
Gallagher, J. R. (2020). *Update culture and the afterlife of digital writing*. Utah State University Press.
Galloway, A. R. (2012). *The interface effect*. Polity Press.
Gerring, J. (2017). *Case study research: Principles and practices*. Cambridge University Press.
Harvey, D. (1989). *The condition of postmodernity: An enquiry into the origins of cultural change*. Blackwell Publishing.
Hine, C. (2005). *Virtual methods: Issues in social research on the internet*. www.loc.gov/catdir/toc/ecip056/2005001815.html\nwww.loc.gov/catdir/enhancements/fy0621/2005001815-b.html\nwww.loc.gov/catdir/enhancements/fy0621/2005001815-d.html.
Hine, C. (2009). How can qualitative internet researchers define the boundaries of their projects. In A. N. Markham & N. K. Baym (Eds.), *Internet inquiry: Conversations about method* (pp. 1–20). Sage Publications.
Holmes, S. (2017). *The rhetoric of videogames as embodied practice: Procedural habits*. Routledge.
Jagadish, H. V., Chapman, A., Elkiss, A., Jayapandian, M., Li, Y., Nandi, A., & Yu, C. (2007). Making database systems usable. *Proceedings of the 2007 ACM SIGMOD International Conference on Management of Data—SIGMOD '07*, 13. https://doi.org/10.1145/1247480.1247483.
Karizat, N., Delmonaco, D., Eslami, M., & Andalibi, N. (2021). Algorithmic folk theories and identity: How TikTok users co-produce knowledge of identity and engage in algorithmic resistance. *Proceedings of the ACM on Human-Computer Interaction, 5(CSCW2)*, 1–44. https://doi.org/10.1145/3476046.
Kendall, L. (2009). A response to Christine Hine's "defining project boundaries". In A. N. Markham & N. Baym (Eds.), *Internet inquiry: Conversations about method* (pp. 21–25). Sage Publications.
Kennedy, K. (2016). Textual curation. *Computers and Composition*, 40, 175–189. https://doi.org/10.1016/j.compcom.2016.03.005.
Law, J. (2004). *After method: Mess in social science research*. Routledge.
Matheson, C. (2014). Procedural rhetoric beyond persuasion: First strike and the compulsion to repeat. *Games and Culture*, 10(5), 1–18. https://doi.org/10.1177/1555412014565642.
Nieborg, D. B., & Poell, T. (2018). The platformization of cultural production: Theorizing the contingent cultural commodity. *New Media and Society*, 20(11), 4275–4292. https://doi.org/10.1177/1461444818769694.

Nielsen, R. K., & Ganter, S. A. (2022). *The power of platforms: Shaping media and society*. Oxford University Press.

Noble, S. U. (2018). *Algorithms of oppression: How search engines reinforce racism*. New York University Press.

O'Neil, C. (2016). *Weapons of math destruction: How big data increases inequality and threatens democracy*. Crown.

Oudshoorn, N., Rommes, E., & Stienstra, M. (2004). Configuring the user as everybody: Gender and design cultures in information and communication technologies. *Science Technology and Human Values*, 29(1), 30–63. https://doi.org/10.1177/0162243903259190.

Pasquale, F. (2015). *The black box society: The secret algorithms that control money and information*. Harvard University Press.

Pickering, A. (1995). *The mangle of practice: Time, agency, and science*. University of Chicago Press.

Piekkari, R., Welch, C., & Paavilainen, E. (2009). The case study as disciplinary convention. *Organizational Research Methods*, 12(5), 567–589.

Pink, S., Horst, H. A., Postill, J., Hjorth, L., Lewis, T., & Tacchi, J. (Eds.). (2016). *Digital ethnography: Principles and practice*. Sage Publications.

Powers, D. (2017). First! Cultural circulation in the age of recursivity. *New Media & Society*, 19(2), 165–180. https://doi.org/10.1177/1461444815600280

Ragin, C. (1992). Introduction: Cases of "what is a case?" In *What is a case? Exploring the foundations of social inquiry* (pp. 1–18). Cambridge University Press.

Raley, R. (2016). Algorithmic translations. *CR: The New Centennial Review*, 16(1), 115–138.

Ridolfo, J., & DeVoss, D. N. (2009). Composing for recomposition: Rhetorical velocity and delivery. *Kairos: A Journal of Rhetoric, Technology, and Pedagogy*, 13(2).

Sanscartier, M. D. (2020). The craft attitude: Navigating mess in mixed methods research. *Journal of Mixed Methods Research*, 14(1), 47–62. https://doi.org/10.1177/1558689818816248.

Shepard, M. (2022). *There are no facts: Attentive algorithms, extractive data practices, and the quantification of everyday life*. MIT Press.

Simons, H. (2012). Case study research in practice. In *Case Study Research in Practice*. Sage Publications. https://doi.org/10.4135/9781446268322.n1.

Spinuzzi, C. (2023). What is a workplace? Principles for bounding case studies of genres, processes, objects, and organizations. *Written Communication*, 40(4), 1027–1069. https://doi.org/10.1177/07410883231185875.

Stake, R. E. (1995). *The art of case study research*. Sage Publications.

Swanborn, P. (2010). *Case study research: What, why, and how?* Sage Publications. https://doi.org/10.1136/eb-2017-102845.

Tang, G., Wu, K., Wu, Y., Liao, H., Guo, D., & Wang, Y. (2020). Quantifying low-battery anxiety of mobile users and its impacts on video watching behavior. *ArXiv*. http://arxiv.org/abs/2004.07662.

Thomas, G., & Myers, K. (2015). *The anatomy of the case study*. Sage Publications. https://doi.org/10.1093/acprof:oso/9780199230136.003.0002.

Thomer, A. K., & Wickett, K. M. (2020). Relational data paradigms: What do we learn by taking the materiality of databases seriously? *Big Data and Society*, 7(1). https://doi.org/10.1177/2053951720934838.

Woolgar, S. (1990). Configuring the user: The case of usability trials. *The Sociological Review*, 38(2), 58–99. https://doi.org/10.1111/j.1467-954x.1990.tb03349.x.

Yin, R. K. (2009). *Case study research: Design and methods*. Sage Publications.

Ziewitz, M. (2015). Governing algorithms: Myth, mess, and methods. *Science, Technology, & Human Values*, 41(1), 3–16. https://doi.org/10.1177/0162243915608948.

3 Collection practices for digital case studies

This chapter is broken into two distinct sections on data collection, theoretical issues and practical methods respectively. Part I discusses breaking down the binary between digital and "real-world" contexts and then argues for a conceptual approach to data collection based on a Wittgensteinian notion of family resemblance. Part II of this chapter discusses the granular, practical details of digital collection practices and procedures. Here I examine observations, fieldnotes, interviews, and document collection via qualitative and web scraping methods. I conclude with brief remarks about when to stop collecting data and *post hoc* collection.

Part I: Theoretical stances

Digital case study collection practices require a flexible stance toward data that updates, but does not discard, existing theory regarding traditional case study research. Yin's (2009) approach to case study data collection, with five different editions and multiple book-length spin-offs, established specific conditions for case research that have been largely cited and followed without retheorizing for our networked, digital world that blurs boundaries. The most pressing consequence is Yin's construal of case studies as events within *real-life context* where "the boundaries between phenomenon and context are not clearly evident" (2009, p. 18). Yin (2009) elaborates on the implications for data collection practices:

> You will be collecting data from people and institutions in their everyday situations, not within the controlled confines of a laboratory, the sanctity of a library, or the structured limitations of a survey questionnaire. In a case study, you must therefore learn to integrate real-world events with the needs of the data collection plan.
>
> (p. 83)

Yin goes on to describe the wide range of qualitative activities with real-world research, including being available for interviews, being equipped

DOI: 10.4324/9781003402169-4

for a wide array of field experiences, and anticipating unexpected events (p. 85). The real-world assertion is so wide-ranging that case study researchers sometimes begin their books with Yin's passage above (Duff, 2008, p. 22; Woodside, 2010, p. 2). Other researchers have picked up on the idea of the "real worldness" of case study research but without citing Yin (Dyson & Genishi, 2005, p. 18).

This passage is notable for its widely applicable practicality but occluded philosophical positivist underpinnings. The idea of real-life context is attractive for researchers who want to study uncontrolled data. But, as Michael Bassey (1999) notes in the following passage:

> The interpretive researcher cannot accept the idea of there being a reality "out there" which exists irrespective of people, for reality is seen as a construct of the human mind. People perceive and so construe the world in ways which are often *similar* but not necessarily the *same*. So there can be different understandings of what is real. Concepts of reality can vary from one person to another.
> (p. 43)

Above is an explicit criticism of the positivism of *real-world* thinking and, in my view, an implicit criticism of Yin's position. To be fair to Yin, he is attempting to separate case study research from laboratory contexts of controlled procedures. In setting up "real-world" contexts, Yin inadvertently misses a broader point: there are multiple ways of constructing reality. This point is even more important with respect to emergent technologies that blur boundaries between electronic mediated realities and corporeal, flesh-based realities. Our use of networked devices already blurs this boundary to a great extent. In fact, this was a hotly discussed topic in the 1990s and early 2000s (see Bolter & Grusin, 2000, pp. 230–265) and will be reignited in the 2020s and beyond as artificial intelligence, big data, augmented reality, virtual reality, mixed reality, and wearable technologies become firmly integrated into society. Real-world contexts, as conceptual scaffolding for case studies, are too binary and risk leaving out rich detailed data. Yin's own concept might leave out laboratory work as real world, which we know is itself contested and Janus-facing (Latour & Woolgar, 1986).

Entity, the schema introduced in the previous chapters, describes the multiple realities of a digital case: "real world" becomes real world*s*. Multiple data sources are necessary and require tracing the processes of data. These tracings move between online and offline contexts as well as mediated and face-to-face situations. The data collection phase of digital entities could be understood as *the creation of entities*.

Framing data collection as creating entities—rather than discovering or uncovering them—provides digital researchers with five benefits. First, it decenters any specific source of data. Multiple data sources are given priority. Second, data is not "out there" to be discovered, but rather is co-constructed with participants, researcher(s), and other elements. Data is not something to be extracted from participants. Third, it acknowledges that there are multiple realities, and that *the researcher is not privy to all of them*. Fourth, it allows for a more reflexive stance toward data. The researcher is more likely to question their own assumptions and biases. One important implication of this shift is that digital case study researchers must develop content management techniques for being reflexive in their data collection practices, especially regarding their sources of data. Researchers need to self-critique their own collection practices and instruments through memos and other documentation. As Bartlett and Vavrus (2017) advise,

> We recommend that you do a great deal of memoing—writing of notes to yourself—to help you think about the ways that the archival material you find might help you develop a temporal understanding of the phenomenon of interest to you.
>
> (p. 98)

Fifth, it allows for a creative approach to data collection. The researcher is not limited to traditional methods but can use a variety of methods to create data.

Data collection as creation of entities

Collecting data creates entities but there is no set way of doing this or even a "core" dataset. Instead, we can apply Ludwig Wittgenstein's notion of family resemblance to case study data collection. Wittgenstein (1968) developed the notion of family resemblances. Family resemblance is a set of metaphors and analogies for describing the fuzzy borders around categories, notably language games. Wittgenstein uses the concept to avoid looking for stable elements of an idea; instead, there are series of vaguely related elements. In Wittgenstein's original formulation, these shared similarities can be understood as family resemblances.

> I can think of no better expression to characterize these similarities than "family resemblances"; for the various resemblances between members of a family: build, features, colour of eyes, gait, temperament, etc. etc. overlap and criss-cross in the same way.—And I shall say: "games" form a family. And for instance the kinds of number form a family in the same way. Why do we call something a "number"? Well, perhaps because it has a—direct—relationship with several things that have hitherto been called number; and this can be said to give it an indirect relationship to other things we call the same name. And we extend our concept of number as in spinning a thread

we twist fibre on fibre. And the strength of the thread does not reside in the fact that some one fibre runs through its whole length, but in the overlapping of many fibres.

(Wittgenstein, 1968, p. 32 [PI 67])

For Wittgenstein, a thing or concept may have no unified core or Platonic form but rather possess shared fibers. Bain et al. (2022) clarify Wittgentsein's meaning:

> [Family resemblance] is a tool of analogies for describing the fuzzy borders around categories. Wittgenstein observes that language games are often unaligned and subject to change. When comparing games, certain elements drop out, and new ones arise arbitrarily. However, there is seemingly no underpinning attribute across them all. Words and games are too unrelated and multifaceted to support a logical or clear-cut definition. Instead, games' and words' meanings have likeness, which Wittgenstein refers to as family resemblance. In other words, there are degrees of belonging to a category where elements in each set share some common attributes.
>
> (p. 3)

As an analytical tool, *family resemblance* is useful for thinking about the data collection process when creating entities for case studies. There is no core to any entity but instead a set or sets of fibers allowing researchers to build and develop ("weave") a case study from the available data. Because cases are selections of reality with boundaries, as well as attempts to represent multiple realities, the analogy of family resemblances and metaphor of fibers aptly describes what researchers are doing. An entity is a series of relations.

Family resemblance equips case study researchers with three analytical techniques for data collection. First, there are no set templates for case studies. There is no set way to conduct a case study but rather sets of practices with overlapping similarities. Data is not collected to fit a specific form but is instead gathered and then analyzed from a stance of epistemological openness. This inductive approach is more flexible and can allow for a sense of creativity in the research process. Second, family resemblance frames data collection as significantly recursive and iterative sets of processes. Third, family resemblance offers the idea of entanglement. Different elements within the case study are connected and cannot be understood independently from one another. This is different from reductionism, which would seek to understand the case study by breaking it down into its component parts. Instead, understanding the case study as an entangled whole can give researchers a holistic understanding of the phenomenon under study. Data collection is thus less about atomistic elements and more about collecting data in multiple, iterative ways that aim at holistic description and understanding.

Family resemblance and digital collection

Data collection is a process of evidence representations. Representation, and thus legitimation, undergird data collection's ideology. Duff (2008) writes,

> Representation refers to how we represent or position our participants, data, and interpretations, and also, perhaps indirectly, how we position ourselves as researchers in relation to those studied. Legitimation is the basis for the warrants or claims we make about our data and the authority of our reports.
>
> (p. 109)

Family resemblance, as an analytical tool for data collection, provides a way for *representation* and *legitimation* to avoid essentialism and determinism. Researchers do not need to represent a core or some universal trait in their case studies because this would rely on some type of neo-Platonic form. There needs to be no single piece of evidence, or even type of evidence, that a case study researcher must collect to describe or represent the case study. Rather, family resemblances can occur between the various data collected to produce the case study. There is no essential component or determining piece of evidence that "finally" produces the case study.

Family resemblance has three important implications for *digital* research and data collection. First, digital researchers often encounter data that is rapidly changing, both in terms of technicalities (the data type, for example) and appearance (formatting of a website, etc.). Case study researchers don't need to collect one type of data or even need a consistent type or format of data. This point of view is quite practical in that it recognizes the constructivist nature of all research including digital. Data collected is a product of research and is not natural, ahistorical, or permanent. This understanding of digital phenomena can help to avoid reification, or the treating of phenomena as if they are static and unchanging. Second, due to the scale and circulation of digital phenomena, it is possible to build a case study from any number of data points. As such, digital case studies are part of a larger web of relations. Third, "family resemblances" as a conceptual schema may assist—but does not guarantee—researchers in challenging essentialist assumptions about data, including racist, gendered, ableist, and homophobic assumptions, because there is no "core" or essential element to datasets.

Iterative collection phase and circulation and distribution for digital research

Practically, a family resemblance approach necessitates identifying, collecting, and describing data at different times because no single piece of data or evidence is the linchpin. Instead, researchers iterate through data collection. The process of collecting, tracing, and confirming data provides a way to verify the data collected represents research goals. This process offers a way to improve the reliability and validity of the data collected. The data collected in each cycle of data collection can be used to build on data collected in previous cycles.

Iterative data collection, for any case study, enables the multiple realities of a holistic case study to be described *cyclically*. Cycling encourages tracking changes in the case study across time, spaces, locations, and other dimensionalities. Cycling, too, may help identify patterns and relationships that could otherwise be hidden or occluded. For example, if a case study is conducted over the course of a year, seasonal changes may impact the results. By collecting data iteratively through cycles, these seasonal changes can be described and determined if they are relevant to the study. Another example could include interviewing different members of a particular community during each iterative cycle. This would allow for a more detailed understanding of the community, as different members would have different perspectives. It might also lead researchers to identify "cracks" in the community or edge users to see where multiple realities and competing perspectives exist.

Iterative collection is critical for networked, digital case studies, including elements such as users, interfaces, website development, computer code, software/applications, databases, computational models/algorithms, and infrastructure because these elements have dramatically different *distribution* and *circulation* mechanisms. Traditional data, such as print texts and physical media, have limitations to their distribution and circulation. A physical video or image can be exchanged physically. On the other hand, media in networked environments have potentially unlimited distribution and circulation. Social media networks amplify texts, images, and video to the point where their distribution and circulation is not limited by any economic cost (Rifkin, 2015; Zuboff, 2019) but rather by user and algorithm attention. While the economic and societal implications of such networked distribution and circulation are outside the scope of this book, iterative collection accounts for the ease, speed, acceleration, and amplification of information by trying to collect data repeatedly and determine if the distribution and circulation change the case's contexts, including the transformation of information as it spreads across various digital and non-digital spaces. For example, when images become memes and those memes virally transform across spaces, we see the need to account for distribution and circulation through interactive data collection cycles.

Distribution and circulation for networked technologies reshape production processes of digital data. As digital case study researchers, connecting production to distribution and circulation helps to formulate critical queries, such as examining why certain information circulates or how distribution shapes the production of content creation. Content creators on social media, for instance, consider how algorithms will distribute and circulate their content. As a result of the presence of algorithms, content creators will change the content, even sometimes using the humorous phrases "Like, comment, and subscribe!" or "Ring the bell for notifications." These phrases are reminders that content creators are aware of necessary attention metrics as well as attendant algorithms and their role in circulating content on platforms. These algorithmic-inflected conventions are made more complicated in that technical processes of algorithms are generally occluded by either proprietary reasons or functional illiteracies (Burrell, 2016). Content production is then guided by perceptions of algorithms, which is then subject to algorithmic lore, gossip, and mythologizing (Bishop, 2019, 2020; Cotter & Reisdorf, 2020). Ultimately, then, data collection needs to be iterative to account for these digital contexts and their intricate contours.

Front- and backstage processes

Practically, as digital researchers begin to collect data for their cases, the dramaturgical metaphors of the façade and its components of the stage (Goffman, 1956) describe the mediated, performative aspects of networked technologies, including content as it is distributed and circulated throughout social networks. The façade is made up of the personal (people and actors) and the stage (the equipment and settings). The "stage" is comprised of two factors: front (public) and back (private). These elements create a performance out of which roles are created, reinforced, and challenged.

> Performances are constructed with an awareness of societal and institutional expectations. In other words, interaction relationships are "organised in particular by the use of shared resources and communication rules" (Serpa and Ferreira, 2018: 74). These rules are learned through repetition by drawing on factors that already exist within our repertoire. Masquerades are performed until the roles have been mastered. Teachers and pupils, nurses and patients, footballers and fans, all assume a role based on preconceived expectations of appropriate communication and behaviour.
>
> (Kilvington, 2021, p. 259)

The frontstage is where most users produce their data and certainly their content, as it is the public-facing interface of platforms. The frontstage is also where users present themselves to other users and algorithms, and where interactions take place. Frontstage digital data often takes the form of content that users generate, such as posts, comments, and likes. The backstage, on the other hand, is the private, "behind-the-scenes" area of the social media platform, including where users manage their account settings and privacy controls. The backstage includes more occluded and black-boxed practices. Backstage data often take the form of data that are generated by platforms or websites, such as user, cursor, and click data, as well as other types of metrics.

There are two distinct frontstages and backstages with networked and social media (Figure 3.1). Such data will appear differently depending on which category researchers inhabit themselves and their level of access.

For the frontstage category, there is the public user view that other users view when logged in. The other frontstage, the platform view, is the public view, which includes when users are not logged into a platform or the view of the platform without any data in it, e.g., wireframing or empty state pages. The primary difference between these views is the presence of algorithms and the customization algorithms provide. The home screen of a user can be dramatically different from the public platform view. Users are provided custom recommendations, meaning that data collected could be different from the case study based on spatial, temporary, and relational factors. Researchers should therefore be prepared to test and experiment with a variety of frontstage views—a milieu of family resemblances. They could log in themselves while testing a variety of other user views to determine the validity and structure of their data. Experimenting with these views may reveal to what extent algorithms shape the data researchers are exposed to.

The backstage of social networks and websites, similarly, contain two versions of the private view. The first is the less public version of digital technologies, such as the user version of websites, including chat functions and messages, to which the user has access. The other backstage is infrastructural, which the user generally does not have access to. This data is often stored differently from the other digital front- and backstages in that it is stored as database files.

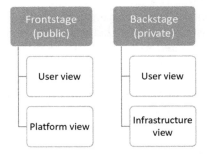

Figure 3.1 A hierarchical matrix of the front- and backstage of many (but not all) social networks and websites

Part II: Practical methods for data collection

In terms of qualitative digital case studies, traditional methods still apply. Observations and fieldnotes, interviews, focus groups, questionnaires, surveys, and documentation are all viable and could be used for digital concerns. To ensure the case studies represent multiple realities, multiple data sources should be used. The main quantitative method I discuss in this chapter, web scraping, can automate data collection procedures. Scraping provides a standardized method for collecting data. This data can then be analyzed with either qualitative and/or quantitative approaches. The second half of this chapter consequently examines these collection methods and addresses concerns specific to mediated environments and digital networks.

Digital observations and fieldwork

Digital observations and fieldwork, and the fieldnotes that arise from these observations, should include elements of traditional observations and fieldnotes. Ethnographic observations are critically important as they are "the gold standard for the study of processes" (Murphy & Dingwall, 2007, p. 2230). Such practices include immersion in situations and contexts, active and ethical participation when and where necessary, talking to participants, and interacting within researcher boundaries—all while taking descriptive notes on those observations.

Mediated environments and digital networks add complexity to observations, including real-time interactions, discursive affective engagement, automated processes, and infrastructural concerns (see Table 3.1). In practice, digital observation can be conducted of text, video, screenshot, multimodal, or a combination of these methods. The affordances of each method enhance the multiple realities of the case study.

Two case study examples are helpful here. First, digital case studies often have users as their entity. Users may livestream videos on a variety of platforms (YouTube, TikTok, and others) that researchers can collect. Let's assume the content is a common activity such as gardening, cooking, or sporting events. A researcher may also record the content producer. There is a distinction here between the participants recording themselves when compared to a researcher recording participants in the same activities. While in both activities, there is a level of performance, personal fronting (Goffman, 1956), and face work (Goffman, 1967), participants are recorded through the mediation of the platform.[1] Triple mediation here thus exists: the participants recording themselves via video, the platform's interface mediates the video, and the video then becomes distributed, circulated, and amplified through a variety of networks. Platforms add to these videos an ability to interact (comments and metrics) while providing affective engagement (permanent and/or real-

Table 3.1 Elements of digital observation and fieldwork

Element	Examples
Real-time interactions	• Live streamed video and audio • Live exchange of text (e.g., commenting) and symbolic interactions (e.g., emojis and "likes") • Amplification techniques (e.g., sharing and retweets)
Discursive affective engagement	• Affective metrics and qualitative affordances (reactions such as "likes") • Graphical interchange format (GIFs) • Electronic buttons of dis/approval (upvotes, etc.)
(Observations of) Automated processes	• Actual algorithms (the equations) • Perceptions of algorithms • Deliberate use of automated processes (e.g., gamifying algorithms)
Infrastructural concerns	• The use of technological networks in the physical world • Physical computing and embodiment • The Internet of Things

time, ephemeral reactions). Interactions and engagements provide automated processes, typically through algorithmic sorting, to distribute and circulate the videos on the platform or in the network. In turn, these elements reshape the user's style and approach to livestreaming. Knowing that these features of the platform or network are present, users will rethink the ways they produce the video.

The second example is that of an open-source code database. Researchers need to collect the code itself while tracking the development of the code, including obsolete code and comments. As with the user livestreaming video, the code is embedded in an interface mediating interacting with the code in the same way a smartphone app is embedded in a smartphone interface. In the code, there are real-time interactions, affective engagement, automated processes within the code and external to the code (how the repository uses automated processes, for example), and the way the code is implemented in infrastructures.

In both examples, jottings and other fieldnotes remain important (Emerson et al., 2011), but fieldnotes may also constitute real-time recordings, including the ability to annotate screenshots and videos. Ephemeral digital objects and data require longitudinal documentation, which can take the form of fieldnotes as well as text files and multimedia sources. Digital ephemera can be defined as any digital content with a short shelf life, including objects from text posts, such as tweets and

Snapchat stories, or website cookies and cached data. Because digital ephemera are so transient, they can be difficult to preserve and document. One way to think about digital ephemera is in terms of the "enduring ephemeral." This concept, coined by Chun (2011), refers to the way in which digital media is always in a state of flux, with information appearing and disappearing rapidly. While the ephemerality of digital media can be frustrating to preserve or document, it provides a unique opportunity to capture the transient moments that make up our online lives.

Two useful digital collection field work strategies for accounting for the elements above as well as enduring ephemerality are what I call *mockup wireframing* and what S. A. Riddick (2019) has labeled *deliberate drifting*. Together these collection strategies highlight the stable and temporary aspects of data. Mockup wireframing centers the stabilizing and coercive force of contemporary screen interfaces (most people do not produce their own interfaces). Data travels through interfaces and can be altered or otherwise changed. Deliberate drifting is a collection method for capturing—or making a good faith effort to do so—temporary and ephemeral interactions, exchanges, and other digital data. In both strategies, researchers revisit the collection site multiple times. Researchers document changes to the data to better capture the multiple realities of their case and to remain holistic about the entity under study.

Mockup wireframing refers to the act of sketching out how the interface looks without any user data entered. In design terms, these types of interfaces are called empty state pages (ESPs). As I have written elsewhere:

> ESPs refer to the default of an interface prior to the encounter between interface and user. As a cursory illustration, imagine a blank Facebook profile page without seeing any personalized content in the standardized profile categories, such as "Work and Education," "Family and Relationships," or "Places You've Lived." Industry discourse characterizes this pre-user input stage as a "zero data" or "null data" interface, hence, the reason for the use of the "empty state" moniker. ESPs present users with data-less fields that are inscribed with instructions on how and what kind of information to input. As an understudied part of design, ESPs permeate our screen-infused world and guide our actions by cultivating recurring prescribed or constrained rhetorical actions. Each time a user logs into Facebook, for example, she is greeted with the status update element of Facebook's ESP (a box labeled with the query "What's on your mind?").
> (Gallagher & Holmes, 2019, p. 271)

One could do this by hand, sketching out empty boxes and buttons or using a variety of other tools. If researchers have the time and energy, they might sketch out more elaborate and detailed mockups. The individual methods matter less than describing how the interface draws on the elements of real-time interactions, discursive affective engagement, automated processes, and infrastructural concerns. Visualizing the wireframing of technological interfaces enables researchers to conduct digital observations of a variety of case studies, ranging from an interface itself to identifying and tracking UX habits that websites and developers aim to inculcate in their users.

Deliberate drifting refers to a flexible type of observation "designed to track live online audience engagement, as well as other types of ephemeral activity in digital fields" (Riddick, 2019, p. 2). Deliberate drifting is a field method used to capture and describe the precarious work of observing live video-streaming. The researcher deliberately engages in ephemeral and temporary digital activities to capture data that would otherwise be lost. This strategy could involve participating in online chats, following hashtags on social media, or taking screenshots of websites that are about to disappear. It also stresses, in keeping with the theme of this book, cyclical iteration when encountering data that may disappear: "the researcher is able to study the field as a recursive site, wherein they can revisit, recontextualize, and reexamine an otherwise ephemeral field" (p. 2). Drifting is not a one-time event, but a continuous, active process, requiring constant effort, attention, and engagement. I have found deliberate drifting to be most useful when watching videos with live text or reactions streamed across the video. These types of videos occur across a range of contexts but most often happen with influencers and politicians. Screen-recording these reactions helps to reinscribe temporal and spatial relations that could be lost if researchers were to rely on text-based fieldnotes only.

Fieldnotes

Fieldnotes have no prescriptive format or one correct format. The audience for these notes can be the researcher(s), present and future. I have never found generalizable strategies for taking fieldnotes. For these reasons, it's useful to take a flexible stance toward fieldnotes. For fieldnotes in general, I suggest:

- Explicitly identify your purposes for taking notes. Recall your research goals and guiding questions.
- Be flexible in your approach to fieldnotes and be willing to experiment with different formats and strategies.
- Remember that fieldnotes are for your own benefit, so make sure to write them in a way that makes sense to you.
- Embrace contradictions and confusion. Writing fieldnotes in the moment does not require immediate analyses or "puzzling" through conundrums. If there are moments of confusion, I record my confusion and embrace it.

- Be willing to revise fieldnotes as your research progresses.
- Make notes of the ways that participants and users label you, the researcher. The construction of the researcher provides you with multiple perspectives for constructing multiple realities of the case.
- Continually question how your presence alters the observed phenomena ("the observer effect" or "Hawthorne effect").

I heed Annette Markham's advice about questioning the nature of a digital field:

> In social media, we need to ask not only how to collect this, but ask more basically: What is naturally occurring discourse? What forms does it take? If we broaden the idea of "discourse" to mean anything that can be read as having communicative meaning, what might it include?
>
> (2013, p. 439)

In terms of digital concerns, I remind myself of the following:

- Collect URLs in a spreadsheet, noting both alive and dead hyperlinks.
- Document software and hardware specifications.
- Take notes on advertisements and spam. While there is going to be a lot of random information, these notes can shed insight into how algorithms position users within networks and websites.
- Pay attention to the site design and how it affects your and participants' experiences.
- Describe, if possible, how an algorithm sorts content at a particular moment in time. Returning to these notes may help researchers to determine or evaluate how an algorithm was being "gamed," which is when users seek to manipulate a system for their own gain.
- Take notes on technical documentation of devices, websites, and networks. Downloading them to take notes as documentation helps see the backstage processes more readily. Download often and systematically.
- Notes can be in a variety of modalities.
- Observe the *timing* between online interactions. Take notes on timestamps and other metadata about when texts, images, and videos are exchanged and posted.

When I study a specific online community, for instance, I take notes on the following:

- The community's stated purpose(s) and norms
- How members self-identify
- How new members are welcomed (or not)

- What kind of support, if any, is offered to members
- What content is discussed and disseminated/circulated
- How members interact with one another

Interviews

To highlight the affordances of digital interviews (the medium) and interviews about digital phenomena requires a brief incursion into interviewing more generally. There is perhaps no qualitative data collection method more common than interviewing. The interview is a *metacommunication event*. The anthropologist Charles Briggs notes in *Learning how to ask* (1986) that the interview is a communication event that is about other communication, notably recall. As Briggs writes:

> Interviews provide examples of metacommunication, statements that report, describe, interpret, and evaluate communicative acts and processes. All speech communities possess repertoires of metacommunicative events that they use in generating shared understandings with respect to themselves and their experiences... Unfortunately, researchers seldom gain competence (in Hymes's [1974a: 92–97] sense of the term) in these repertoires, relying instead on the metacommunicative routine that figures so prominently in their own speech community—the interview. This practice deprives the researcher of an adequate sense as to how the information she or he obtains fits into broader patterns of thinking, feeling, and speaking.
>
> (1986, p. 2)

Briggs goes on to argue that the interview systemically suppresses phatic expressions and repertoires of speech exchanges in which naturalistic knowledge is learned in a coproduced manner. Opening exchanges, such as small talk or personal stories, are often not part of the official interview. These opportunities could facilitate the interview and guide how interviewees answer (or not) questions from the interviewer but are instead considered not the focus of the interview. The interview is about a spatial-temporal experience not present in the interview setting. In terms of new knowledge, the interview is prefigured and structured by the interviewer setting up the event for the sake of a research project.

The interview is a site of knowledge production, one that draws on the interviewee's reflection and recall. Whatever the interviewee answers is prompted by what the interviewer asks while *also* a recall of their own experiences. These experiences are not a direct reflection of reality and instead are a conventionalization of the experience. In my work, for example, I asked about "communication issues" interviewees had when "communicating about machine learning." My case study participants took "issues" to mean problems. Most of them had issues, I can report, not only because they experienced issues, but also because I asked them to report those issues. As an interviewer, I might have actualized issues into existence or turned neutral experiences into issues. I asked several follow-ups during the interviews but the interview was the site of the creation of these problems. The answers I received were thus routinized. It was, in fact, only through interviewing that these issues could be routinized for participants because they likely never took notes on communication issues. To understand the answers as routines, produced by the interviews, is a different epistemological treatment of the interview as a site of knowledge production rather than a reflection of some reference treated as ground truth.

Consequently, the interview as a metacommunication event has four key frameworks that are often tacit. First, it's a participatory creation of the interviewer. The practical takeaway here is that minor shifts in interviewing questions (word choice, form, timing) are of consequence. Interviewers should plan out their questions and practice them—even hedges. Second, the interview is an open well or mine of referentiality. Interviewees may even misinterpret the goal of the interview or conflate it with a different sort of activity (Koven, 2014). There are many opportunities for miscommunication and areas for learning. Interviewers need to be prepared for the latter, as well as the former. It's for this reason that interviews should, in my view, have an open-ended segment or, if structured interviews are being performed, a follow-up should be scheduled. Third, knowledge generated from interviews is dependent on the interviewer's positionality, which is not clear until this positionality is altered in some way. The power rests in the interviewer, who directs the interviewee. Finally, an interview shows gaps where other types of methods are necessary.

In broad strokes, interviews are either unstructured, semi-structured, or structured. Unstructured interviews have no established interview protocol, i.e., a list of questions asked in a specific order. A semi-structured interview has a protocol of interview questions, but the interviewer can ask follow-up questions or clarifying queries. During a semi-structured interview, interviewers make real-time adjustments to maximize what they can learn. A structured interview uses a protocol and does not deviate from that protocol. There are benefits and drawbacks to the three approaches (Table 3.2).

Unstructured interviews are the least common type in my experiences for case studies but still useful, especially when the interviewer has established relationships with the participants and is looking to have an open-ended conversation. But there should still be established goals for the interview. Semi-structured is the most common interview type and is useful for eliciting tacit and implicit knowledge of a case study. Asking follow-ups is crucial for clarification of terms, identifying contradictions, and so forth. Structured interviewing enables more valid statistical

Table 3.2 Benefits and drawbacks to unstructured, semi-structured, or structured interviewing

Interview	Benefits	Drawbacks
Unstructured	• Interviewer's language and queries do not prefigure the interview • Lack of question formatting enables a wide range of questions and in-depth conversation • Knowledge from unstructured interviews tends to be treated more contextually than structured interviews	• Interviews are not comparable; each interview is a unique instance of conversational exchange • No statistical evidence
Semi-structured	• Interviews can be compared and some statistics determined (validity and reliability may be measurable) • Situational queries can be asked but must be couched in the protocol	• Interviewers may be tempted to measure statistical inferences despite variation in queries administered • Structures interviewees' language through protocols
Structured	• Interviews can be compared and statistics/meta-analytics determined	• Lacks flexibility for follow-up questions • Cannot account for dynamics of interviewees misunderstanding of questions • Inhibits elaborations of context

analyses. Because there is no deviation between questions asked, the answers are comparable and can be collated more readily with other types of interviewing. While structured interviewing benefits quantitative analysis most, it is useful for teams of qualitative researchers to ensure team members ask a standard set of questions. For a case study methodology, semi-structured interviews are likely to be the most productive. Because case studies need to represent phenomena multi-dimensionally, structured interviewing is unlikely to represent the multiple realities of a case or describe the entity in ways that a semi-structured interview could. That said, for case study research, unstructured interviews are useful for a follow-up to the semi-structured interview because they allow the researcher and participant to navigate the messiness of a case study.

Interview modality

There is unlikely to be any interview modality that is most effective for case studies—digital or not. Whether it's face-to-face, phone, messaging, or video, no universal best practices exist (Table 3.3 for strength and weaknesses). In terms of maintaining a case study methodology, one that upholds the elements of a case study, it's probably most effective if researchers conduct multiple interviews with a participant across a range of modalities because interviewees may be willing to share different types of information when the modality changes. While there are obviously drawbacks to interviewing participants multiple times, such as willingness of the participants, the researcher's time, or pressure to publish, engaging in multiple interviews across modalities helps ensure the case study represents multiple realities.

Recording face-to-face or video interviews provides a record of gestures, visual cues, and other embodied activity (Olinger, 2020). If possible, multiple recording angles of the interviewer and interviewee can triangulate gesture or visual cues to determine their relationship to answers. Recording in these ways stresses *real-time embodied* (RTE) data collection. RTE data collection is designed to capture, during an interview as well as an observation, the interaction between people and their environment as they act and react to the world. RTE captures embodied activity in a naturalistic way while acknowledging the construction of that activity.

When interviewing participants about digital cases, asking about perceptions of algorithms and motivations for joining a network or community often reveals "cracks" in the case study or unsettles the case study without needing to determine if the interviewees' perceptions are accurate or not. In other words, interviewees do not need to understand an algorithm or factually perceive a network or community to offer interesting or challenging viewpoints on the case. A case study of an algorithm, for instance, needs to investigate the algorithm itself as well as the *mythologizing* around the algorithms, thereby emphasizing users' perceptions and the lore they create. Awareness of the algorithm shapes the input data into the algorithm, thereby reshaping the functionality of the algorithm.

Taking notes during interviews assists researchers in keeping track of what was said, identifying important points, developing follow-up questions, and organizing their thoughts. When I conduct face-to-face interviews, I take notes while trying to avoid interfering with the flow of conversation. For telephone interviews, I have found note taking may be more difficult due to holding multiple instruments, including the phone and writing devices, but it is still possible to jot down key points. For messaging interviews (e.g., text messaging and instant messaging), note taking may appear to be built into the platform but, as noted above,

Table 3.3 Strengths and weaknesses of synchronous interview modalities

	Face-to-face	Phone	Messaging	Video
Benefits	• No collapsing of time space • Body language • Allows for the use of non-verbal communication, which can be helpful in building rapport and understanding the interviewee • Can provide personal rapport more than other modalities	• Highly transportable • Single modality (aurality)	• Multimedia object • Punctuation • Can allow for a more relaxed conversation, as the interviewee can take their time to compose their responses • Use of emojis and complex emotions	• Can interview across distances • Less taxing on the interviewee (see Oliffe et al., 2021) than in-person
Drawbacks	• Not transportable • May be expensive • Time consuming • Can be taxing on interviewees, notably vulnerable populations	• No visual cues • Non-verbal cues are missing • Glitches • Signal reception issues	• Lack of tone and body language • Unclear how to interpret pauses and vernacular syntax	• Glitches • Space is compressed to two dimensions

timing should be recorded and, if necessary, clarified with a follow-up question. For video interviewing, I suggest taking notes on where gestures take place on the screen and if references appear on other screens or if messages and links are exchanged. Finally, reflecting on your performance as a researcher *during the interview* could fall under the broad category of note taking, a suggestion backed up by other researchers (Oliffe et al., 2021). If there was a hedge or qualification, I suggest jotting this down. I try to reflect on what I said in addition to what the interviewee(s) said.

Questionnaires and surveys

In this section, I provide some general guidelines for questionnaires and surveys and then move on to specific digital concerns. In terms of data collection, using questionnaires or surveys may appear to be a methodological mismatch for case study research, with some even seeing them as contrasting approaches because case study research is holistic whereas questionnaires or surveys are reductionist (Verschuren, 2003, p. 125). While it is true that questionnaires and surveys are not the most common method for digital case studies, especially of single users, websites, or forums, they help augment digital case studies in a variety of ways that aim to *scaffold* a holistic case study approach. Questionnaires and surveys can elaborate on an entity and provide expansive insights into the functioning of the case.

Questionnaires and surveys complement interviews by identifying backstage activities (Goffman, 1956) that are not explicit in digital spaces. If the case is a website, forum, or community, for example, it = questionnaires and surveys can be used to collect information about members' experiences. If the case is an algorithm, questionnaires and surveys can provide perceptions of the algorithm on a broader scale than interviews. Surveys can be used to collect qualitative data about users' experiences of a forum website or community to make statistical claims if the population is properly sampled. In terms of basic principles of questionnaires and surveys, Krosnick and Presser's (2010, p. 264) well-received general advice still stands:

1 Use simple, familiar words (avoid technical terms, jargon, and slang).
2 Use simple syntax.
3 Avoid words with ambiguous meanings, i.e., aim for wording that all respondents will interpret in the same way.
4 Strive for wording that is specific and concrete (as opposed to general and abstract).
5 Make response options exhaustive and mutually exclusive.
6 Avoid leading or loaded questions that push respondents toward an answer.
7 Ask about one thing at a time (avoid double-barreled questions).
8 Avoid questions with single or double negations.

Qualifications on the advice in items one through four are necessary for the particularity and granularity of case studies. Technical terms, jargon, and slang are acceptable in my experiences if those terms are defined or given a range of meanings, such as using "e.g.," or "i.e.," although whatever is listed in these constructions must be accounted for when analyzing responses. Technical terms should not be avoided if the questionnaires and surveys are targeting a population that uses those terms, i.e., the language is emic. Jargon and slang could be deployed, too, if the researcher is trying to determine the *uses* of that jargon or slang.

For digital inquiry, using jargon or slang that originates in a network or online community might be an essential consideration for questionnaire and survey design. It can be useful to match syntax, or the arrangement and order of words, to the community, group, or network. When trying to determine meaning, it might be that avoiding ambiguous meanings is necessary; however, when case studies are meant as information gathering and learning about the entity under study, e.g., instrumental case studies (Stake, 1995, p. 3), intentionally leaving certain question items ambiguous can yield a wider range of responses and may prompt multiple perspectives of the case.

Order of questions matters, too. Krosnick and Presser (2010, p. 264) again provide excellent advice on optimizing question order:

1 Early questions should be easy and pleasant to answer, and should build rapport between the respondent and the researcher.
2 Questions at the very beginning of a questionnaire should explicitly address the topic of the survey, as it was described to the respondent prior to the interview.
3 Questions on the same topic should be grouped together.
4 Questions on the same topic should proceed from general to specific.
5 Questions on sensitive topics that might make respondents uncomfortable should be placed at the end of the questionnaire.
6 Filter questions should be included, to avoid asking respondents questions that do not apply to them.

Krosnick and Presser go on to discuss satisficing, which is a problem when respondents provide answers they believe researchers desire or when respondents answer in a way that makes it easier and/or faster for them to complete the questionnaire or survey. For digital case studies, the problem of satisficing increases due to the scale of online survey respondents.

Documentation

Documentation refers to a panoply of evidence and the term itself has a complex history. While such a history is outside the scope of this book, documentation developed through a tension between being a written text on paper to semiotic inscription on an object (Buckland, 1997). In terms of digitality, documentation is influenced by technology:

> Each different technology has different capabilities, different constraints. If we sustain the functional view of what constitutes a document, we should expect documents to take different forms in the contexts of different technologies and so we should expect the range of what could be considered a document to be different in a digital and paper environments. The algorithm for generating logarithms, like a mechanical educational toy, can be seen as a dynamic kind of document unlike ordinary paper documents, but still consistent with the etymological origins of "docu-ment," a means of teaching—or, in effect, evidence, something from which one learns.
> (Buckland, 1998, p. 229)

Documentation does not stand alone or separate from an investigation. Rather researchers need to determine what kind of documentation their research questions need and the media of that documentation.

Producing documentation from web-scraping

While some of the nascent and emergent documentation cannot be easily collected and collated, one important strategy for documentation and artifact collection is web scraping. Web scraping is the act of taking information from a website and placing it into a file for later analysis. There are different levels of scraping from using manual copy and paste to extracting data using a programming language (see Table 3.4). As others have written of the technique:

> Scraping, to state this quite formally, is a prominent technique for the automated collection of online data. It is one of the most distinctive

Table 3.4 Types of web scraping with their respective levels of automation

Level of automation	Type of web scraping
Manual	Copy and paste
Partially automated	Using XML query language to pull information based on (X)HTML tags; using scraping software
Readily automated	APIs (application programming interface; not always accessed through computer programming, but often advanced programming skills are required)
Fully automated	Computer programming to engage full automation (Python or R are most common)

practices associated with current forms of digital social research, those that are marked by the rise of the Internet and the new ubiquity of digital data in social life. Scrapers, to say it more informally, are bits of software code that makes it possible to automatically download data from the Web, and to capture some of the large quantities of data about social life that are available on online platforms like Google, Twitter and Wikipedia. Scraping is widely seen as offering new opportunities for digital social research: it promises to enable the development of new ways of collecting, analysing, and visualising social data.

(Marres & Weltevrede, 2013, p. 313)

From a technical standpoint, most web scraping uses the markup language of a website, such as HTML, to identify the desired area of a web page. For instance, if researchers aimed to extract the text of the headers or paragraphs on a website, they would identify the corresponding tags (<header> or <p>). They would then determine a location on a local hard drive for that text to be placed. This information is then typically stored in a comma-separated value (CSV) file. Often, researchers scrape hundreds, thousands, or millions of web pages, targeting a specific field on the website (Gallagher & Beveridge, 2021, p. 3).

According to Chasins et al. (2018), web scraping has two main elements: (1) extraction, such as "finding an element with a given semantic role (a title, an address), extracting a table of data," and (2) data access, such as "loading a URL, clicking a link, filling and submitting a form, using a calendar widget, autocomplete widget, or other interactive component" (p. 964). In addition to being a data extraction tool, web scraping is a practice that asks researchers to think about how data are stored for later analysis. Web scraping tends to be targeted, focusing on websites and even specific tags. Web scraping can also refer to the use of application programming interfaces (APIs). Unlike web scraping that targets specific HTML or CSS tags to collect data, API scraping accesses already available data, often delivered in JavaScript Object Notation (JSON). However, API scraping can be slower and less accurate than code-based scraping (Dongo et al., 2020; Freelon, 2018). API scraping is not as effective, either, at accounting for website changes (Dongo et al., 2020).

As a scalable method, web scraping supports sustainable document collection for case studies in four ways. First, web scraping supports transparent and data-driven methods, allowing researchers to share scraping programs and rapidly produce datasets. Second, web scraping can be iterated to generate new variations of data or extend already available archives through community collaboration. Third, web scraping procedures can be documented with instructions for software or available scraping programs; this documentation might lead to a stronger sense of trust in research designs and results. Fourth, web scraping can yield either a random sample or a complete sample of website content and metadata.

Web scraping is an effective complement to the typical case study methods, such as interviews, surveys, experiments, usability tests, document reviews, and ethnographic work. Web scraping augments interview and survey methods through verification or evaluation of user responses. If researchers have interview results or survey answers about websites, they can scrape a website to determine if the perceptions are aligned with actual behaviors. For example, if researchers are interested in the number of times users tweet, they may augment their survey methods by also collecting public data on user activity to compare to survey responses.

There are four drawbacks to web scraping in my experience. If a website does not use a consistent front-end architecture or framework, then an automated web scraper might not yield complete or consistent data. For example, if a blog uses manually crafted paragraph tags (<p>) and inconsistently uses CSS classes, then any automated program could miss key aspects of a website. While this is less of a concern when scraping the websites of large organizations with automated systems for building websites, e.g., corporations and institutions, scraping the websites of smaller organizations with manually produced websites might produce incomplete or inconsistent data. Because websites can have high variability in their architecture, researchers may need to develop "independent scraping protocols" based on individual websites (Freelon, 2018, p. 666). Therefore, effective web scraping requires qualitative work, such as spot-checking, to ensure that scraped data is consistent.

Second, I have found a need to exercise patience with web scraping programs and techniques. If information is pulled too quickly, and if the program makes too many server requests ("pings"), it is possible to accidentally simulate a distributed denial of service (DDoS) attack. Researchers could end up shutting down a smaller website or being denied access to larger websites that block the researcher's IP address. Researchers should follow best practices in accessing a website's architecture to see if the site has a preferred page visit delay time for scraping the site.

Third, information scraped from a website looks very different from the way it appears in file format. Researchers need to determine the extent of such changes and consider how the transition from web page to dataset affects the research design of the project. Researchers need to weigh to what extent scraped data differ from the source content that was rendered in a browser. This determination depends on which content is scraped from a site and how it addresses a particular research question.

The fourth drawback is related to training. Web scraping requires an understanding of the HTML and scripting languages used to create the webpages, as well as the data structures that can be used to store and manipulate the scraped data. Technical proficiency with languages such as Python, JavaScript, and SQL is essential for successful web scraping projects.

Corrupt data and corporate algorithms

A related but distinct topic to missing data is corrupt data. By corrupt data, I do not mean glitchy or buggy data. Those errors are usually possible to identify or spot if researchers go through the data manually or with a refined procedure. Rather, I use corrupt data to make legible the influence of corporate algorithms on users and the production of data. As a brief example, social media platforms use algorithms to sort content. These algorithms are almost always programmed to maximize time spent on these applications while exposing users to targeted advertising. Users consequently produce data that is shaped by algorithms themselves as well as algorithm *gossip* and *lore* (Bishop, 2020; Bucher, 2012; MacDonald, 2021). Because data are seen as capital, and there is an insatiable drive for more capital (Srnicek, 2017), platforms have made their data proprietary, which means that researchers cannot verify the accuracy or trustworthiness of data or if that data is reflective of any trends online. In fact, platforms themselves might *create* the trends that data emerge from. While there are no quick or easy fixes for addressing corrupt data, I try to examine the user interface and place myself into the position of a user to determine how the platforms shape what users write and the data they are encouraged to produce. Doing so allows me to better think about how the collected data should be analyzed, a topic that is the focus of the next chapter.

Conclusion: When to stop collecting?

Regardless of whether dealing with missing or corrupt data, I always find it difficult to decide when to stop collecting data. It can also be difficult to determine which data to include in the final analysis. To avoid needing to answer these questions after the fact, I suggest setting a stopping *point* or stopping *criteria* for the project and documenting the decision-making process.

When I'm interviewing, for instance, I set up a target number of contacts or interviews. However, I usually commit to interviewing participants as long as they still respond to my contact emails. In a case study project about machine learning, I had a participant contact me several months after I stopped interviewing, but I made the effort to interview him. In terms of practical questions to remember, I suggest asking:

- What are the research questions?

- What data has been collected and what will more data help to answer about the research questions?
- Practically, how much time is there left to collect data?

This last question relies on data analysis, as the time a researcher has to collect is intimately tied up with how much time and resources you have to analyze the data, which is the subject of the next chapter.

Note

1 Platforms could be considered the basis of a digital type of *footing* (Goffman, 1956).

References

Bain, R., Festa, A., Lee, G. Y., & Zhang, A. (2022). Wittgenstein's philosophy of language the philosophical origins of modern NLP thinking. *ArXiv*, 1–21.

Bartlett, L., & Vavrus, F. (2017). *Rethinking case study research: A comparative approach*. Routledge.

Bassey, M. (1999). *Case study research in educational settings*. Open University Press.

Bishop, S. (2019). Managing visibility on YouTube through algorithmic gossip. *New Media and Society*, 21(11–12), 2589–2606. https://doi.org/10.1177/1461444819854731.

Bishop, S. (2020). Algorithmic experts: Selling algorithmic lore on YouTube. *Social Media + Society*, 6(1), 1–11. https://doi.org/10.1177/2056305119897323.

Bolter, J. D., & Grusin, R. (2000). *Remediation: Understanding new media*. MIT Press.

Briggs, C. L. (1986). *Learning how to ask: A sociolinguistic appraisal of the role of the interview in social science research*. Cambridge University Press.

Bucher, T. (2012). Want to be on the top? Algorithmic power and the threat of invisibility on Facebook. *New Media and Society*, 14(7), 1164–1180. https://doi.org/10.1177/1461444812440159.

Buckland, M. (1997). What is a "document"? *Journal of the American Society for Information Science*, 48(9), 804–809.

Buckland, M. (1998). What is a "digital document"? *Document Numérique*, 2(2), 221–230.

Burrell, J. (2016). How the machine "thinks": Understanding opacity in machine learning algorithms. *Big Data & Society*, 3(1), 1–12. https://doi.org/10.1177/2053951715622512.

Chasins, S. E., Mueller, M., & Bodik, R. (2018). Rousillon: Scraping distributed hierarchical web data. *The 31st annual ACM symposium on user interface software and technology—UIST '18*, 963–975. https://doi.org/10.1145/3242587.3242661.

Chun, W. H. K. (2011). *Programmed visions: Software and memory*. MIT Press.

Cotter, K., & Reisdorf, B. C. (2020). Algorithmic knowledge gaps: A new dimension of (digital) inequality. *International Journal of Communication*, 14(January), 745–765.

Dongo, I., Cadinale, Y., Aguilera, A., Martínez, F., Quintero, Y., & Barrios, S. (2020). Web scraping versus Twitter API: A comparison for a credibility analysis. *Proceedings of the 22nd international conference on information integration and web-based applications & services*, 263–273. https://doi.org/10.1145/3428757.3429104.

Duff, P. (2008). *Case study research in applied linguistics*. Lawrence Erlbaum Associates.

Dyson, A. H., & Genishi, C. (2005). *On the case: Approaches to language and literacy research*. Teachers College Press.

Emerson, R., Fretz, R., & Shaw, L. (2011). *Writing ethnographic fieldnotes* (Vol. 2). University of Chicago Press.

Freelon, D. (2018). Computational research in the post-API age. *Political Communication*, 35(4), 665–668. https://doi.org/10.1080/10584609.2018.1477506.

Gallagher, J. R., & Beveridge, A. (2021). Project-oriented web scraping in technical communication research. *Journal of Business and Technical Communication*, 36(2), 231–250. https://doi.org/10.1177/10506519211064619.

Gallagher, J. R., & Holmes, S. (2019). Empty templates: The ethical habits of empty state pages. *Technical Communication Quarterly*, 28(3), 271–283. https://doi.org/10.1080/10572252.2018.1564367.

Goffman, E. (1956). *The presentation of self in everyday life*. University of Edinburgh. https://doi.org/10.2307/258197.

Goffman, E. (1967). *Interactional ritual*. Doubleday.

Kilvington, D. (2021). The virtual stages of hate: Using Goffman's work to conceptualise the motivations for online hate. *Media, Culture & Society*, 43(2), 256–272. https://doi.org/10.1177/0163443720972318.

Koven, M. (2014). Interviewing: Practice, ideology, genre, and intertextuality. *Annual Review of Anthropology*, 43(1), 499–520. https://doi.org/10.1146/annurev-anthro-092412-155533.

Krosnick, J. A., & Presser, S. (2010). Question and questionnaire design. In P. V. Marsden & J. D. Wright (Eds.), *Handbook of survey research* (pp. 263–313). Emerald Group. https://doi.org/10.1097/01.PRS.0000074494.47391.BE.

Latour, B., & Woolgar, S. (1986). *Laboratory life: The construction of scientific facts*. Princeton University Press.

MacDonald, T. W. L. (2021). "How it actually works": Algorithmic lore videos as market devices. *New Media and Society*. https://doi.org/10.1177/14614448211021404.

Markham, A. N. (2013). Fieldwork in social media. *Qualitative Communication Research*, 2(4), 434–446. https://doi.org/10.1525/qcr.2013.2.4.434.

Marres, N., & Weltevrede, E. (2013). Scraping the social? Issues in live social research. *Journal of Cultural Economy*, 6(3), 313–335. https://doi.org/10.1080/17530350.2013.772070.

Murphy, E., & Dingwall, R. (2007). Informed consent, anticipatory regulation and ethnographic practice. *Social Science & Medicine*, 65, 2223–2234. https://doi.org/10.1016/j.socscimed.2007.08.008.

Oliffe, J. L., Kelly, M. T., Gonzalez Montaner, G., & Yu Ko, W. F. (2021). Zoom interviews: Benefits and concessions. *International Journal of Qualitative Methods*, 20, 1–8. https://doi.org/10.1177/16094069211053522.

Olinger, A. R. (2020). Visual embodied actions in interview-based writing research: A methodological argument for video. *Written Communication*, 37(2), 167–207. https://doi.org/10.1177/0741088319898864.

Riddick, S. A. (2019). Deliberative drifting: A rhetorical field method for audience studies on social media. *Computers and Composition*, 54, 1–27. https://doi.org/10.1016/j.compcom.2019.102520.

Rifkin, J. (2015). *The zero marginal cost society: The Internet of Things, the collaborative commons, and the eclipse of capitalism*. St. Martin's Griffin.

Srnicek, N. (2017). *Platform capitalism*. Polity Press.

Stake, R. E. (1995). *The art of case study research*. Sage Publications.

Verschuren, P. J. M. (2003). Case study as a research strategy: Some ambiguities and opportunities. *International Journal of Social Research Methodology*, 6(2), 121–139. https://doi.org/10.1080/13645570110106154.

Wittgenstein, L. (1968). *Philosophical investigations*. Basil Blackwell.

Woodside, A. G. (2010). *Case study research: Theory, methods, practice*. Emerald Group.

Yin, R. K. (2009). *Case study research: Design and methods*. Sage Publications.

Zuboff, S. (2019). *The age of surveillance capitalism*. Public Affairs.

4 Analysis for digital cases

Analyzing digital case studies requires the consideration of multiple factors and the use of different techniques. The size and scale of social media datasets, for example, makes analysis time consuming. The availability of qualitative and quantitative techniques and tools, while providing researchers with a wide range of analytical options, presents complications related to overload (see Chapter 1). The question of what collected digital data *represent* remains an open inquiry because such data may have unclear referents, such as the affordances of digital interfaces. After all, what does a "like" or "share" mean when a user deploys them? Does it matter if other users do not share the same meaning of those affordances? This chapter, aware of difficulties such as these, outlines principles and conceptual schemas for digital case study analysis, as well as practical analytical techniques, but the different sections are meant to be read out of order and consulted while engaging in digital case study analysis.

This chapter has four parts. The first part describes seven facets of digital data to consider after initial collection but before engaging in direct analysis: atomization, structures, attention, networks, power users, vocality, and distribution/circulation. This stage "between" collection and analysis accomplishes three goals: (1) it allows for collection to resume if the case needs to do so; (2) it allows for marination and percolation of ideas, thereby allowing researchers to develop impressions without the formal investment of analysis; (3) it provides for ways of "re-seeing" data in different ways. Part II provides a four-part framework for developing a workflow when performing analysis: task definition and specification, needed tools and technologies, efficient processes, and automation of processes (if possible). The third part discusses "cleaning," pre-processing, and processing data. While this is often discussed with respect to quantitative methods, I apply cleaning and wrangling approaches to qualitative digital case studies. The fourth part of this chapter discusses practical analytical techniques for digital case study analysis. Here, I discuss a broad constellation of practices ranging from completely inductive, open, and qualitative (grounded theory) to automated techniques for creating categories and themes in case study data, including topic modeling, named entity recognition, and sentiment analysis.

DOI: 10.4324/9781003402169-5

Before continuing, I want step in less formally and offer my perspective on mentorship and its critical role in case study analysis. Analyzing case studies has been considered "the most difficult and least developed or described aspect of conventional [case study research]" (Morgan et al., 2017, p. 1064). Yin (2009) has argued analytical strategies are the "least developed" aspect because researchers may not know what to do with their data or how to start the process. The case study researcher is a teacher, advocate, evaluator, biographer, and interpreter, taking on numerous analytical roles during this stage (Stake, 1995, pp. 91–99). Consequently, researchers have written that experienced case study researchers are at an advantage over novice case study researchers (Yin, 2009). As such, any inexperienced case study researcher should consider seeking out a mentor when initiating analysis. Even experienced case study researchers may benefit from seeking out mentors from different domains and who may have access to different tools, programs, and approaches. I recommend finding a mentor.

Part I: Facets for digital analysis between collection and formal analysis

When writing this book, I struggled with what to place into the data collection chapter and this chapter on analysis. That struggle is representative of the intimate relationship between collection, "getting to know" data, and analysis. This "getting to know" your data is, in my view, a nebulous region between collection and analysis that I often jokingly call data marination. Several of my mentors have called this "sitting with the data." Researchers also call this stage "play" (Yin, 2009, p. 129) which I tend to agree with, although when researchers use *play*, it often implies a rigorous version of iteration. In my formal and informal observations of scientists and engineers, some call it thinking, while others call it playing. Whatever the label for this process, it's an important step to learn about the data before conducting more formal or structured analysis because researchers can spend quite a bit of time wrestling with the data before attempting to analyze it. The seven facets I discuss in this section are thus meant to function as guideposts for thinking about messy, real-world data.

Atomization

Atomization is the process of breaking down a complex phenomenon to better understand its constituent parts. Atomization involves manually or automatically breaking down data into smaller chunks or data points. The concept of atomization, when analyzing case study data, provides scaffolding for thinking through data in bounded segments. Many aspects of this book and other digital methods related to social media aim to examine large datasets. Atomization is an alternative way of thinking at *smaller* and *micro* scales. For example, researchers can take interview transcripts or collect text data and break them into phrases or chunks they deem important. These segments can be related back to larger segments and codified into preliminary patterns or emergent themes. In my experiences, atomization encourages thinking about segments in non-linear and iterative ways that *connect* collection and analyses. Atomization can be used when examining chunks of digital texts, such as online comments. Comments could be on any social media site, text messaging, or question and answer forums. In terms of collection, comments are typically collected as clusters of text without much differentiation between them, other than a user has simply entered text into an interface. However, these comments can be radically different in length. Think here of a comment that simply states "Thanks!" while another comment may be a lengthy disquisition on politics. Researchers could *atomize* comments down into smaller segments, such as the first sentence of comments, initial ngrams of comment, and so forth.

Structures

Examining data structures may prompt researchers to revisit or reconsider the collection process while providing added context to the data itself as they are prepared. Structures may refer to literal structures out of which data emerges, such as online interfaces, electronic and physical infrastructures, or embodied contexts, as well as implicit structuring elements, which may include website user agreements, organizational policies, or other influential elements. Examining literal and implicit structures may provide explanations for patterns or biases in data, thereby allowing for case studies to learn more about data context. Taking fieldnotes about these structures may allow researchers to identify potential weaknesses in a data collection pipeline *after* some data has been collected, which once again shows the non-linear movement between data collection and analysis.

To revisit my previous examples of comments, or more broadly a social media post, the structure of a commenting box will have demonstrable effects on the data. A comment box could have, for instance, character limits, design affordances, and design/layout. Character limits may constrain the length and complexity of comments, while design affordances limit or create possible responses, influencing how users express their opinions. Twitter, for years, had a 140-character limit which constrained the data in highly specific and coercive ways. An interface that is prominently displayed with clear directions may encourage more participation and engagement, while an interface with difficult navigation may discourage users from participating or slow them down. Many such unethical design choices that aim to trick users with unclear design layouts are called "dark patterns" (e.g., Bringull, 2018; Trice & Potts, 2018).

Attention

Attention is a key currency that users seek in digital networks. Social media platforms, too, create incentives, both positive and negative, around attention. Attention therefore structures data, operating through a variety of mechanisms, including algorithms, personalized feeds, notifications, and affordances, such as likes, retweets, shares, comments, and other amplification metrics. Some researchers, for example, have found that these metrics incentivize and create the opportunity for certain risky content, including young people posting pictures of themselves drinking (Goodwin et al., 2016). Users compete for attention because the more attention content receives, the wider the audience. Attention is crucial, too, for organizations to reach their target audience, increase their visibility, and achieve their key performance indicators, which are simply sets of metrics. When analyzing data, digital case study researchers should examine how attention *distributes* and *circulates* data within the digital networks and social media platforms.

Attention enhances *discoverability* (McKelvey & Hunt, 2019). For example, content creators are incentivized to talk, write, and communicate (e.g., gestures) in ways that garner attention, thereby allowing for more discoverability. Case study researchers might consider identifying, if possible, what data contains *attention incentives* because those incentives are not necessarily contained within the data themselves. Therefore, asking participants via interviews, surveys, email, or other qualitative inquiry as well as attending to backstage processes (see previous chapter) will solidify queries about attention and its role in shaping datasets.

Networks

As I noted in the introduction and first chapter, case studies are bounded systems. Networks make those boundaries porous. Networks allow attention to flow, thereby creating a complex web of interactions that can be difficult to trace and understand. Networks therefore enable or disable flows of attention, and information more broadly, including how events or trends on one platform shape another. For example, trends on TikTok and Twitter may reshape a case study of a user or of an organization contending with competing or complementary trends. More specifically, since most case studies fit within a network or are embedded in multiple networks, researchers should account for the type of network when beginning their analysis and cleaning/processing the data.

Facebook and Reddit provide useful examples of centralized and decentralized networks. Facebook is a centralized platform, meaning that it is controlled by a central authority (i.e., the corporation) and the flow of information is controlled and monitored by the company. Users must have accounts to access and share information, and the platform has mechanisms in place to prevent web scraping. Nodes in a centralized network are likely to be more surveilled and controlled while being linked to centripetal elements. In the case of Facebook, these are proprietary algorithms and personalized newsfeeds. Reddit, on the other hand, is decentralized, allowing users to move freely between groups, and non-users to still consume content. Reddit is also straightforward to scrape data, although it charges for that privilege. Nodes in a decentralized network are less likely to be surveilled or monitored while being linked to centrifugal factors. In the case of Reddit, these are user creator forums with volunteer content moderators. Of course, since the relationship between centralized and decentralized networks is more of a spectrum, and not a binary, elements can be shared.

A crucial consideration here of the "between" collection and analyses is whether data comes from networks that are forum- or feed-based. Forum data is often contained to a community while feeds are more porous. Since the introduction of algorithmic sorting in the 2010s, feeds are generally no longer organic but instead sorted according to attention principles. The type and distribution of users who actively participate in forums and feeds is the next consideration, often referred to as the Pareto principle or power users.

Pareto principle and power users

In terms of users, the Pareto principle, or a Pareto distribution, refers to the likelihood of a distribution of a small number of users in a population being responsible for a large amount of activity. Less formally, and in internet contexts, the concepts gesture at an informal 80/20 rule or even a 1% rule wherein a small number of users are responsible for a large amount of content or a large number of data points. In an analysis of comments from *The New York Times*, for example, my team and I found that the top 100 commenters were responsible for over 43,000 comments (.1% of commenters made almost 10% of the comments) (e.g., Gallagher et al., 2020). Researchers have sought to theorize this distribution for online users, referring to them as power users. These power users often intersect and overlap with the concept of influencers and content creators.

Pareto distributions, and the resulting power users, are both produced by patterns of attention or engagement and produce those same patterns. As a result, as researchers identify where their cases fall on a distribution curve, they can either return to data collection to determine what other data should be collected or they can continue with their analysis, understanding to what degree their cases, such as a user, are power users or part of a larger population that is not as active or resource rich. Content itself also follows a Pareto distribution, meaning that most posts or pieces of content do not receive much attention in the network. Rather, a small percentage of posts or content receives attention. Determining where collected content falls on the distribution curve thereby allows researchers to make informed analysis about the significance (or lack of significance) the content has with respect to research questions.

Considering the Pareto principles and power users may be useful when analyzing the data (explored in this chapter) and for writing up findings as a narrative (see Chapter 6). If one has a case of a power user, this indicates the user likely has extra attention and resources that will establish a higher rate of activity, and possibly the number of data points. Conversely, if the user is part of the longer tail, the user may have fewer resources and data points, which could indicate that the user has less power and represents a more marginalized viewpoint or a viewpoint with less attention.

Vocality

The Pareto distribution and power users raise issues of power and who has authorization to speak, write, and communicate in digital venues. In the context of digital research, "vocality" refers to the presence of voices in the data being analyzed. As Anderson (2014) writes, vocality is "a peculiar category of sound that attends speech but also exceeds it, and as a mediated material that pushes the boundaries of human embodiment and agency" (par. 3). Many others have examined vocality, noting it is a mediated process (e.g., Milner, 2013; Schlichter, 2011) which can reflect gender performativity (Schlichter, 2011). In the context of this book, *vocality* generally refers to the mediated presence of voices or perspectives in data being analyzed. More specifically, and practically, it can refer to "a person'[s] *vocality* in the online UX community by their degree of activeness in the community, indicated by their number of posts or number of comments" (Kou et al., 2018, p. 2071, emphasis in original). *Monovocality* refers to a single voice or perspective, often dominant and reflective of someone in power or with power, in the data, while *polyvocality* refers to heterogeneous voices or perspectives in the dataset(s). Identifying vocality in data may help researchers develop a categorization schema in their workflow.

Considering the distribution and circulation in relation to the production of data

The distribution and circulation, as noted in previous chapters, of data play a crucial role in how digital data is produced. Distribution refers to the process of a product, data, or information, as a type of delivery mechanism for that product, data, or information. Distribution is often intentional and aligns with consumer or user information with a more bureaucratic or institutional valence. Circulation refers to the movement of products, data, or information with a less intentional delivery mechanism. For digital case studies, the delivery and circulation of digital information may be as important as its production. When conducting a case study of an application, the application must be studied not only for its essential elements but also how it is used and how users take it up, accounting for a heterogeneous range of outcomes. The circulation of the application is critical to a case study in addition to the "nut and bolts" of the application. With respect to a case study of a user's social media activity, tracing their activity may illuminate how algorithms distribute that activity and the ways audiences circulate the activity. The distribution and circulation of a user's activity will also shape how the user perceives their own activity. Asking the user about the information flow *after* data is collected may thus impact how future data is collected.

Accounting for distribution and circulation in relation to the production of content on social media illustrates this point. When users post content on a platform, such as TikTok or Instagram, they are more likely to post additional content if those videos go viral and garner attention in one or more networks. They then look at the attributes of the content and produce content that is similar. The distribution and circulation of data will shape the production of *future* content.

There are undeniable implications of distribution and circulation related to economics, specifically the role of profit in a capitalistic, global economy. As Pulver (2020) notes, circulation is "about understanding the circulation of texts and information in dialectical relation with the circulatory demands of capital and how this process inevitably conditions all other circulatory processes" (p. 21). Case study researchers can collect any type of data without specifically focusing on the economic aspects or "layers" of the data during the collection process. Nevertheless, this layer may be—and likely should be—considered at some point either when revisiting the collection phase or during analysis. In particular, the economic aspect deserves investigation when dealing with social media corporations that black box their proprietary data (Pasquale, 2015; Zuboff, 2019). Researchers and the general population do not have established ways to determine whether data has been warped by monetized incentives from a corporate platform. How content is distributed and circulated requires some detective work to identify if patterns in delivery elements are organic and grassroots or if they are corporate patterns resultant from monetization processes. These should be accounted for in a workflow routine.

Part II: Workflows for digital case study analysis

Developing a cogent, written workflow produces a stabilizing structure for case study creation. For digital cases, specifically, a documenting workflow (see Gentle, 2012) for social networks enables data to be corralled in manageable, organizational flows while remaining flexible and responsive to the entity under study. Case study practitioners have addressed developing a workflow with substantive variation in terms of language. It has been presented, to name a few examples, as analytic strategy (Yin, 2009), protocols (Stake, 1995), and analytical models along with resource maps and handoff chains (Spinuzzi, 2018). "Pipeline" is also used frequently with data heavy projects. The field of technical writing has a wide array of strategies for creating documentation with regards to managing content of research projects (e.g., Anderson, 2014; Hart-Davidson et al., 2007) and how networked globalized economies and workplaces complicate content management (e.g., Batova & Clark, 2015). Information design and data visualization studies use workflow to describe the process of creating visuals from data (e.g., Kirk, 2016, pp. 53–60). For academic researchers, workflows have been found to facilitate four themes: (1) information literacy, (2) information management, (3) knowledge management, and (4) scholarly communication (Ince et al., 2022).

This book uses "workflow" to account for the dynamic and complex activities within and around case study analysis (for overviews of workflow, see Hollingsworth, 1995; Ince et al., 2022; Lockridge & Van Ittersum, 2020; van der Aalst & van Hee, 2004). Using workflow, on one hand, locates doing analysis *as labor* and highlights some of the laborious activity involved with analyzing data. On the other hand, workflow raises a relationship to business, business processes, task definition and creation, efficiency, and automation.

> Workflow is often aligned with business or computing jargon, and its proximity to that discourse points to connotations of labor, capitalism, and manufacturing… In this light, workflow might point to contemporary capitalism and the business push to replicate tasks, to distribute tasks among workers, or to industrialize a process so that manufacturing can proceed without the expertise of a single worker.
> (Lockridge & Van Ittersum, 2020, n.p.)

While framing case study research as business-centered can be unpleasant, especially with the naturalistic inquiry a case approach brings (Stake, 1995), there are some benefits to thinking about this relationship. Because case study research can be a "mangle of practice" (Pickering, 1995), one in which living and non-living things interact in subtle and multifaceted ways, analysis might simply constitute "doing stuff." In fact, Clay Spinuzzi alludes to this in *Topsight 2.0* (2018). He opens his chapter on analytical models with an anecdote from *The Simpsons*:

> In one *Simpsons* episode, the Simpsons are reflecting on recent events. Marge proposes several morals to the story, but Homer concludes there was no moral, "It's just a bunch of stuff that happened." At this point, you might feel like Homer. You've designed a study,

> gathered data, and characterized it. You may have seen some patterns emerging. But you're probably having a hard time getting the big picture... Do the data tell you anything? And if they do, how will you know?
>
> (Spinuzzi, 2018, p. 185)

Analysis in case study research can feel similar to what Spinuzzi describes above. Where do you begin when you likely have not only a wealth of data but also multiple types of data? What kinds of approaches should be avoided, and other processes targeted?

Workflow answers these questions by prodding us to think about the distillation of cases. Workflows "trim" the bounded systems of a case study and may prompt the following questions:

1. What kinds of tasks must be defined?
2. What tools and technologies are needed to perform these tasks and how do these tools and technologies shape the tasks?
3. How can a researcher create efficient processes?
4. What processes can be automated?

These questions are, invariably, about researcher habits, and require flexibility for the inquiry under study.

Workflow habit 1: Task definition and specification

The sheer variety of ways to analyze digital case study data requires identifying necessary tasks, typically across a continuum between ideal, likely, and possible tasks. Task definition allows digital researchers to focus on specific elements of their data while avoiding analytical overload. *Modularization* of activities—or the breakdown into manageable units of work—can provide researchers with ways of deciding on what tasks and decisions might need to be continued or stopped. Modularization allows researchers to attend to different tasks when it's most convenient for them, even being able to schedule tasks if the modular task can be estimated in terms of time. There is an uncomfortable issue here with tracking one's labor, but I am by no means advocating for a bureaucratic vision of case study research, only as a workflow for accomplishing tasks that can be overwhelming, both in terms of time and emotion burden.

The concept of content illustrates why task specification is crucial for digital case study analyses. As a term, content is historically what occurs between advertising. Content is a vessel for selling other things. It is a *fluid* and *conditional* concept.[1] With apps and websites,[2] content still has this meaning and is highly commodified. Content can be defined as:

digital assets, conditional in their shape and value, that are assembled within and pushed out to networks, where human and machine audiences will assess them, assign value to them, consume them, appropriate and repurpose them, extract from them, and push them into other networks.

(Dush, 2015, p. 178)

This flexible definition provides thorny problems for case study analysis: What analytical tasks are required of data that is conditional by definition and can be reshaped by circulation and distribution methods? To grapple with this question, researchers need to define tasks related to the tools, technologies, and techniques they use to perform analysis.

Workflow habit 2: Needed tools and technologies

Tools order reality (Law, 2004, p. 122). They mediate and modify analyses based on their affordances. Tools and technologies determine, partially, the kind of analysis researchers can perform. I have found taking series of notes and observations about the available tools and software provides opportunities to reflect on task specification. When analyzing screenshots, for instance, the ability to annotate images enables a different range of analyses (with a PDF editor) than if those images can be completely edited with more fully functional software (advanced image editing software that uses vectors). The task definition, and subsequent workflow, is altered by the tools.

It may be important, however briefly, to examine the history of the tool or technology being employed, including how those technologies are remediated from previous types of media (see Bolter & Grusin, 2000). When information is documented, it is remediated and transformed by the analytical tool. Unless the tool was designed specifically for the research project, the gap between the case study and the tool(s) should be addressed, if only at the workflow stage. Addressing practical and ideological gaps between tool and case within the workflow provide opportunities and interventions for iteration to occur, thereby allowing the multiple realities of a case study to be described.

For example, PDFs, a frequent source of data documentation online, are part of the broader history of documents, one that involves remediations through printing, typograph, and copying in the last two centuries. The PDF was, in fact, preceded by failed attempts at similar technology (Gitelman, 2014). As a tool, PDFs have a specific ideology of capturing the image of the document, including format. The format is integral to the content. As many digital researchers are aware, when PDFs are broken into texts, that image as a gestalt is lost. Using PDFs as a tool of analysis, then, foregrounds an image-oriented type of analysis that favors gestalt analytical models.

Workflow habit 3: Efficient processes

While efficiency is often a language that case study researchers try to avoid, myself included, there are invariably instances when we should consider ways to make our analyses more efficient. Guarding oneself against ongoing data streams can help from feeling as though the project will never end and making little to no progress despite sinking time and effort into the project. Online comments, as a source of data, illustrate these considerations. Online comments will never really cease production. They function as sources of revenue for digital venues, including newspapers and social networks (Gallagher, 2020). As a result, platforms and networks are designed to encourage users to comment continuously. Researchers of online comments, such as myself, have learned to accept that our datasets need to stop at some point even through the data is being produced on a continuous basis. Instead, I set goals for stopping collection. In terms of post-data collection but before extensive analysis, I examine the structure of the data and learn how to manage these procedures early. Some of the efficiency procedures I've established are identifying the kinds of comments that need to be eliminated, such as very short comments (less than say seven characters), thereby allowing me to reduce my workload.

The process of transcribing, for example, can be broken into several different steps with specific tasks, all of which need to be weighed in terms of efficiency. When transcribing, researchers need to determine, via criteria likely chosen based on their research questions and disciplinary backgrounds, which parts can be transcribed as partially verbatim, i.e., eliminated fillers words, stutters, and repeated words, or full or "true" verbatim, including fillers such as *like, um,* and *ah* (McLellan et al., 2003 offer a useful discussion of transcription processes). Other moments of the transcript may not be transcribed, including preliminary parts of the interview wherein interviewer and interviewee negotiate consent, or the conclusion of the interview in which personal exchanges may not be covered by consent. Seemingly other trivial steps, such as capitalization and spelling in transcripts, need to be decided to keep data preparation efficient for future analysis. Transcript analysis is labor intensive in terms of cognitive focus and time, so it is important to make even small parts of the process efficient. When analyzing transcripts, researchers might decide that one of their questions was especially important and prioritize participants' answers in that area of the transcript. From that decision, they could go in two directions: identifying topics and themes in the transcript data with a qualitative approach, such as grounded theory (Strauss & Corbin, 1998) or with a more automated approach.

Workflow habit 4: Automation

Automation may not be available to all researchers, particularly those who are trained in the complexity of qualitative research. Automation takes time. There is no reason to establish automated procedures if there are only a few data points to analyze. That can be accomplished manually. However, when possible, and the data can be properly processed, automating processes can save time and it might provide insight that granular and manual processes could overlook. Establishing clear and assistive templates can enable automation in workflow routines. These templates can function as instructions for the researchers, notably for their future selves. In other words, the audience for these templates can be the researcher downstream in the project. The templates can also serve to standardize procedures.

One area especially open to automation for case study research is the thematic identification of qualitative data, such as interview transcripts. Specific methods for automation include topic modeling, clustering, sentiment analysis, or other types of classifications. Any number of automation techniques exist for identifying emergent themes from text data. In terms of a workflow, researchers might start with an initial attempt at thematizing with software or applications, rather than *grounded theory* (Strauss & Corbin, 1998). While grounded theory can find truly emergent themes in data, these themes are usually influenced by the researcher's own interests, disciplinary stance, and available tools. Automation may allow the researcher to adopt some perspectives they are biased against. An important caveat here is that any automated system should be transparent and avoid black boxing of how themes or analyses occur. Algorithmic processes, too, come infused with their programmers' ideologies and power dynamics that researchers must account for in their analyses. Just as important, while these automated themes may not hold true at the end of the case study, the themes can be useful as a starting point to help sift through data.

Part III: Pre-processing data

Alongside the establishment of a workflow routine is the iterative pre-processing and processing of data. Pre-processing and processing use a variety of terms, including cleaning, refining, standardizing, transforming, and wrangling. There are benefits and drawbacks (Table 4.1) with each capturing some but not every important element of data processing. Regardless of the term, processing data is integral to digital case studies as there is a high likelihood of large datasets, unstructured datasets, data from diverse sources, and multiple data formats, especially with the help of web scraping. In fact, web scraping can turn a qualitative case study into both a qualitative and quantitative case study even if the case is of a single entity.

This book uses wrangling for two reasons. First, because case studies are often qualitative and messy, wrangling tends to fit as an apt metaphor slightly better than the others. Second, wrangling implies that the data is

Analysis for digital cases 105

Table 4.1 Benefits and drawbacks of terms for data pre-processing

Term	Benefits	Drawbacks
Cleaning	• Implies removal of items or data that should not be present • Implies labor and manual effort • Emphasizes removing errors	• Lacks the transformative power that processing can entail • Gendered historical association
Refining	• Implies data can be improved • Implies increasing value in the data through change	• Implies that changes make the data better • Implies the data loses some aspect or dimensionality
Standardizing	• Implies consistent processing procedures	• Does not fully capture the entire data processing pipeline
Transforming	• Implies data can be worked with and identified in different ways	• Implies data is not acceptable in its current format • Lacks the social activity involved with processing
Wrangling	• Implies working with messy and complex data • Implies data is active and "moving"	• Implies data may have agency outside how the researcher collects it • May not imply the need for consistency

still alive and there is a connection between the researcher ("wrangler") and data ("the wrangled"). Wrangling could fit into a chapter on data collection, but I choose to place it in the analysis as it involves thinking about data in a variety of ways and choosing how to represent data. These choices are all part of analysis, even if they are dependent on collection.

For case studies, wrangling contains five steps. First, *inspecting* involves observing data to identify any issues such as missing values, duplicates, inconsistencies, or mistakes. Second, *cleaning* involves removing or correcting errors. Third, *transforming* involves modifying the data to answer research questions, which can include converting data from one format to another or turning one category of data into another. Fourth, *integrating* is the process of combining multiple data sources into a dataset that can cohere into a case study. Fifth, *reducing* the data means to make the dataset into something able to be written about. Reduction often leaves out important features but this is a practical outcome if datasets are inordinately large.

While researchers have devoted entire books to pre-processing and data wrangling, both conceptual and practical, I choose to highlight four questions related to pre-processing and wrangling salient to digital case study research. First, what are the formats of the data and how will these formats *interact*? Because digital cases are likely to draw on text, image, observation notes, wireframe, and other formats, these data cannot all be compared readily. Considering what format types are outliers (or inliers) may prompt researchers to turn their attention to, or away from, those outliers. Second, what kind of wrangling process is needed for the data? For many qualitative researchers, wrangling may not be needed at all or even desired. That said, if such a process is needed, will you need an existing data-cleaning process or create a custom process? There are many computational packages available without needing to develop highly specialized pipelines. Third, how will data be labeled? Labeling data *is* analysis. Labeling is often an overlooked element. Fourth, researchers need to consider the ethical implications of their data collection and processing. While I will discuss ethics in the next chapter, important elements of processing data include anonymization of user data (if applicable and/or warranted), misidentifying data, and self-critiquing the data processing stage as a *part* of analysis.

Part IV: Analytical techniques for digital case study analysis

Up to this point, I've largely avoided positioning this book as qualitative or quantitative in nature because the qualitative and quantitative divide breaks down, somewhat, with digital case study research. While case study research often emphasizes a connection between domain and methodological paradigm, such as government scholars drawing on quantitative approaches (e.g., Elman et al., 2016; Gerring, 2017) or education researchers drawing on qualitative methods (e.g., Bartlett & Vavrus, 2017; Bassey, 1999; Dyson & Genishi, 2005; Herrington & Curtis, 2000; Merriam, 1998; Stake, 1995), contemporary case study research in the latter 20th and early 21st centuries appears to accept both paradigms as not only effective but also as possibly productive when applied in synchronicity (e.g., Blatter & Haverland, 2012; George & Bennett, 2005; Seawright & Gerring, 2008; Smith, 1994; Tietje & Scholz, 2002). Digital case studies in fact can benefit from a further union of qualitative and quantitative approaches when it comes to analysis. With web scraping, for instance, digital research enables large datasets to be collected. If these sets are large enough, quantitative approaches could be warranted even if the case is qualitative. In my own research, I've collected enough data on single users that I could start making descriptive statements about their habits, including the frequency with which they post and the timing of their posts.

Even with quantitative analysis, though, case studies often call for the fine-tuned, manual work of human beings. The framework that I advocate for in this book, then, is to view qualitative and quantitative analyses as a spectrum or gradient, ranging from completely inductive qualitative analysis to deductive quantitative analysis. Because no analytical framework can be complete, I instead emphasize digital analysis techniques that are related to social media platforms and networks.

There is a general analytical strategy common to many qualitative case studies. The general approach is identifying (or creating, depending on epistemic positioning) patterns in the data. These patterns are typically carried out through the activity of tagging or labeling (first cycle), qualitative coding[3] (second cycle), and thematizing (third cycle). The themes are generally then rethought and reorganized to identify relationships between themes at a broader level (fourth cycle, combining earlier cycles). Researchers may then take these broad themes and engage in hierarchicalization to determine which categories and concepts connect back to their theories while making judgments about importance. There are many versions of this time-intensive process that, despite the labor involved, yields high-quality case studies that reflect the complex nature of the entity under study. This process is messy and requires being transparent[4] about how ideas were developed throughout the analytical process, including how these stages are iterative and recursive.

One of the most common approaches is grounded theory, which attempts to avoid casting a pre-existing theory on data. Grounded theory opts for an open and inductive approach to answering research questions. Concepts emerge from the "ground up" in this methodology. Indebted to sociologists,[5] grounded theory is practically described as an initial process of open coding that progresses to axial coding. Connecting axial code to theory and creating broad categories, ones that may appear in final research products, such as journal articles or reports, is known as selective coding. Teston (2017) summarizes the grounded theory approach succinctly:

> the collection, coding, and analysis of data happen iteratively, or co-occur. This approach ensures that any substantive theory built as a result of said investigations are inductively derived from and closely resemble actual real-time happenings. With a grounded theory approach, data are not retrofitted into a predetermined theory.
>
> (p. 29)

Grounded theory can be critiqued epistemically in that researchers bring their own perspectives to bear on the data; emergent ideas, concepts, or themes are in this sense driven by the research questions. No analysis emerges *ex nihilo* out of data. Nevertheless, grounded theory, as a specific example of case study analysis, provides methodological flexibility for unexpected findings to emerge.

Qualitative techniques

Interface analysis

Perhaps the most qualitative element of digital case study research is interface analysis. Rather than examining interfaces from a design perspective, that is to build them, tracing the design of pre-existing interfaces enables analysis. Analyzing interfaces requires a multidimensional approach that accounts for basic wireframing of the interface, users entering information into the interface, and the information entered in the interface. In practice, this often means analyzing the website interface and the method of user input, as well as the input itself. Interface analysis involves, too, determining normative prescriptive behavior with non-normative descriptive user behavior: "The interface makes a normative claim; it is not an omnipotent system" (Stanfill, 2015, p. 1061). Stanfill offers the concept of discursive interface analysis (DIA), which "takes sites' affordances as such a general intervention they reflect, and help establish, cultural common sense about what Users do (and should do), producing the possible and normative rather than acting on any particular individual" (p. 1061). DIA examines three parts of interface: functional, sensory, and cognitive affordances. Functional affordances are what things do, cognitive affordances are what users know a thing can do, and sensory affordances are what a user can sense in a thing, i.e., sight, sound, taste, touch, and smell. These affordances enable a powerful heuristic for analyzing the various interfaces of digital technologies, corporate platforms, and social networks.

Interface analysis informs the researcher about the experiences users might have with the interface. A case study, therefore, could be of the interface and its development over time. Alternatively, the interface could *inform* a case of a user or many users, including how they cope with norms and expectations of the interface. Such a critical outlook helps to guard against understanding the interface as something that should be overlooked and made invisible (Carnegie, 2009). A key component here is *describing* images, wireframes, and other design schematics. In my experiences, composing these designs firsthand and describing them helps identify user behavior while revealing functional, sensory, and cognitive affordances that I was not necessarily aware of while I collected the data. In fact, this may build a critical consciousness on the part of researchers (Arola, 2010, p. 7).

In addition to the above affordances, interface analysis can include examining subtypes of functional affordances, specifically amplifying and circulatory affordances. Amplification and circulatory affordances are essentially buttons or other qualitative elements that move information between users and other interfaces. In concrete terms, this might be the act of sharing content on a platform or between social networks. What distinguishes these two types of affordances is they move beyond a single interface and emphasize how information moves between interfaces. Digital media are designed to move (i.e., circulate) between artifacts and things, such as software applications, as well as changing the size of audience engagement with content (i.e., amplification).

Integration of text, image, emojis, stickers, GIFs, and other semiotics

In any study, there is likely to be a wide combination of multimodal data, including plain text, images, emojis, digital stickers, GIFs, and videos that require analysis. Accounting for these types of data through coding schemas requires translation of the individual example as well as their meaning when they occur in combinations. In some situations, for instance, emojis need to be translated for their meaning when they appear at the end of a sentence in a stand-alone sequence. Imagine here collecting text messages or in-game exchanges of users who rapidly use emojis to represent their emotional state. Emojis might also need to be translated when they are replacements, surrogates, or substitute for words, phrases, or even events.

Analyzing emojis and other multimodal semiotics requires balancing prescriptive meaning with descriptive usage. By way of illustration, emojis have stated, prescriptive Unicode meaning, which is the organization that standardizes emojis across electronic devices. Researchers could use a reliable emoji dictionary or reference guide, such as Unicode's full emoji list.[6] While Unicode has a problematic history of racial bias,[7] this list provides an updated comprehensive list of emojis and their meanings. Yet, emojis have a descriptive meaning that depends on context, positionality within sentence, frequency, and repetition. Analyzing the frequency and patterns of emojis used in the case study's dataset offers insights into the underlying emotions, attitudes, and communication patterns of the participants. Asking participants either through interviews or casual exchanges the meaning of the emojis is a way to confirm or disavow certain meanings.

In terms of concrete methods, coding emojis with both stated and ambiguous meaning creates a framework for determining the multiplicity of meaning with such semiotic communication.[8] One might add, if feasible, how participants defined the meaning and how their audiences understood the meaning (Table 4.2). Single usages and combinations of emojis should also be coded for their complexity of meaning. A smiley face (☺) might simply mean a smile. But the see-no-evil monkey (🙈) may represent a complex idea. A combination of emojis could serve to create a complex chain of events, such as throwing up (🤢🤮) or traveling by plane (🧳✈).

The complexity of this coding is made more difficult when text, GIFs, stickers, images, and videos are integrated. While the process is often *ad hoc* and particular to the data, I have found that re-establishing connections with participants or their audiences, if possible and applicable, helps to determine meaning here. This process could be undertaken with a brief correspondence, e.g., sending an email or message. Nevertheless, analyzing the multiple modes of data is a salient concern for digital researchers and likely requires a more embodied approach to analysis.

110 *Analysis for digital cases*

Table 4.2 Sample template of coding emojis and their ambiguity (answers provided are for illustration only). Coding meanings from both participants and their audiences provides analytical structure when trying to understand emotions, attitudes, and social cues in multimodal, semiotic meaning. This step can be particularly important in cross-cultural, cross-device, and cross-identity digital studies in which the same emoji may be interpreted in divergent ways

Emoji	Stated meaning (Unicode)	Possible meanings (researcher interpretations)	Participant meaning (confirmed via interview or correspondence)	Audience meaning (confirmed via interview or correspondence)
😬	Grimacing face	Discomfort, unhappy, awkward, disgust	Discomfort	Awkward
😵	Dizzy face	Confusion, under the influence of alcohol and other drugs, surprised	Surprised	Intoxicated
🙃	Upside-down face	Sarcasm, pointing out ridiculous nature of statement, humorous passive aggressive way of stating disapproval	Sarcasm	Unsure
👍	Thumbs up	Approval, acknowledgement, ending conversation, passive aggressive end to conversation	Approval	Annoyance

Describing embodiment while analyzing data

One way to account for the complexity of analyzing these various forms of digital communication is to reframe them as *embodied action*. Rather than adopt the perspective that digital interactions are disembodied, digital interactions can be understood as discursively embodied through text, GIFs, stickers, images, and videos. This perspective has been written about extensively by black and feminist internet researchers (e.g., Coffey & Kanai, 2021; Dobson, 2015; Nakamura, 2008; Steele, 2021; van Doorn, 2011). In digital spaces, "Bodies matter differently in this space because of its continued presence in mediating interactions and communications, whilst being not physically visible" (Coffey & Kanai, 2021, p. 4). Embodiment cues and initiates how digital spaces are shaped, enacting discursive norms while disabling others (Coffey & Kanai, 2021, p. 5). Integrating embodiment extends to the important process of transcribing interviews, which is in my experience an overlooked site of analysis and learning. A complex analytical schema includes the multifaceted transcription pioneered by Jefferson (1979) as well as more traditional transcriptions (Hepburn & Bolden, 2017).

There are significant benefits to adding this complexity to transcription, including "the interactional relevance of adding in elements of speech delivery and timing, as well as some basic visual information" (Park & Hepburn, 2022, p. 3). Other elements crucial to coding for embodiment are:

> nonverbal vocal qualities (intonation; volume; tempo; audible in- and out-breaths; sounds like laughter, disgust, and crying) and nonvocal bodily movements and positions (eye gaze; facial expressions; head and body positions and movement; interaction with aspects of the environment; gestures).
>
> (Olinger, 2020, p. 174)

These embodied elements occur not only in interviews but may also in social media data. Intonation, volume, and tempo, to name a few delivery components, apply to viral social media videos and GIFs as much as they would apply to transcriptions. Likewise, movement and spacing are key features in GIFs, videos, and images on social networks and in digital spaces. While this can be overwhelming for digital case researchers, especially as our datasets begin to scale, I have often tackled these issues by returning to my design (see Chapter 2) and recalling my bounded systems and research questions. There are, however, ways of coping with complex data as it begins to scale, including quantitative analytical techniques.

Quantitative techniques for generative thematizing

In this section, I discuss three quantitative techniques meant for use in digital case study research: topic modeling, named entity recognition, and sentiment analysis. These techniques could be for single or multiple case studies and are useful for qualitative case studies when datasets from digital sources become large enough that quantitative approaches become possible. Descriptive and inferential statistics are useful here, too, but are likely familiar to readers and thus outside the scope of this book. However, these statistics are useful for initial analysis of data so that trends can be identified.

Generative thematizing: Topic modeling

There are many computational techniques that can benefit a case study approach, including topic modeling (TM hereafter). TM is a methodological technique in natural language processing (NLP) and information retrieval. It automatically uncovers, or creates depending on theoretical perspective, underlying word associations or "topics" present in the collection. It essentially reverse engineers themes in data by *assuming* themes exist: "Topic modeling is a way of extrapolating backward from a collection of documents to infer the discourses ('topics') that could have generated them" (Underwood, 2012, par. 4). The general goal of TM is to identify topics in large datasets of text. The main benefit of TM is to avoid manual categorization.

The most used algorithm for TM is Latent Dirichlet Allocation (LDA) (Blei et al., 2003). LDA is a generative probabilistic model that assumes that each document in a corpus is a mixture of topics and that each topic is characterized by a distribution of words. The model works by randomly assigning words in each document to topics. The model then iteratively adjusts assignments until the model converges on the most likely set of topics for each document. The result of this process is a set of topics that are representative of common relationships or "topics" in the dataset. Researchers can set the number of topics in a collection; depending on the number of set topics, the topics may change given the algorithm. TM is essentially like a statistical table of contents about a collection of texts. A table of contents can tell you a lot about the collection.

While not an instinctive match, TM is a well-suited technique for case studies, in both theory and practice, because *the case provides a construct around which topics can cohere*. One of the weaknesses of TM is that the topics from a collection of text do not have a central construct around which to cohere. The tool creates topics about the collection, but the collection may simply be an unstructured set of documents collected. In terms of theory, then, case studies provide the entity around which that coherence can occur. The topics tell us about the case study's entity and provide insight into possible topics that qualitative processes may miss or overlook.

Practically, TM assists with identifying initial themes within large sets of textual data, such as interview transcripts, documents, and fieldnotes. This thematizing can help uncover implicit patterns within the data, which can inform subsequent analysis and interpretation of the case study (qualitative or quantitative). In a less structured sense, TM can help brainstorm ideas about the data. TM is a more efficient and systematic way to analyze qualitative data when compared to manual coding. However, TM can be understood as a qualitative process because researchers set the number of topics, which in turn will affect the topics.

Let's use three digital examples to concretize this discussion. First, let's say that researchers conduct a case study of a single piece of media, such as a viral tweet, YouTube video, or newspaper article. With each piece of viral media that is a case, there are likely to be thousands of user engagements in the form of comments and replies. Reading thousands of responses and categorizing them manually not only takes a great deal of time, expense, and labor but some themes in the data might be overlooked through bias or ignored by a research framework. Using TM enables an initial categorization to guide researchers, who can then iterate between automated topics and their manual tagging, categorization, and coding schemas to better understand the data. Second, the case study could be of a specific user in an online community. The researcher has interview data, user texts scraped from their profiles, responses to the user's texts, and observation memos. Analyzing these data sources could take a great deal of time; with TM, thematizing the data will speed this up. Third, the case could be of an entire internet community, such as a massive slack channel with thousands of users. The sheer amount data could be overwhelming, exposing the researcher to overload. With TM, researchers could identify salient patterns about the channel, using the topics to make generalizable claims about the community or using the topics as a guide for looking at individuals who possess varying degrees of power and influence within the community.

Generative thematizing: Named entity recognition

Named entity recognition (NER) is an NLP technique that identifies named entities in a text into categories, including people, places, and things. Marrero et al. (2013) write, "Named Entities have been defined as proper nouns, or common names acting as proper nouns, because this grammatical category designates beings and unique realities with identifying function" (p. 483). To be clear, the entity referred to in NER is not the same as the theoretical construct I have used throughout this book. NER can be used to extract the people, places, and things within a dataset to produce initial categorization and thematizing in ways similar to TM. NER can also be used to guide TM, selecting different relevant topics based on named entities or using topics to re-identify entities and determine their importance. NER "plays a very important role in other Information Extraction tasks such as identification of relationships and scenario template production, as well as other areas such as semantic annotation, ontology population or opinion mining, just to name a few" (Marrero et al., 2013, p. 488). Identifying positions of named entities can thus provide some starting points for which entities have agency in a dataset.

As with TM, NER benefits from a case study framework because the named entities have a construct (the case) about which they refer. The case study provides the context for understanding named entities, providing a conceptual centripetal force around which entities can be identified and described. In fact, pairing NER with case studies sidesteps the central issue with the technique: the uniqueness of a named entity. Much of the assumptions built into NER draw on Kripke's philosophical notion of rigid designator.[9] Kripke writes:

> Let's call something a *rigid designator* if in every possible world it designates the same object, a *nonrigid* or *accidental designator* if that is not the case. Of course we don't require that the objects exist in all possible worlds... When we think of a property as essential to an

object we usually mean that it is true of that object in any case where it would have existed. A rigid designator of a necessary existent can be called *strongly rigid*.

(Kripke, 1980, p. 48)

The problem that occurs in NER is a neo-Platonic recreation of an undergirding form that named entities rely upon. The "uniqueness" element of entities means they are difficult to define for a collection of documents because the collection may have repeated words that represent different entities. As a result of this difficulty, NER researchers therefore divide named entities into two categories: generic (e.g., person, place, or thing) and domain-specific (e.g., disciplinary or domain specific words) (Li et al., 2021, p. 50). Case studies allow named entities to have a coherence to them, that is they are about the case, while providing a flexibility to thinking about different ways that named entities could be understood within the multiple realities of a case study.

Generative thematizing: Sentiment analysis

Sentiment analysis (SA) is an NLP technique that measures the emotional tone of a text, such as a post, tweet, online review, or comment. SA uses machine learning algorithms to classify text as either positive, negative, or neutral based on words, phrases (ngrams or sequences of multiple words), and context. Sometimes, SA techniques can measure more complex tones or emotions. Typically, SA uses a five-point scale (-2, -1, 0, 1, 2). These measures are usually automated by assigning pre-existing word or phrases with specific emotional measures. The weaknesses of SA are, of course, many, including a binary approach to emotion (positive or negative sentiment) and misassigning the complex fabric of human emotion, including parody and irony. SA also does not work at the scale of individual texts. However, SA has the advantage of identifying a snapshot of emotion at a large scale, such as with a large collection of texts.

SA is most often used in customer service and marketing, such as measuring how customers or users feel about a particular product, for example using movie reviews to gauge audience response to the movie. However, the technique can be used to measure the emotion within a case study, or it can be used to compare the feelings of cases studies to one another. Two examples illustrate the applications of SA for case studies. First, for a case study of a user over time, SA can be measured to understand how the user feels at specific moments in the data. The researcher could take a variety of text posts and measure the sentiment of the user as they react to events or responses. Second, for a case study of an online community, SA can be used to determine the feelings of the community with respect to events or at a time, with SA being used to measure how different segments of the community feel longitudinally.

SA analysis is useful to integrate at the three stages of analysis. First, in the above and other examples, SA can be combined with other techniques, such as TM and NER, to *initially* tag, code, and thematize data. Second, SA could be used *after* initial and opening coding to confirm and contest the preliminary themes and findings. Third, SA could be weaved throughout the process, much in the same way abduction is used (e.g., Johansson, 2003; Nair et al., 2023; Thomas, 2010).

Generative machine learning

As with the techniques of TM, NER, and SA, machine learning can more generally augment initial processes. Generative computational modeling and machine learning is a relatively new analytical framework that has unexplored benefits for digital case study analysis. As I have tried to emphasize, the primary advantage of this approach is that it is much faster and less labor-intensive than manual coding approaches such as grounded theory. However, a disadvantage of machine learning is that it can be difficult to understand and interpret the results generated by the algorithms. One innovative way of using machine learning for case study research is to *test* and *refine* qualitative categories and themes. Qualitative analysis, such as grounded theory (e.g., Strauss & Corbin, 1998), involves generating theories from the data, but the themes generated might not hold true with respect to other aspects of the case or when examining the multiple realities of the case. Shepard (2022) writes, "machine learning algorithms are better understood in terms of experimental processes of perceiving, recognizing, and attributing that which resides beneath and beyond the perceptual threshold of human" (p. 13). Machine learning classifiers and word embeddings can augment these themes to either support or contradict the theory. This fusion of qualitative and quantitative analysis could lead to improved theories, more transparent findings, and better understanding of the case.

Conclusion: Analysis as a type of ethics

These quantitative techniques may provide ethical opportunities for case study researchers. Machine learning and other computational techniques, such as topic modeling, named entity recognition, and sentiment analysis, can for example address bias in qualitative analytical processes. Using topic modeling during initial stages allows the data to "speak for itself" rather than relying on preconceived notions of what the data ought to show. Named entity recognition may ensure that researchers accurately identify the relevant people, places, and things within their data that they may overlook due to personal or professional assumptions. Because sentiment analysis provides an external measure of the sentiment, it could challenge a researcher's interpretation of the data.

The steps of the analytical process are rife with ethical choices, with missteps and mistakes quite possible. The scale, scope, and size of digital datasets can amplify the harm resultant from mistakes made during the analytical stage. Transparency and honesty, in the form of note taking and documentation, about analytical steps taken is generally a habit I've found useful. The workflow I discussed earlier in this chapter is meant to function as an ethical signpost to prevent the scale of data from overwhelming analysis processes and causing possible harm. The next chapter thus more capaciously addresses ethics.

Notes

1 As technical communication scholar Lisa Dush writes, "Content has a core conditional quality, fluidity in terms of what shape it may take and where it may travel, and indeterminacy in terms of who may use it, to what ends, and how various uses may come to be valued" (2015, p. 176).
2 Content is also traditionally understood as what happens within a website's infrastructure of "what happens between the HTML tags."
3 See Saldaña (2021).
4 For an exemplar, see the appendix in Prior (1998) as well as Herrington and Curtis (2000).
5 See Glaser and Strauss (1967).
6 https://unicode.org/emoji/charts/full-emoji-list.html
7 "Beginning in 2013, the Unicode Consortium—the US based, international standards body responsible for the encoding and maintenance of emoji—came under fire for the racial homogeneity of the original emoji set: minus two 'ethnic' characters, the people emoji in Unicode 7.0 were entirely light-skinned in a way that read as White. This lack of equitable representation understandably upset users whose full participation in the emoji phenomenon was constrained by their exclusion" (Miltner, 2021, p. 517). Unicode has made strides to be more inclusive, including opening up its process for new emojis to the public. In fact, there are now organizations dedicated to creating more inclusive emojis (Gallagher & Avgoustopoulos, 2023).
8 "Emojis could be inherently distinct from words in terms of bottom-up encoding processes, while still being used similarly to words when top-down contextual processing is needed" (Homann et al., 2022, p. 268).
9 "Several works on NER keep citing Kripke's definition of rigid designator from Theory of Names as an essential part of the NE definition, though they recognize that this definition is loosened sometimes for practical reasons" (Marrero et al., 2013, p. 484).

References

Anderson, E. (2014). Toward a resonant material vocality for digital composition. *Enculturation*. https://enculturation.net/materialvocality

Arola, K. L. (2010). The design of Web 2.0: The rise of the template, the fall of design. *Computers and Composition*, 27(1), 4–14. https://doi.org/10.1016/j.compcom.2009.11.004.

Bartlett, L., & Vavrus, F. (2017). *Rethinking case study research: A comparative approach*. Routledge.

Bassey, M. (1999). *Case study research in educational settings*. Open University Press.
Batova, T., & Clark, D. (2015). The complexities of globalized content management. *Journal of Business and Technical Communication*, 29(2), 221–235. https://doi.org/10.1177/1050651914562472.
Blatter, J., & Haverland, M. (2012). *Designing case studies: Explanatory approaches in small-N research*. Palgrave Macmillan.
Blei, D. M., Ng, A. Y., & Jordan, M. I. (2003). Latent Dirichlet Allocation. *Journal of Machine Learning Research*, 3(4–5), 993–1022. https://doi.org/10.1016/b978-0-12-411519-4.00006-9.
Bolter, J. D., & Grusin, R. (2000). *Remediation: Understanding new media*. MIT Press.
Bringull, H. (2018). *Dark patterns*. https://darkpatterns.org/.
Carnegie, T. A. M. (2009). Interface as exordium: The rhetoric of interactivity. *Computers and Composition*, 26(3), 164–173. https://doi.org/10.1016/j.compcom.2009.05.005.
Coffey, J., & Kanai, A. (2021). Feminist fire: Embodiment and affect in managing conflict in digital feminist spaces. *Feminist Media Studies*. https://doi.org/10.1080/14680777.2021.1986095.
Dobson, A. S. (2015). *Postfeminist digital cultures: Femininity, social media and self-representation*. Palgrave Macmillan.
Dush, L. (2015). When writing becomes content. *College Composition and Communication*, 67(2), 173–196.
Dyson, A. H., & Genishi, C. (2005). *On the case: Approaches to language and literacy research*. Teachers College Press.
Elman, C., Gerring, J., & Mahoney, J. (2016). Case study research: Putting the quant into the qual. *Sociological Methods & Research*, 45(3), 375–391. https://doi.org/10.1177/0049124116644273.
Gallagher, J. R. (2020). The economy of online comments: Attention as economic motivation in digital public spheres. In S. Ross & A. Pilsch (Eds.), *Digital age: Histories of digital textual labor* (pp. 172–184). Routledge.
Gallagher, J. R., & Avgoustopoulos, R. E. (2023). Emojination facilitates inclusive emoji design through technical writing: Fitting tactical technical communication inside institutional structures. *Journal of Technical Writing and Communication*. https://doi.org/10.1177/00472816231161062.
Gallagher, J. R., Chen, Y., Wagner, K., Wang, X., Zeng, J., & Kong, A. L. (2020). Peering at the internet abyss: Using big data audience analysis to understand online comments. *Technical Communication Quarterly*, 29(2), 155–173. https://doi.org/10.1080/10572252.2019.1634766.
Gentle, A. (2012). *Conversation and community: The social web for documentation*. XML Press.
George, A., & Bennett, A. (2005). *Case studies and theory development in the social sciences*. MIT Press.
Gerring, J. (2017). *Case study research: Principles and practices*. Cambridge University Press.
Gitelman, L. (2014). *Paper knowledge*. Duke University Press.
Glaser, B. G., & Strauss, A. (1967). *The discovery of grounded theory: Strategies for qualitative research*. Aldine.
Goodwin, I., Griffin, C., Lyons, A., McCreanor, T., & Moewaka Barnes, H. (2016). Precarious popularity: Facebook drinking photos, the attention economy, and

the regime of the branded self. *Social Media + Society*, 2(1), 1–13. https://doi.org/10.1177/2056305116628889.

Hart-Davidson, W., Bernhardt, G., McLeod, M., Rife, M., & Grabill, J. T. (2007). Coming to content management: Inventing infrastructure for organizational knowledge work. *Technical Communication Quarterly*, 17(1), 10–34. https://doi.org/10.1080/10572250701588608.

Hepburn, A., & Bolden, G. B. (2017). *Transcribing for social research*. Sage Publications. https://doi.org/10.4135/9781473920460.

Herrington, A. J., & Curtis, M. (2000). *Persons in process: Four stories of writing and personal development in college*. National Council of Teachers.

Hollingsworth, D. (1995). *Workflow management coalition: The workflow reference model*. The Workflow Management Coalition.

Homann, L. A., Roberts, B. R. T., Ahmed, S., & Fernandes, M. A. (2022). Are emojis processed visuo-spatially or verbally? Evidence for dual codes. *Visual Cognition*, 30(4), 267–279. https://doi.org/10.1080/13506285.2022.2050871.

Ince, S., Hoadley, C., & Kirschner, P. A. (2022). A qualitative study of social sciences faculty research workflows. *Journal of Documentation*, 78(6), 1321–1337. https://doi.org/10.1108/JD-08-2021-0168.

Jefferson, G. (1979). A technique for inviting laughter and its aubsequent acceptance/declination. In G. Psathas (Ed.), *Everyday language: Studies in ethnomethodology* (pp. 79–96). Irvington.

Johansson, R. (2003). Case study methodology. In *Conference on methodologies in housing research*. www.psyking.net/htmlobj-3839/case_study_methodology-_rolf_johansson_ver_2.pdf.

Kirk, A. (2016). *Data visualisation: A handbook for data driven design*. Sage Publications.

Kou, Y., Gray, C. M., Toombs, A. L., & Adams, R. S. (2018). Knowledge production and social roles in an online community of emerging occupation: A study of user experience practitioners on Reddit. *Proceedings of the 51st Hawaii International Conference on System Sciences*, 2068–2077. http://dx.doi.org/10.24251/HICSS.2018.261.

Kripke, S. (1980). *Naming and necessity*. Harvard University Press.

Law, J. (2004). *After method: Mess in social science research*. Routledge.

Li, J., Sun, A., Han, J., & Li, C. (2021). A survey on deep learning for named entity recognition. *IEEE Transactions on Knowledge and Data Engineering*, 34(1), 50–70. https://doi.org/10.1109/TKDE.2020.2981314.

Lockridge, T., & Van Ittersum, D. (2020). *Writing workflows: Beyond word processing*. University of Michigan Press.

Marrero, M., Urbano, J., Sánchez-Cuadrado, S., Morato, J., & Gómez-Berbís, J. M. (2013). Named entity recognition: Fallacies, challenges and opportunities. *Computer Standards & Interfaces*, 35(5), 482–489. https://doi.org/10.1016/j.csi.2012.09.004.

McKelvey, F., & Hunt, R. (2019). Discoverability: Toward a definition of content discovery through platforms. *Social Media + Society*, 5(1), 1–15. https://doi.org/10.1177/2056305118819188.

McLellan, E., MacQueen, K. M., & Neidig, J. L. (2003). Beyond the qualitative interview: Data preparation and transcription. *Field Methods*, 15(1), 63–84. https://doi.org/10.1177/1525822X02239573.

Merriam, S. B. (1998). *Qualitative research and case study applications in education*. Jossey-Bass.

Milner, R. M. (2013). Pop polyvocality: Internet memes, public participation, and the occupy Wall Street movement. *International Journal of Communication, 7*, 2357–2390.

Miltner, K. M. (2021). "One part politics, one part technology, one part history": Racial representation in the Unicode 7.0 emoji set. *New Media and Society, 23* (3), 515–534. https://doi.org/10.1177/1461444819899623.

Morgan, S. J., Pullon, S. R. H., Macdonald, L. M., McKinlay, E. M., & Gray, B. V. (2017). Case study observational research: A framework for conducting case study research where observation data are the focus. *Qualitative Health Research, 27*(7), 1060–1068. https://doi.org/10.1177/1049732316649160.

Nair, L. B., Gibbert, M., & Hoorani, B. H. (2023). *Combining case study designs for theory building*. Cambridge University Press.

Nakamura, L. (2008). *Digitizing race: Visual cultures of the internet*. University of Minnesota Press.

Olinger, A. R. (2020). Visual embodied actions in interview-based writing research: A methodological argument for video. *Written Communication, 37*(2), 167–207. https://doi.org/10.1177/0741088319898864.

Park, S. H., & Hepburn, A. (2022). The benefits of a Jeffersonian transcript. *Frontiers in Communication, 7*, 1–4. https://doi.org/10.3389/fcomm.2022.779434.

Pasquale, F. (2015). *The black box society: The secret algorithms that control money and information*. Harvard University Press.

Pickering, A. (1995). *The mangle of practice: Time, agency, and science*. University of Chicago Press.

Prior, P. (1998). *Writing/disciplinarity: A sociohistoric account of literate activity in the academy*. Routledge.

Pulver, C. J. (2020). *Metabolizing capital: Writing, information, and the biophysical environment*. Utah State University Press. https://doi.org/10.7330/9781607329688.

Saldaña, J. (2021). *The coding manual for qualitative researchers* (4th ed.). Sage Publications.

Schlichter, A. (2011). Do voices matter? Vocality, materiality, gender performativity. *Body & Society, 17*(1), 31–52. https://doi.org/10.1177/1357034X10394669.

Seawright, J., & Gerring, J. (2008). Case selection techniques in a menu of qualitative and quantitative options. *Political Research Quarterly, 61*(2), 294–308.

Shepard, M. (2022). *There are no facts: Attentive algorithms, extractive data practices, and the quantification of everyday life*. MIT Press.

Smith, M. L. (1994). Qualitative plus/versus quantitative: The last word. *New Directions for Program Evaluation, 1994*(61), 37–44. https://doi.org/10.1002/ev.1666.

Spinuzzi, C. (2018). *Topsight 2.0: A guide to studying, diagnosing, and fixing information flow in organizations*. CreateSpace.

Stake, R. E. (1995). *The art of case study research*. Sage Publications.

Stanfill, M. (2015). The interface as discourse: The production of norms through web design. *New Media & Society, 17*(7), 1059–1074. https://doi.org/10.1177/1461444814520873.

Steele, C. K. (2021). *Digital black feminism*. New York University Press. https://doi.org/10.18574/nyu/9781479808373.001.0001.

Strauss, A., & Corbin, J. (1998). *Basics of qualitative research: Techniques and procedures for developing grounded theory*. Sage Publications.

Teston, C. (2017). *Bodies in flux: Scientific methods for negotiating medical uncertainty*. University of Chicago Press. https://doi.org/10.7208/chicago/9780226450834.001.0001.

Thomas, G. (2010). Doing case study: Abduction not induction, phronesis not theory. *Qualitative Inquiry*, 16(7), 575–582. https://doi.org/10.1177/1077800410372601.

Tietje, O., & Scholz, R. W. (2002). *Embedded case study methods: Integrating quantitative and qualitative knowledge*. Sage Publications.

Trice, M., & Potts, L. (2018). Building dark patterns into platforms: How gamergate perturbed twitter's user experience. *Present Tense: A Journal of Rhetoric in Society*, 6(3), n.p.

Underwood, T. (2012). *Topic modeling made just simple enough*. https://tedunderwood.com/2012/04/07/topic-modeling-made-just-simple-enough/.

van der Aalst, W., & van Hee, K. (2004). *Workflow management: Models, methods, and systems*. MIT Press.

van Doorn, N. (2011). Digital spaces, material traces: How matter comes to matter in online performances of gender, sexuality and embodiment. *Media, Culture & Society*, 33(4), 531–547. https://doi.org/10.1177/0163443711398692.

Yin, R. K. (2009). *Case study research: Design and methods*. Sage Publications.

Zuboff, S. (2019). *The age of surveillance capitalism*. Public Affairs.

5 Ethical habits in a digital world

One of the great strengths of a case study approach is flexibility. Cases have complex, iterative histories that are typically not random but *purposive* (Nair et al., 2023, p. 4). They require making honest choices (Stake, 1995, p. 103) about the selection of the bounded system and how to create the case from the entity of inquiry. Complicating these choices is that case study methodologies can adopt any number of research designs, tools, and concepts, sometimes at the risk of appropriating theories into contexts where they may not entirely be appropriate. The entities at the center of a case study are studied in their real-world contexts, possibly necessitating any number and type of tool use, theoretical framing, and disciplinary approach.

This flexibility, when it comes to ethical decision-making, may give researchers pause. Ethical decision-making presupposes a normative framework rather than a descriptive one. In contrast to descriptive frameworks—the ways things are—normative frameworks make claims about how people *should* or *ought* to act. With respect to case studies, in general and digital, there aren't any universal ethical normative frameworks. There are of course ways of framing high-quality case study work, such as when Yin (2009) argues that good case studies are significant, complete, consider alternative perspectives, use sufficient evidence, and are written in an engaging manner (pp. 185–190). This type of framing, though, poses the thorny question of what each of these five exemplary characteristics means when trying to figure out how one should *create* case studies, as opposed to looking at completed case studies. In one of the older references to the impossibility of an ethics code in case study research, Bromley (1986) identifies a similar conundrum:

> It is hardly possible to specify in detail an ethical code suitable for carrying out psychological case-studies. A code which attempts to set up ideal standards is too demanding and vague; a code which attempts to specify detailed practical rules is too cumbersome, sometimes not applicable, and not enforceable. What is needed is more collective agreement on basic principles and practical

DOI: 10.4324/9781003402169-6

procedures, with an increased awareness of what issues are ethically important, what conflicts of interest are likely to arise, how ethical issues can be raised as matters of collective debate, how "bad" or "poor" practices can be replaced by "good" or "better" practices, how to handle malpractice—whether in major or minor matters…

(p. 307)

While Bromley writes specifically about psychology case studies, he articulates the bind facing case study researchers more broadly: ideal standards, such as those referenced by Yin, must be so generalized that they are either coercive within the individualized, historical case study or ethical issues are so specific that they are not transferrable between case studies.

Digital research intensifies these concerns by blurring meaning across geopolitical and cultural boundaries. Just to gloss a few examples: online communities can be accessed by a variety of users, including users who have a different understanding of social mores; augmented reality quite literally creates multiple realities for the case study researcher to investigate; and online celebrity and influencing raise issues around identity and branding that pose questions of authenticity for case study researchers attempting to triangulate phenomena in "real-life" contexts. Making decisions about these difficult situations requires us thinking beyond the scope of regulations, such as with institutional review boards (IRBs), because many of these situations are not covered or considered by administrative apparatuses.

The difficult and complex situations above may give rise to the feeling and perception—one I feel often—that ethics is simply a personal preference for right and wrong. As a result of these feelings and perceptions, we may feel an urge to jettison the search for guiding ethical frameworks. To give up on a search for ethical paradigms, however, would be to give in to emotivism, or the notion that ethics is an expression of personal preference: "Emotivism is the doctrine that all evaluative judgments and more specifically all moral judgments are nothing but expressions of preference, expressions of attitude or feeling, insofar as they are moral or evaluative in character" (MacIntyre, 1984, pp. 11–12). Emotivism offers a theory that if our moral expressions are personal beliefs, then discussions of ethics will ultimately end in interminable debates (MacIntyre, 1984, p. 12). These debates can prompt the view that ethics is really about aesthetics.

Emotivism is an attractive option in our twenty-first century, digital, globalized, and networked world. Ethical frameworks become tricky when applying principles to changing circumstances that vary so widely; we as researchers might be tempted to give up such pursuits. After all, performing case studies in China will have vastly different cultural and ethical expectations than in Russia or the United States. The problem of emotivism is exacerbated in our digital era, rife with misinformation, online hatred and vitriol, and viral cruelty. Software applications have rules and expectations that differ by location, country, and usage. Norms and expectations of online communities vary immensely; some members may want no part of a research project while some communities may desire attention and expect the research to provide more attention than typical from a research publication. For reasons such as these, we might be tempted to say that ethics is contingent and leave our decisions to the specific situations of our case studies.

How then could case study researchers conduct ethical inquiry in this milieu without resorting to emotivism? Answering this question requires a *normative yet contingent framework*. The framework needs to be normative because *should* or *ought* claims are only necessary when *the correct answer is not clear*. When participants in private online communities, for example, desire not to be studied, rejecting a researcher's inquiries, the correct answer is clear: the researcher should cease study. Alternatively, in the case of a UX case study that tests whether an interface accounts for colorblindness, researchers should have colorblind participants. Only when the answer is unclear does normativity play a role: "the normative question arises when our confidence has been shaken, whether by philosophy or by the exigencies of life" (Korsgaard, 1996, p. 40).

An archetype of unambiguously unethical practices in digital research was Facebook's study of social contagion (Kramer et al., 2014). The study manipulated the newsfeeds of users on the social network Facebook:

> Using specialized software, Kramer, Guillory and Hancock manipulated the News Feeds of 689,003 Facebook users. For one week in 2012, half of these participants had some negative stories posted by their friends removed from the Feed, and the other half had some positive stories removed. This means that for seven days over 300,000 Facebook users had either much more positive or much more negative News Feeds than usual. For all they knew, their friends were having either really good weeks or really bad weeks. The results showed that those in the "negative" group tended to then post negative stories themselves, and those in the "positive" group tended to post positive stories.
>
> (Shaw, 2016, pp. 29–30)

Criticized rightfully for ignoring consent, causing possible harm to unconsented participants, and choosing a massive sample for unclear reasons (Shaw, 2016), the study violates the expectations of IRB guidelines[1] and most likely harmed children. While not a case study, Kramer et al. (2014) is an extreme example of possible ethical harm—in fact, it is generally agreed upon that this was unethical to varying degrees.[2] We generally do not need an ethical framework to judge this study to be unethical.

Let's take two far stickier cases from my own research, one about user location in online comments and the other about using participant identities, that do not have clear answers. First, in my past research (Gallagher & Holmes, 2019; Gallagher et al., 2020), I've worked extensively with comments from *The New York Times* (NYT). We performed a case study of the NYT commenting function. Comments are publicly accessible, and the NYT allows them to be freely web scraped. There is no expectation of comments not being read and, in fact, the entire *purpose* of comments is to be read by strangers on the internet. Nevertheless, users do not expect these comments to be aggregated into a large searchable corpus that includes a location field (often with a city and town). This location field is required to be filled out but is not required to be truthful. The occasional humorous commenter filled in the field with "hell" or "The 9th Circle." My co-authors and I discovered that we could use the location field to accurately plot commenters' location generally—sometimes with surprisingly specific accuracy. Unsure of how to protect this location data, we made the decision to analyze the data in aggregate and map by states in the US. But we did not release individual data locations. This would protect the location of the individual commenter, despite the public availability of the data. Our rationale was that users had an expectation of their comment being read but not necessarily of the locations being mapped.

Second, in my case studies of redditors and Amazon reviewers, many desired attention for their work. Counter to my previous experiences with participant protection, many participants *wanted* to use either their real names or their screen names. In the literature on digital ethics, there is often a thoughtful discussion about how to protect participant identities. Yet I have found few discussions about how to help participants *gain* attention.

The rest of this chapter develops a *normative yet contingent framework*. Such an ethical framework in our digital age must exhibit flexibility to accommodate the diverse range of digital technologies and the unique situations they engender, while simultaneously avoiding overly broad, universalizing principles. To do so, I first present a comprehensive analysis of the prevailing ethical epistemologies—deontology, consequentialism, postmodern ethics, and virtue ethics—emphasizing each paradigm's respective advantages and drawbacks. After this review, I endorse virtue ethics as a viable framework for case study research. However, each framework is useful in its own right. Next, I provide specific examples of how to cultivate digital habits that align with virtue ethics principles for case study research. By integrating these ethical habits into digital case study research, researchers can navigate the complex landscape of digital technologies in a manner that is ethically responsible and sensitive to context.

Four ethical paradigms

Generally, there are four ethical paradigms available to case study researchers: deontology, consequentialism, postmodern ethics, and virtue ethics. The first two paradigms often receive the most discussion, as they are the most common (Salganik, 2017). In brief, "ethics was defined in Western philosophy by one of the two preeminent moral theories, the so-called 'Big Two': deontology, the ethics of rules and obligations, and consequentialism, the ethics of outcomes and results" (Duffy, 2017, p. 12). Third, postmodern ethics, though not a unified body of scholarship, attempts to critique existing socio-political structures and institutions to reveal underlying problems:

> A good number of postmodern (and poststructuralist) approaches take the form of examining systems of meaning with the goal of identifying how universal or naturalized truths, goods, or belief systems have only ever supported particular and frequently inegalitarian ideological systems such as patriarchy, capitalism, eurocentrism, racism, ableism, homophobia, and transphobia. These approaches are obviously motivated by ethical concerns, even if they are not framed in such language.
>
> (Colton & Holmes, 2018, p. 7)

Postmodern ethics, too, seeks to "challenge naturalized metanarratives" (p. 8) and reject grand narratives about the nature of reality. Lastly, virtue ethics emphasizes character or dispositions for finding ethical or "right" action, notably through exemplars of virtues, such as courage, friendliness, honesty, and patience. Rather than rules or outcomes, virtue ethics begins by asking what a virtuous exemplar, i.e., a person, would *do* in a situation; how would they act? In discussions of digital research, the latter two have received less discussion. In my view, the lack of attention is due to: (1) postmodern and virtue ethics are not as easily juxtaposed as deontology and consequentialism, and (2) having four paradigms reveals the complex overlap and intersections between ethical thinking.

Deontology

Deontology is a normative ethical framework for understanding right action as one of duty or obligation. It is often summarized as a type of rule-based ethics in that certain actions are intrinsically good or "right." Rather than focusing on outcomes, it focuses on the decisions or duties for executing an action. Perhaps the most influential deontological philosopher is Immanuel Kant, who argued in *Groundwork of the Metaphysics of Morals* (1785/2012) that moral actions are guided by the principle of the "categorical imperative." The categorical imperative argues an action is morally correct if it can be universally applied as a rule without contradiction.

Strengths of deontology for digital case study research

There are three main strengths, in my view, of deontology for digital case study research: consistency, protecting individuals, and duty to the law or similar type of institution. First, as a duty-centered or rule-based approach, deontology emphasizes *consistency* in ethical decision-making. Consistency helps frame agents as impartial and objective in their judgments. While case study researchers know such impartiality and objectivity are not possible, deontology tries to get closer to such concepts. If one follows strict adherence to rules, in theory objectivity can be more closely—though never fully—achieved. In terms of case studies writ-large, deontology could help researchers develop a set of rules around consistent boundary production, notably if researchers are producing multiple case studies and plan to compare those cases. If researchers are part of a team, rules might be set about collection and analyses such that the collaborators achieve better communication between their decision-making processes and procedures.

For digital research, consistency has multiple advantages, three of which I discuss here. Online communities may trust researchers with transparent and explicit procedures, such as written consent forms or data management plans. I have found that participants trust me more if I have the appropriate paperwork. In fact, a redditor once quipped lightheartedly during an interview that my project was "official" because of the consent form I provided. Many participants have told me that the forms instill a sense of trust when agreeing to engage in an interview. These documents and procedures, in my experiences, tend to create a more trustworthy ethos on the part of the researcher. Consistency, too, may reveal some of the biased content to which researchers are exposed via algorithms. In turn, researchers might write these experiences into a positionality statement (see the next chapter).

Second, deontology frames individuals and their rights as inherently valuable because the agent has a duty to other people (see Korsgaard, 1996). These duties are typically prioritized over outcomes or results. Practically, for researchers, this can mean prioritizing duties to participants and their data over the *results* of the study. In medical fields, for example, researchers have a duty to avoid doing more harm than good, regardless of the possible outcome, such as with medical trials. For case studies, this means emphasizing a duty to the entity over the final narrative. Digital case studies may emphasize duty to the communities or people under study more than the corporate platforms that host such communities or people.

Third, deontology emphasizes duty to laws and institutional procedures and guidelines. Examples of such guidelines include IRB protocols, mandated reporting, and certifications from administrative training modules, such as the Collaborative Institutional Training Initiative. Adherence to guidelines, as I noted earlier, may increase the *ethos*, trustworthiness, and credibility of researchers. Being consistent about institutional procedures, I believe, also provides researchers with incentives—though no guarantees—to make their record keeping better, which in turn can yield higher quality case studies.

A timely example of deontology is related to artificial intelligence writing technologies (AIWT), such as the generative pre-trained transformers (GPTs) released by the company OpenAI. Let's imagine a case study of AIWT, such as ChatGPT, and briefly sketch out how such a framework would help ethically guide the design of a digital study. A deontological framework would emphasize the rules and obligations that make up a GPT technology; a deontological-oriented researcher would stress how ChatGPT is developed through rules and the processes of those rules rather the consequences of its use. Studying the developers would be especially important in such a case study as the developers likely have a set of procedures they are implementing into the system—and indeed OpenAI wrote out many of those procedures (Brown et al., 2020; OpenAI, 2023). The safety measures taken by the developers would be integrated into the study, including principles and rules programmed into the algorithms. The training data, too, would be a critical part of the case study because, within the context of machine learning, the models are learning principles and "duties" from the data. I will revisit this example shortly.

Drawbacks of deontology for digital case study research

The main drawbacks of deontology are essentially different perspectives on its strengths.

First, consistency can be overly rigid and dogmatic, ignoring potentially harmful or unintended outcomes. A well-known misapplication of consistency is the avoidance of lying; generally, most people know that in some instances, lying is warranted, such as when saving a life. Another drawback with consistency directly applicable to case study research is the lack of situational awareness and context. To return to my earlier example, if I adopted the deontological, consistent rule that all participants, such as the redditors or Amazon reviewers, needed their identities protected, then I would overlook that some participants would actually like their identity—really more like their digital brands—broadcast to as broad an audience as possible. Due to the highly context-dependent nature of case studies, this weakness of deontology can make it complicated for researchers to adopt.

The second drawback is that rules, duties, and obligations can conflict with one another, which in turn can lead to conundrums and, somewhat ironically, inconsistencies. These types of conflicts are common with digital research, such as needing to account for different government policies regarding data management, such as human subject data. Researchers might encounter website- or technology-use policies that conflict with responsibilities to participants or institutional obligations—or even government differences. I've encountered this when trying to read through website terms of service, for example. Alternatively, participants in case studies may use artificial intelligence technologies, such as ChatGPT, to produce texts, thus raising conflicting questions about what constitutes collected data from a participant.

Third, an emphasis on rules and guidelines may ignore consequences while not accounting for *variability* in the application of such rules and guidelines. Consequences in deontology are generally de-emphasized when considering "right" or "wrong" ways of acting. To be fair to the deontological framework, this perspective is due to the claim of being unable to predict consequences or outcomes on the part of agents. Vague guidelines or rules can lead to misapplications and misunderstandings. Digital researchers, for example, might encounter this drawback if they follow terms of service for technology that has ambiguous language. Other examples would be how geopolitical laws apply to researchers studying platforms and people. Case studies of content moderators in the Philippines, for instance, may require different application of guidelines than studies of content moderators in the United States. The study of algorithms, too, may amplify this weakness: algorithms are a series of exacting rules and do not consider outcomes. A case study researcher may thus need an alternative framework for studying such technology, such as consequentialism.

Consequentialism

The second main ethical paradigm is consequentialism, which determines "good" or "right" action by emphasizing outcomes or consequences. According to typical consequentialist thought, an ethical action produces the best overall consequences for the maximum number of people rather than following rules or obligations. The most well-known consequentialist approach, in my view, is John Stuart Mill's utilitarianism, which is "a philosophy of pragmatism and common sense, most often framed simply as the ends justify the means, in which the means are justified if the end is deemed the greater good" (Colton & Holmes, 2018, p. 23). Another consequentialist approach is rule-consequentialism, which attempts to reconcile the rigidity of rule-based ethics while emphasizing the best overall outcomes (e.g., Hooker, 1990, 2003). Preference utilitarianism (e.g., Singer, 2011) emphasizes that some preferences may be considered alongside, or even against, outcomes, such as a person in chronic pain choosing to die, i.e., euthanasia.

Strengths of consequentialism for digital case study research

Consequentialism has three main advantages applicable to digital case study research: (1) an emphasis on outcomes allows for situational flexibility; (2) outcome-focused decision-making tends to be more centered on communities and society than on individuals and their rights; and (3) understanding that *some* negative consequences may be inevitable. First, digital researchers need adaptable frameworks for their work on social networks and digital platforms. Moving across platforms, using new technologies, and moving between digital and corporeal contexts reveals the need for situational flexibility. The rules or duties of deontology may not be applicable in these fast-moving digital situations. Second, a focus on outcomes or consequences likely means the decision makers, in this case the case study researchers, are less focused on their own selves and more focused on communities or groups of people. From this point of view, online communities and groups of users may be the entity under study. If digital researchers are guided by this paradigm, then they could choose to produce case studies that have the most equitable outcomes for participants. Third, consequentialism has the capacity for practical action due to its capacity for understanding that some negative consequences are *inevitable*. The paradigm, as I see it, seeks to *maximize* positive outcomes. This perspective is particularly useful—though difficult in practice—for social media case studies in which researchers must seek to maximize the benefits of their participants, even if there may be drawbacks to participating in the study.

Let's return to AIWT and ChatGPT for a concrete example. A consequentialist case study framework would argue that the rules of AI systems are less important than their output, i.e., consequences. When designing a case study of AIWTs such as ChatGPT, researchers would collect and examine the outputs of the machine as well as how a variety of users wrote prompts and then use the prompts. Developers would be backgrounded as an inquiry, although their decisions would factor into the study with respect to the consequences—unintended or not—of the output rather than the rules and obligations the development team followed. Very broadly, a consequentialist case study would also investigate the outcomes of AIWT on communities and society, such as whether information provided by these technologies is accurate or the impact of public discourse on social networks. With respect to social impacts and outcomes, consequentialist researchers could analyze a wide range of demographics of AIWT users to determine how the technologies impact access, inclusivity, and diversity.

Drawbacks of consequentialism for digital case study research

As with deontology, the same strengths of consequentialism could be framed as weaknesses. A general problem with a consequentialist paradigm is that an emphasis on outcomes and consequences requires an ability to *predict*:

> Consequentialist ethics asks us to turn to the results in a particular context to judge morality—it asks us to consider consequences. Considering the ethics of an algorithm by considering its consequences demands that we trace its instantiation in actual situations, or at least imagine them. We must therefore understand the web of associations and interconnections that algorithms have with other technologies and people.
>
> (Sandvig et al., 2016, p. 4981)

Put simply, we live in a complicated, complex world in which outcomes cannot always be predicted. And, if an outcome could be predicted with relative clarity, I argue that the decision then ceases to be ethical precisely because the decision would be certain. In our digital world, filled with changing algorithms on social networks and shifting geopolitical laws and strategies, predicting outcomes becomes immeasurably complex.

More specifically, the situational flexibility of consequentialism (the first strength) could lead to *ad hoc* ways of making choices in which, famously, *the end justifies the means*. Consequentialist case studies on social networks might simply adopt any ways to bound an entity that fit a preconceived notion at the outset of the study. This might include neglecting (to invoke deontology) rights and obligations to users. Finally, weighing beneficial outcomes with drawbacks begs the question of "according to whom?"

If case study consequentialists weigh benefits against drawbacks, they must be careful to think about benefits for the entities and not their own study. For digital case studies, specifically, I think there are simply too many variables, such as algorithms, platform policies, and communities, to predict outcomes with a high degree of accuracy.

Postmodern ethics

Deontology and consequentialism are readily compared and contrasted but not easy to reconcile. Often, technology ethicists try to look for the strengths of each paradigm in order to build a practical and pluralistic approach for the ever-changing realities of digital tools and the ever-present screens and networks in a world of rapid information exchange (e.g., Ess, 2009). Considering the strengths and weaknesses of both paradigms often forces ethicists to become skeptical of truths—which once again returns us to the problem of emotivism. The third paradigm, postmodern ethics, emerges as a response to the weaknesses, failures, and irreconcilability of deontological and consequentialist frameworks. Consequently, in this paradigm, no single set of ethical rules will apply to all people and "right" or "wrong" outcomes vary depending on context. Postmodern ethics frame objective truth as not possible and stress the relativism of knowledge. Institutions and structures, in this paradigm, are constantly being remade by power dynamics, without any stability underneath those dynamics.[3] History is contingent, too, written and determined not by truth but by those in power. As Duffy (2017) writes, "the postmodern ethos is primarily one of fragmentation, irony, positionality, and contingency" (p. 58).

In this sense, postmodern ethics is less an analytical framework and more a constellation of practices that some have termed a "process of inquiry" (Porter, 1998, p. 29). Postmodern ethics hails from a variety of disciplinary approaches, most typically associated with interpretive traditions.

> Many canonical theorists associated with this [postmodern ethical] movement (Derrida, Jameson, Haraway, Hutcheon, Foucault, Levinas, etc.) offer dramatically different theories, emphasizing Marxism, Heidegger, postcolonialism, Foucauldian archaeology, Lacanian psychoanalysis, poststructuralism, indebtedness to the Other, and other theoretical and philosophical approaches. Nevertheless, it is not an overgeneralization to state that advocates affiliated with postmodernism share a commitment to vocabularies of respect for cultural difference and multiplicity, specifically advocating the value of creating or recognizing the spaces, discourses, and identities that have been historically marginalized or negated by dominant meta-narratives such as capitalism, patriarchy, racism, religion, and homo- and transphobia, among others.
> (Colton & Holmes, 2018, p. 27)

Drawing on a historical perspective of language, writing, and discourse, notably the instability of language, postmodern ethics stress uncertainty and ambiguity around ethical decisions. (I think this is one of its great appeals.) To address uncertainty, this paradigm focuses on *who* makes ethical decisions, these agents' power to make decisions, and how that power shapes an individual's and societies' experiences. In digital case study research, this focus might examine how power dynamics shape users' behavior, platforms' policy decisions, and algorithm programming choices. With postmodern ethics, too, there is an effort to deconstruct and challenge "grand narratives." By performing this critique, postmodern ethicists believe they can reveal ideologies and latent power structures.

Strengths of postmodern ethics for digital case study research

The strengths of postmodern ethics include plurality and diversity of perspectives that lead to an acceptance, and sometimes an embrace, of ethical uncertainty. As a result, postmodern ethicists tend to emphasize interrogating themselves and their inquiries for uncertainties, developing reflexivity and self-awareness. Practicing reflexivity can enable case study researchers to better interrogate our biases and assumptions, thereby increasing our sensitivity to accepting and rejecting perceived truths from their data.

For digital platforms, a postmodern ethicist may refuse to accept certain designs and interfaces as "ground truth," instead opting to see those structures as sources of power dynamics that influence users of the platforms. Consider TikTok's highly addictive algorithms that keep users on the application for many hours per day. One might conduct a case study of power dynamics of this platform, such as how the platform provides different settings for users in China versus the United States. The app is called Douyin in China and limits teenagers to only 40 minutes per day (Madhok, 2021). Moreover, the Chinese government provides digital protection for minors whereas the US government does not. A postmodern perspective is less interested in the rules or obligations of TikTok and the outcome of the applications than in how power shapes participants' perspective on societal and individual scales. A case study of this platform would include how the power structures and people in positions of authority exert power over users and their communities. Part of this investigation would attempt to describe, deconstruct, and criticize the ways such power is transmitted and translated from authorities to online communities via algorithmic procedures.

While most digital researchers do not use the label "postmodern," a clear postmodern case study approach can be found when applying casuistry to internet ethics (McKee & Porter, 2009). A method derived from ancient rhetorical methods, casuistry is an ethical method that advocates analyzing specific case studies and then developing judgments that may be applied to other cases. It emphasizes practical reasoning, personal experience, and context-sensitive judgments rather than rules/obligations or outcomes. Casuistry considers the specific context and circumstances of each case, allowing for a flexible decision-making process that accounts for the complexities of real-world situations.

To return to the example of AI writing technologies, a casuistry approach could analyze each technology, such as ChatGPT and Google's AI program Bard, as a case study to understand the ways in which these companies, i.e., OpenAI and Google, shape the power dynamics between users and communities, as well as the interfaces and affordances of the technology. For example, AI writing technologies are mediated through a *chat interface*, likely to imbue the technologies with a sense of authority and power. Within this paradigm, the researcher studies these AI technologies through algorithms, interfaces, and training/decorum policies (i.e., what the model can and cannot write) to describe how these technologies are influenced by, and in turn influence, power dynamics and their influence on user behavior.

Drawbacks of postmodern ethics for digital case study research

The postmodern ethics approach is an attractive paradigm for digital case study researchers because it embraces context and contingency of social networking and digital technologies as an inherent feature of ethical decision making. The weaknesses of a postmodern ethical paradigm, however, primarily involve a lack of guiding principles or productive ways of making ethical decisions due to an emphasis on deconstruction and critique. Literary scholar Rita Felski (2015) argues that interpretive postmodern and poststructuralist critique, of which postmodern ethics is a part, engages in "the hermeneutics of suspicion," which is a deconstructive approach that searches for ambiguous interpretations, hidden ideologies, and latent power dynamics (pp. 14–51). The hermeneutics of suspicion *assumes* hidden meanings. With respect to case study research, then, it leads to an assumption of decision-making around design and collection about a never-ending search for hidden meanings.

In a digital world without clear obligations or ability to predict consequences, the postmodern framework can lead to ethical relativism, wherein ethical decisions are understood as subjective and dependent on the specific context or individual perspective. Establishing ethical guidelines for methodological designs and approaches, such as effective ways to collect data, becomes almost impossible except *after the fact*. As a result, in perhaps the most devastating drawback, this framework could result in a *post hoc* construction of case studies in which researchers confirm a pre-existing narrative they had at the start of the case, defeating the entire purpose of conducting any study.

For case studies, and digital cases specifically, this framework can result in two distinct weaknesses: (1) lack of consensus around design, collection, and analysis; and (2) fragmentation of case studies. First, due to the absence of firm ethical principles, postmodern ethics can lead to a lack of consensus among researchers about what is ethical or unethical in case studies. There are no sources of normativity, which can result in *post-hoc* inconsistency about design, collection, and analysis. Second, by emphasizing analysis of power dynamics and specific contexts, case study researchers may run the risk of fragmentation. With a casuistry framework, for example, case studies can be contrasted but any principles of comparison end up as critiques of power dynamics. Case studies thus become isolated inquiries without an ability to build a broader knowledge base except for descriptive or exploratory case studies.

Virtue ethics

The fourth and final ethical paradigm—virtue ethics—is perhaps the oldest paradigm, originating with ancient Greek philosophers, e.g., Aristotle, and revived by twentieth- and twenty-first-century ethicists (e.g.,

Annas, 2011; Anscombe, 1958; Hursthouse, 1999; MacIntyre, 1984). Unlike deontology or consequentialism, which fundamentally ask the question, "What should I do?" virtue ethics asks the question, "What sort of person should I be?" (Duffy, 2017).[4] To answer this question, virtue ethics emphasizes the development of ethical character traits, or virtues, as a foundation for ethical action. Rather than focusing on rules or consequences, as deontological and consequentialist theories do, virtue ethicists argue that virtues guide us in our ethical actions. Virtues can include, but are not limited to, courage, temperance, generosity, and orderliness. Virtues act as guides for actions and exemplars of those virtues, i.e., people, provide concrete models of the virtues. Virtues are cultivated via practice and habituation of the virtue, emulation of the exemplar, and developing a sense of unity between acting in a virtuous manner and the correct feeling of the virtue (see Hursthouse, 1999). Exemplars are determined by communities (MacIntyre, 1984; Zagzebski, 2010), allowing the virtue ethics framework to be normative *and* contingent.[5] The goal of virtue ethics is to actualize human flourishing or *eudaimonia*. Virtue ethics seeks practical wisdom to achieve flourishing.

For the purposes of the case study as a methodology, exemplars provide a way of making ethical decisions without resorting to rules or outcomes while still providing a way to practically act without resorting to a mode of critique or *post-hoc* decision justification. The contingent yet normative framework of exemplars enables researchers to inculcate habits that are responsive to context yet prescriptive, i.e., supplying a "should" or "ought" claim.

> Exemplars are those persons who are most imitable, and they are most imitable because they are most admirable. We identify admirable persons by the emotion of admiration, and that emotion is itself subject to education through the example of the emotional reactions of other persons.
> (Zagzebski, 2010, p. 52)

Exemplars of case study research could include (1) the cases themselves, and (2) the case study researchers. Looking for admirable case studies, including their principles of selection, composition of the entity under study, methodological design, and data collection/analysis, could take the form of an exemplar. Related, the case study researcher could function as the exemplar. Here we might look to canonical researchers, such as Bartlett and Vavrus (2017), Flyvbjerg (2006), Stake (1995), Yin (2009), or any number of well-cited researchers if citation is understood as a form of admiration or condoning the approach. Exemplars do not need to be exemplary in *every* virtue. One exemplar could demonstrate orderliness while another exemplifies compassion while yet another might demonstrate honesty. With the scale of research in our digital age, this kind of flexibility allows us to search for a variety of exemplars and virtuous agents.

Strengths of the virtue ethics approach for digital case study research

There is a particular quandary with ethics in digital worlds: how do we ask normative questions about information technology (IT) while understanding that "these questions are inseparable from the particular empirical contexts of IT use" (Vallor, 2016, p. 160).

> Virtue ethics is, arguably, the best and perhaps the only solution to this quandary, for while it does reject the use of *a priori* criteria for ethical decisions, that is, criteria that transcend the concrete conditions of human flourishing, it still allows us to speak of sound ethical choices within such contexts, choices that reflect shared normative principles of broader significance and application.
> (Vallor, 2016, p. 160)

Virtue ethics addresses the intractable problems of pluralism and emotivism in a world that can be scaled and amplified to wider audiences due to social media.

The strengths of the virtue ethics approach thus include at least three factors. First, it values a holistic approach, accounting for character, motivations, and intentions together when making an ethical decision while still not devaluing the outcomes. Second, virtue ethics acknowledges that ethical adjustments and adaptations need to be made for contexts such as social networks, online communities, AI, mixed realities, and technologies. Third, because virtue ethics emphasizes "the good life," it has a diachronic component, meaning it encourages individuals to improve their lives over the course of time. To adapt this element for case study research means that case studies can be designed with improvements. Past choices made, if they were flawed, may offer opportunity for reflecting on how the habitation of virtues might need to change for future case studies. Third, virtue ethics offers guidance when tricky and difficult situations arise, such as with the complexities and ambiguities of digital case studies, when guidelines and regulations are not clear, and consequences cannot be predicted.

Drawbacks of the virtue ethics approach for digital case study research

Virtue ethics has its detractors, such as some who argue that virtue ethicists tend to be simply anti-deontology and anti-consequentialism (Nussbaum, 1999) as well as others who argue there is ambiguity around the criteria of being virtuous (Hooker, 2002). Louden (1984) has argued virtue ethics engages in a kind of utopian ideal about ethical frameworks, namely that there need to be rules, order, and consequences in pluralistic and multicultural societies (pp. 234–235). Our digital technologies amplify these drawbacks, four of which I list here. First, virtue ethics does not provide principles or rules for addressing ethical dilemmas, meaning that researchers are left to make their own judgments about their case studies. Such flexibility, if left to individuals, could lead researchers to make inconsistent judgments. Second, virtue ethics accepts communitarianism (e.g., MacIntyre, 1984) or that communities can develop their own sense of virtues. Communitarianism can lead to insularity between communities. When these communities encounter each other, such as on social networks, conflict can ensue. For case study researchers, virtue ethics offers no resources for addressing such conflict between communities. Third—and this emerges somewhat out of the communitarianism drawback—there is no universally agreed upon type or number of virtues, making it difficult to determine which virtues, or the number of virtues, are applicable to the case study. As social networks change and emerging technologies change, identifying virtues may become an *ad hoc* process.

Fourth, exemplars are rare (Athanassoulis, 2013) due to age (the virtues are developed over time) and recognition of exemplars. Young people generally are not virtuous because they have not inculcated the unity of both feeling and action. Exemplars need to be known enough in a community for there to be agreement about exemplar status. Most people are not exemplars, which can be a difficult concept to accept in cultures of individualism. Critically, exemplars can only exist when there is a strong enough community for there to be agreement about admirable behavior.

Habits and practices

Deontology and consequentialism cannot provide a contingent and normative—prescriptive and context-sensitive—way of approaching case study research, while postmodern ethics suffers from a lack of normative frameworks. Virtue ethics offer such a contingent, normative approach. To address virtue ethics' drawbacks and augment their strength would be to frame virtues as *habits*. Habits-as-virtues has four distinct advantages.

First, habits can be broken. Sometimes, in fact, they must be broken to respond to context. Let's use the common refrain about protecting user privacy when conducting online research. *Protecting user privacy* is a habit most digital researchers have inculcated, likely due to IRB protocols and administrative guidelines. Protecting user privacy could be understood as a demonstration of the virtue of compassion. However, the exemplar of this habit might recognize two important aspects: first, user privacy may need to be broken to protect other people, such as if a participant was going to hurt themselves or others. Researchers are likely familiar with this as it is a requirement of mandated reporters. The second hinges on whether the user wants their identity broadcasted, as I've noted earlier. Protecting user privacy could suggest that a user or organization wants their identity known and, by participating in a study, they hope more people will learn about them. Participants have expressed this desire for amplification in my own work about an organization that proposes new emojis for public use (Gallagher & Avgoustopoulos, 2023), Amazon reviewers and redditors who want to accrue more metrics (Gallagher, 2020), and some machine learning researchers who would like to influence how documents are produced in their field (Gallagher, 2023). Many participants wanted their identities associated with their cases, as there was potential for more attention and, consequently, impact.

Second, habits can be multiple. The participants I turned to in the previous example would not offer an effective habit for designing an effective case study, a habit that might fall under the virtue of orderliness. There can be different virtues, in other words, that can be emphasized at different moments in the case study. I frequently turn to Bartlett and Vavrus (2017), Duff (2007), Stake (1995), and Yin (2009) as exemplars of—and guidance for—orderliness. Exemplars of some habits are not exemplars of others.

Third, researchers can alter their habits but do not need to jettison older habits for entirely new situations. Habits are repeated actions that can be changed when needed to adapt to context, such as with studies of emergent technologies. The habits developed in case studies of users on one platform do not need to be abandoned when studying a different platform. Habits are adjustable yet normative.

Fourth, habits are repeated acts. One of the great strengths of virtue ethics is the recognition that most human beings are "rather poor ethical specimens" (Hursthouse, 1999, p. 233). That is, most human beings are not exemplars. There is an acceptance in a virtue ethics framework that ethical mistakes will be made in practice. For case studies, then, ethics is less about adherence to rules or outcomes and more about enacting the virtuous habits as best we can over the course of our research lives. Our identities are not made of one instance, one case study, one dimensionality, or one ethical success story. Rather, this identity is built on a string of repeated acts made for specific reasons. We know too that mistakes will be made, and our identities can "take a few knocks" (Korsgaard, 1996, p. 103).

IRB applications and participant consent are opportunities where, for example, the virtue of justice can be habituated and practiced, while reworking these habits for digital concerns. First, the IRB process, as a series of checkpoints, is often seen as a deontological, rule-based way to secure justice and beneficence for participants. But as digital sociologist Salganik (2017) argues, the IRB is a floor not a ceiling (pp. 321–322). Filling out, quite literally as a form, an IRB application is an opportunity for habituating and practicing the habit of justice through the process. The process of writing these documents encourages researchers to find other examples of IRB applications and to talk with researchers who have prioritized the benefits of the study, i.e., exemplars. In turn, researchers could design the study to minimize participant risk *and* maximize participant opportunities. Such opportunities could take the form of designing interview questions that would help participants learn about themselves and for the researcher to share insights with the participants such that the participants are better off having contributed to an interview.

Maximizing benefits, as a virtue of justice, still satisfies IRB requirements while accepting the contingency of case study research. Some participants may have different stories and backgrounds where beneficence is measured or understood based on context. Online communities may have shared values for instance, but case studies of members in those communities require researchers to attend to beneficence needs on a case-by-case basis.

The consent process is, too, an opportunity for practicing and habituating the virtue of justice with respect to a person's identity, notably accounting for disability, race, gender, sexuality, and class as well as power distinctions. Consent is a process and needs to be granted in an ongoing, negotiated fashion.[6] Discussing consent forms and expectations of what consent means is a floor, not a ceiling. Developing checkpoints to keep participants updated on the progress of research or providing memos to the participants about their portrayal in case studies are just two instances of practicing justice with *informed* consent.

With the scale of digital data, rapid development of social networks and platforms, and inevitable obsolescence of technologies, better practices of informed consent that go beyond a minimum are a necessity for digital case study researchers. While forms still need to be signed, other consent practices are needed for AI, VR, AR, gaming, and so forth. Such researcher practices could include developing websites or other repositories where participants can control and manage their data, thereby exerting sovereignty over collected data.

A relevant ethical practice here—one of going beyond the minimum—is *glitching* evidence and data when necessary. Glitching evidence is the practice of making certain collected data unsearchable and blurring images. A glitch is a mistake, usually unintentional, typically within software. With glitching, there are two ways of looking at it: looking through the glitch to see what the "correct" version is *or* looking at the glitch for the sake of itself (Boyle, 2015). The ambiguity here creates potential for ethical practices related to consent. Participants may not want their images indexed by a search engine (e.g., Google) or fed into AI-driven web scrapers, such as GPT or Bard. As a result, researchers could integrate noise into their images or other glitches that would cause these machines to overlook or disregard such images. More generally, a glitching approach is an effective contingent normative approach to data collection and preparation because it operates on a case-by-case basis and operates underneath systems of surveillance. But what are the virtues upon which case study researchers should specifically base their habits? Who do we model ethical practices on for case study research? Where do we find such exemplars?

What kind of researcher should we be?

When thinking about the habits and practices of virtuous exemplars, two foundational questions emerge: (1) What kind of case study researcher should I be? (2) What kind of digital researcher should I be? To answer the first, as researchers we aim to be exemplary in our ethical decision-making, though we inevitably fall short, whether due to time constraints, changing contexts, or technological developments. As noted in the previous section, it is through emulation of other researchers in our communities that we can find these exemplars. To find exemplars, case study researchers have a readily and accessible set of ethical habits precisely because of the variability of case studies. We can read through the designs, collection procedures, and analytical approaches of other case study researchers. We can find well-cited and grounded cases. We might, for example, look through the canonical literature on case studies (see Table 1.1 in Chapter 1). For specific disciplinary exemplars, researchers might look to respected scholars at the conferences they attend (Gallagher, 2018). To be clear, though, these exemplars can make mistakes. Virtue ethics, as a framework, recognizes that habits may be occasionally broken, due to extenuating circumstances, extreme conditions, or simply because exemplars are humans and, as such, imperfect.

Based on the scholars I've cited in this book, to be an ethical case study researcher means to practice the virtues of:

- **Openness** and **multiplicity**, which allow researchers to inculcate habits of documenting heterogeneous viewpoints, interpretations, and alternative explanations.
- **Patience** and **persistence**, which are needed due to the time-intensive nature of case studies. These virtues allow researchers to accept failure and address setbacks, as well as the "fits and starts" of case research, including experiences of frustration.
- **Honesty** and **transparency** about case study design, tools, methods, data collection, analysis, and the story/narrative (see the next chapter). Very few case studies are replicable due to their non-experimental nature. Exemplar case study researchers acknowledge limitations of their findings as well as the design of the case studies, which includes the relationship between the researcher and the inquiry.
- **Sincerity**, which means learning from the case study and not merely confirming a pre-existing hypothesis or hunch.

Answering the second question, then, about what kind of digital researcher we should be, does not require any introduction of *new* virtues. Rather, it's about applying these virtues to our digital cases.

Conclusion: The case that's worth having

I have endeavored in this chapter to articulate an ethical framework for making normative decisions—that is decisions about what researchers should or ought to do—for digital case study research. I turned to virtue ethics to allow for that normative framework to be contingent enough to account for the dynamic range of activities in our mediated, networked world.

In virtue ethics, there is a Greek concept called *eudaimonia*, and it's typically translated as happiness. In virtue ethics, *eudaimonia* is the goal of leading a good life. A more accurate translation for *eudaimonia*, as many ethicists have noted, is closer to human flourishing. But what does flourishing mean? Flourishing could be understood as the "sort of happiness worth having" (Hursthouse, 1999, p. 10). When we think of happiness that's worth having, it's the sort of well-being that lasts. Spending meaningful time with loved ones is *eudaimonia*. Spending meaningful time in online communities, learning from them, and not simply moving on after data collection could be another form of *eudaimonia*. We could think about ethical case studies, then, as the type of case study *worth having*. Case study researchers, regardless of the ethical framework chosen, should seek the type of case that's worth having. This may mean the case is not a happy or exciting case. Rather, it's the type of case study that allows the entity to flourish. And this involves telling the story of the case and writing about it, the subject of the next chapter.

Notes

1 According to the editor of the study at the time, the study does not fall under IRB guidelines (Verma, 2014).
2 On March 3, 2023, I conducted a search of the articles citing Kramer et al. (2014). Out of 3851 citing articles, 369 returned for the word "unethical."
3 For a discussion of related discussion of liquid modernity, see Bauman (2000).
4 "[A] virtue-centered view sees character at the core of morality and supposes that the central moral question is not 'What ought I to do?' but 'What sort of person am I to be?'" (Schneewind, 1990, p. 43).
5 "…people can succeed in referring to good persons as long as they, or at least some people in their community, can pick out exemplars" (Zagzebski, 2010, p. 51).
6 For an exemplary study of continuous consent in a medical context, see Allmark and Mason (2006). Qualitative researchers have argued for the consent process to be part of a larger epistemic framework (Klykken, 2022) in which "account[s] for consent practices as an affectively charged and non-idealized engagement, and to approach ambiguous and creative aspects of research engagement with curious attentiveness" (p. 807).

References

Allmark, P., & Mason, S. (2006). Improving the quality of consent to randomised controlled trials by using continuous consent and clinician training in the consent process. *Journal of Medical Ethics*, 32(8), 439–443. https://doi.org/10.1136/jme.2005.013722.
Annas, J. (2011). *Intelligent virtue*. Oxford University Press.
Anscombe, G. E. M. (1958). Modern moral philosophy. *Philosophy*, 33(124), 1–16.
Athanassoulis, N. (2013). *Virtue ethics*. Bloomsbury Academic.
Bartlett, L., & Vavrus, F. (2017). *Rethinking case study research: A comparative approach*. Routledge.
Bauman, Z. (2000). *Liquid modernity*. Polity Press.
Boyle, C. (2015). The rhetorical question concerning glitch. *Computers and Composition*, 35, 12–29. https://doi.org/10.1016/j.compcom.2015.01.003.
Bromley, D. B. (1986). *The case-study method in psychology and related disciplines*. John Wiley & Sons.
Brown, T. B., Mann, B., Ryder, N., Subbiah, M., Kaplan, J., Dhariwal, P., Neelakantan, A., Shyam, P., Sastry, G., Askell, A., Agarwal, S., Herbert-Voss, A., Krueger, G., Henighan, T., Child, R., Ramesh, A., Ziegler, D. M., Wu, J., Winter, C., … Amodei, D. (2020). Language models are few-shot learners. *34th Conference on Neural Information Processing Systems (NeurIPS 2020)*. 1–25.
Colton, J., & Holmes, S. (2018). *Rhetoric, technology, and the virtues*. Utah State University Press.
Duff, P. (2007). *Case study research in applied linguistics*. Lawrence Erlbaum Associates.
Duffy, J. (2017). The good writer: Virtue ethics and the teaching of writing. *College English*, 79(3), 229–250.
Ess, C. (2009). *Digital media ethics*. Polity Press.
Felski, R. (2015). *The limits of critique*. University of Chicago Press.
Flyvbjerg, B. (2006). Five misunderstandings about case-study research. *Qualitative Inquiry*, 12(2), 219–245. https://doi.org/10.1177/1077800405284363.
Gallagher, J. R. (2018). Enacting virtue ethics. *Rhetoric Review*, 37(4), 379–384.
Gallagher, J. R. (2020). *Update culture and the afterlife of digital writing*. Utah State University Press.
Gallagher, J. R. (2023). Lessons learned from machine learning researchers about the terms "artificial intelligence" and "machine learning." *Composition Studies*, 51(1), 149–154.
Gallagher, J. R., & Avgoustopoulos, R. E. (2023). Emojination facilitates inclusive emoji design through technical writing: Fitting tactical technical communication inside institutional structures. *Journal of Technical Writing and Communication*, 1–20. https://doi.org/10.1177/00472816231161062.
Gallagher, J. R., Chen, Y., Wagner, K., Wang, X., Zeng, J., & Kong, A. L. (2020). Peering at the internet abyss: Using big data audience analysis to understand online comments. *Technical Communication Quarterly*, 29(2), 155–173. https://doi.org/10.1080/10572252.2019.1634766.
Gallagher, J. R., & Holmes, S. (2019). Empty templates: The ethical habits of empty state pages. *Technical Communication Quarterly*, 28(3), 271–283. https://doi.org/10.1080/10572252.2018.1564367.
Hooker, B. (1990). Rule-consequentialism. *Mind*, 99(393), 67–77.

Hooker, B. (2002). The collapse of virtue ethics. *Utilitas*, 14(1), 22–40. https://doi.org/10.1017/S095382080000337X.
Hooker, B. (2003). *Ideal code, real world: A rule-consequentialist theory of morality*. Clarendon Press.
Hursthouse, R. (1999). *On virtue ethics*. Oxford University Press.
Kant, I. (1785/2012). *Groundwork of the metaphysics of morals* (M. Gregor & J. Timmermann, Trans.; 2nd ed.). Cambridge University Press.
Klykken, F. H. (2022). Implementing continuous consent in qualitative research. *Qualitative Research*, 22(5), 795–810. https://doi.org/10.1177/14687941211014366.
Korsgaard, C. (1996). *The sources of normativity*. Cambridge University Press.
Kramer, A. D. I., Guillory, J. E., & Hancock, J. T. (2014). Experimental evidence of massive-scale emotional contagion through social networks. *Proceedings of the National Academy of Sciences*, 111(24), 8788–8790. https://doi.org/10.1073/pnas.1320040111.
Louden, R. B. (1984). On some vices of virtue ethics. *American Philosophical Quarterly*, 21(3), 227–236. https://doi.org/10.1515/9781474472845-013.
MacIntyre, A. (1984). *After virtue*. University of Notre Dame Press.
Madhok, D. (2021). *The Chinese version of TikTok is limiting kids to 40 minutes a day*. www.cnn.com/2021/09/20/tech/china-tiktok-douyin-usage-limit-intl-hnk/index.html.
McKee, H., & Porter, J. E. (2009). *The ethics of internet research: A rhetorical, case-based process*. Peter Lang.
Nair, L. B., Gibbert, M., & Hoorani, B. H. (2023). *Combining case study designs for theory building*. Cambridge University Press.
Nussbaum, M. (1999). Virtue ethics: A misleading category? *The Journal of Ethics*, 3(3), 163–201.
OpenAI. (2023). GPT-4 technical report. *arXiv*, 2303. 08774. http://arxiv.org/abs/2303.08774.
Porter, J. E. (1998). *Rhetorical ethics and internetworked writing*. Praeger.
Salganik, M. J. (2017). *Bit by bit: Social research in the digital age*. Princeton University Press.
Sandvig, C., Hamilton, K., Karahalios, K., & Langbort, C. (2016). When the algorithm itself is a racist: Diagnosing ethical harm in the basic components of software. *International Journal of Communication*, 10(June), 4972–4990. https://doi.org/10.1378/chest.110.3.866-a.
Schneewind, J. B. (1990). The misfortunes of virtue. *Ethics*, 101(1), 42–62.
Shaw, D. (2016). Facebook's flawed emotion experiment: Antisocial research on social network users. *Research Ethics*, 12(1), 29–34. https://doi.org/10.1177/1747016115579535.
Singer, P. (2011). *Practical ethics* (3rd ed.). Cambridge University Press.
Stake, R. E. (1995). *The art of case study research*. Sage Publications.
Vallor, S. (2016). *Technology and the virtues: A philosophical guide to a future worth wanting*. Oxford University Press.
Verma, I. M. (2014). Editorial expression of concern and correction. *Proceedings of the National Academy of Sciences of the United States of America*, 111(29), 107779.
Yin, R. K. (2009). *Case study research: Design and methods*. Sage Publications.
Zagzebski, L. (2010). Exemplarist virtue theory. *Metaphilosophy*, 41(1–2), 41–57. https://doi.org/10.1002/9781444391398.ch3.

6 Writing and visualizing the digital case

The most difficult part of case study research may very well be writing up the narrative. The process of turning the study of an entity into a written case study is an *art* (Stake, 1995) as much as a procedure. Moving back and forth between collection and analysis to write a report requires balancing coherence and elegance with transparency and truthful representation of the process. Writing up the case study, too, suggests subjectivity. In 1928, Katharine Jocher noted this:

> It is hardly conceivable that the case study can ever be made wholly objective, for in the very nature of it is inherent a certain subjectivity, not only on the part of those from whom the data are obtained but also in the interpretations of the research specialist.
>
> (p. 205)

Case studies aren't grown in a laboratory. Researchers bring their subjectivities to studying the entities within lived contexts. There are any number of choices to make during the research process.

Such processes are much more fractured with the scale and speed of digital life. Our technologies can change with a software update. Artificial intelligence (AI) can produce misinformation and disinformation on scales and at speeds unprecedented in human history. Social networks can fail rapidly or mutate in ways that make our studies unrecognizable months later—or even overnight. Obsolescence is built into our software. The researcher, then, is not only a storyteller but also the producer of coherence. We need to tell our research narratives in ways that are legible to our audiences in an era of constant change.

However, there is no set normative way of writing up the case study in general, in a similar way that there is no one correct way to collect and analyze data. As Swanborn (2010) writes, "Specific rules for reporting case studies are virtually non-existent" (p. 138). The most practical way to develop writing practices for case studies is to first and foremost write while being guided by exemplars, looking to authors of books, articles, and reports that you most admire for specific characteristics. But we

DOI: 10.4324/9781003402169-7

know that this is an *ad hoc* process, dependent on having the time and energy to write. To this end, I draw on writing advice and suggestions from notable case study theorists as well as theories and studies about writing more generally.

This chapter offers a six-part framework for writing about case studies in general, one that is capacious enough to recognize the arduous task of writing. In the first part, I discuss generalities about case study writing, focusing on audience considerations, forum determination, and digital opportunities. In the second part, I describe methods for using writing as an opportunity for learning called writing-to-learn and its complement, visualizing-to-learn. In Part III, I discuss timing and planning for writing case studies. In Part IV, I discuss revision, cycling, and "passes" in the context of our digital age. In Part V, I discuss the importance of writing the methods section of a case study. In the sixth part, I discuss the role of visualizations for case study research. I conclude with a discussion of dissemination and social media's impact on post-publication processes.

Part I: Generalities

Audience considerations

There is perhaps no greater agreement from case study theorists about the importance of audience consideration when writing up a case study (to cite only a few: Bartlett & Vavrus, 2017, pp. 117–123; Crowe et al., 2011, p. 8; Duff, 2008, p. 182; Merriam, 1998, pp. 221–223; Stake, 1995, pp. 125–126; Yin, 2009, pp. 167–170). Case studies are widely variable in disciplinary framing, practical purpose, and concrete methods; hence the emphasis on audience. As a result, how case studies are written, reported, and presented generally adapts to targeted audiences. Identifying, determining, and researching concrete audiences is incredibly important. Having conversations with colleagues and mentors about audiences provides guidance about writing, including expected sentence structure and word choice as well as organizational framing. Considering audience in practical ways, such as by brainstorming tables about keyword usage, allows researchers to adapt their writing to purpose, situation, and context. For example, policy makers have radically different expectations of document format and source use than academic peer reviewers.

When considering audiences, though, two general questions confront case study researchers as we write our reports and findings. First, what if we do not know who the audience is?[1] This question is tricky because it undercuts one of the primary strategies for writing up research that suggests defining the audience either in particulars (such as editors of academic journals or administrators reading the case) or in generalities (a specialist in field X or Y). This latter solution is especially useful when dealing with peer reviewers of academic research wherein the researchers remain unknown to the writer. Other solutions could include, if the audience is unknown, looking at a targeted forum or venue for the write-up (see the next section). The writer could consider, too, the purposes of their work, including typical conventions used in publications they draw upon. Another solution may involve understanding audiences as organizations or representatives of organizations. For example, when we present case studies to people in bureaucratic positions, these administrators may adopt a role that represents the norms and values of their institutions—and obligations—rather than adopting the values of a discipline. In these situations, examining written guidelines or policies may help researchers write their case studies. These solutions are imperfect, but they provide a starting point when audiences are unknown or occluded from the writer.

The question of unknown audiences is more salient in our technology-saturated lives because unexpected audiences can emerge during the research process in terms of (1) the content of our project, (2) the scholarly conversation and context, and (3) our own online identities. Unexpected audiences might emerge when researching, for example, an online community which suddenly experiences an influx of members (Gallagher, 2018). The audience of the research then must account for these emergent voices and participants. For scholarly conversations and contexts, new research is being conducted and published at an ever-increasing scale. Research questions might need to account for emergent scholarly trends without going astray from the research design. And researchers' own participation online and in social networks may alter their understandings of who reads and consumes their scholarly work.

Second, even if researchers can identify their audiences, how do we avoid pandering to audiences while challenging them as they read? Considering an audience requires balancing telling them what they expect or want to read—such as disciplinary conventions or expected citations—with what they need to read. This balancing act is a writing strategy called addressing/invoking (Ede & Lunsford, 1984; Lunsford & Ede, 1996). *Addressing* an audience implies stressing "the concrete reality of the writer's audience" (Ede & Lunsford, 1984, p. 156), a strategy that accommodates the attitudes, beliefs, and expectations of readers. *Invoking*, on the other hand, emphasizes that writers may not—or cannot—necessarily know the concrete reality of their readers. Instead, "the writer uses the semantic and syntactic resources of language to provide cues for the reader—cues which help to define the role or roles the writer wishes the reader to adopt in responding to the text" (p. 160). Addressing and invoking are twin concepts, with writers often addressing/invoking at the same time. When we write, we are trying to accommodate the readers, as our audiences. But we are also attempting to persuade them to take on the role we wish them to adopt. An implication here is the need to abstain from reporting "idyllic" case studies (Nair et al., 2023, p. 162). We cannot always accommodate audience expectations. Sometimes, we need to challenge the assumptions of our readers.

Genre expectations

Genre expectations are another way to answer these tricky questions about audience. Genres could include books, academic articles, and reports for case studies. If we imagine ourselves writing an academic monograph or academic article, there are different purposes, actions, and ways of writing a book versus an article. For example, in a book, introductions tend to be longer and often offer a vignette. In fact, one of my close colleagues told me that he literally counted the number of paragraphs in the introductions of his favorite academic books. Following this average number (seven, if you're curious), he set about writing a short vignette. Articles, on the other hand, have different genre expectations, or genre moves (Swales, 1990), of their introductions. Reports, too, are a different sort of genre, generally meant to be skimmed by administrators or managers who have less tolerance for academic scaffolding. To add a bit of complexity here, genres can appear within other genres (Auken, 2021), such as if a report appears in the appendix of book, something called *genre systems*. An executive summary, a genre itself, is also part of the genre of a report.

Genre consideration, at a very abstract level, allows researchers to write and draft their case studies if they cannot identify their audiences or audiences are opaque, such as with the case of blinded peer reviewers or unknown bureaucratic readers. Considering genre moves, signals, and systems of previous case studies provides researchers with actionable writing templates that we can follow if the need arises.

Forum determination and digital opportunities

The venue situates the research (Duff, 2008, pp. 183–184). Traditional forums include academic journals, scholarly presses, conference proceedings, and institutional or organizational reports. Venues establish material specifications, often through templates that set word limits, section headers, scope of appendices, and reference specifications. Venues produce genre expectations, language usage, and audience expectations.

In addition to the traditional venues above, *digital* case study researchers have the opportunity to select forums and digital dissemination practices that can have a material effect on how results, findings, and descriptions are produced. eBook formats are becoming increasingly more common and provide more opportunities for *interactive* images, tables, and figures. More emergent publishing opportunities include video-based scholarship, media-rich websites (with interactive modules), and podcasts. Audiobooks, common for public press books, are also a possibility for scholarship, although the use of citations and quotations currently do not have best practices.[2] While the affordances of audiobooks are underutilized (Colbjørnsen, 2015), the audiobook represents, in my view, powerful opportunities for publishing and disseminating.

Digital opportunities, including and beyond medium and mode, related to dissemination and circulation on social networks involve video and audio production. Blogging as a "traditional" new media strategy may allow researchers to share their work and receive feedback during the initial drafting stages. Blogs could be open to public audiences or they could be shared in closed networks. Likewise, video presentations, such as on YouTube or Tiktok, provide opportunities for sharing early reporting and can be shared with hyperlinks only accessible to those who have the precise website address. I will write about this at the end of this chapter.

Part II: Writing-to-learn and visualizing-to-learn

Initial drafting is a non-linear, recursive, and iterative process of case study research. As with design, data collection, and analysis, writing up a case study requires patience, persistence, and consistency. Because case studies are often both a research method and an educational method (Stoecker, 1991, p. 107), accounting for the learning that occurs *during* the writing of a case study should be considered alongside the transactional aspect of writing for publication or dissemination purposes. In my own field, dedicated to understanding writing as a process, one understanding of this initial stage is to reframe the writing away from finished "products," instead thinking about writing process, including as an opportunity to learn, or what we call writing-to-learn (WTL).[3] Writing memos designed for the researcher and not external audiences is an example of WTL and is helpful because the writing becomes a "tangible construction" that allows for thoughts and ideas to "be generated and developed in the interaction between the writer and what is being written that would not be possible if the ideas were left to flower and perhaps fade in the transience of the mind" (Smith, 1994, pp. 16–17).

WTL can be used at any stage in the research process. During the design phase, researchers can produce documents and memos to generate researcher queries, even if those queries do not appear in the final report or narrative. In the collection phase, memos can be used as the data is gathered to reflect on processes that may need alteration. In the analysis phase, memos can be used for analyzing data but they could also be used to log thoughts or analyses that may "dead end" with the possibility of being reintroduced at a later date. WTL can be used during the various stages of writing a case study narrative. During the writing process, WTL can be used to work through frustrations and "writer's block," generating text that may simply be thinking on paper or a screen.

By testing out multiple iterations of interpretations, WTL can facilitate defining and refining the structure of the case study narrative.

The corollary of WTL is visualizing-to-learn (VTL), something many digital case study researchers are familiar with. VTL involves producing multiple graphs, charts, and images to produce the case study. Concept mapping complements VTL by allowing researchers to connect analyses to research conversations in literature reviews. VTL is distinguished from data analyses in that, with respect to VTL, researchers already have the analyses they wish to present and instead seek to try out different visuals to tell the story of the case.

Part III: Time and planning

One of the most frustrating aspects of writing case studies is its time-intensive, recursive nature. As Stake (1995) eloquently puts it, "One should expect that it will take longer to write up than to gather all the data in the first place. Another reason for getting the writing started early" (p. 130). Novice and experienced case study researchers alike may read a well-crafted publication and then, when comparing themselves to the published work, become disappointed and experience anxiety as they write their own initial drafts because finalized research products often do not hint at the arduous revision process that publications undergo. This anxiety can be exacerbated when writing up case studies because the narrative may need to be produced under deadlines and still be true to the case study. There are unfortunately no best timing or planning practices for writing up case studies that can be universally applied, such as a maxim of "Report writing should take X amount of time or X number of weeks to produce." Adding a further element of frustration, *digital* research can change so rapidly that the research might be "aged" or "old news" by the time of reporting and narrativizing the case study. For these reasons, scheduling time and other resources for writing is a vital element for case study research (and research in general).

Time is the epistemological *and* practical resource for determining what to include and exclude when writing up case studies. Time allows us to sift through our writing for relevance by allowing writers to *oscillate into the position of a reader*. As writers of case studies, we need time to process our own manuscripts and reports because we are not simply presenting straightforward results of an experiment. Narratives need to be crafted. Time enables many practices crucial to writing, including the following:

- Scheduling time between drafts ensure that you will come back to the draft with fresh eyes and, perhaps, *different* eyes from things you have learned.
- Time allows you to understand *yourself* as a future audience of your work.

- Time allows you to collaborate with fellow researchers and colleagues willing to read and offer feedback on the work. Even the very act of preparing a manuscript for a colleague may prompt you to revise in necessary and productive ways.
- Time allows you to reflect on the ethical considerations of the case study, including alternative ways it could be written, participant descriptions, and insightful quotations.

When writing, the corollary of time is attention. In my experience, writing up cases can be distracting because there is so much data and so many numerous interesting anecdotes that we want to tell them all. It is easy to start writing up a narrative, then dive back into the data, and become unfocused (I certainly have!). With digital research, becoming unfocused is even more of a problem because the phenomenon is likely changing as we write. In studies of websites and social networks, new data is constantly emerging, tempting us to rethink our cases even as we write. New software updates are released frequently, making analyses sometimes out-of-date. And this is to mention nothing about our own personal distractions while writing on screens.[4]

To break down the time and attention needed for writing and reporting case studies, planning documents can be used, such as Gantt charts, annotated bibliographies, and dissemination strategies. Task articulation within workflows (Chapter 4) can be reoriented for the writing stage, thereby breaking down reporting and writing into manageable discrete tasks to focus more effectively. As part of this planning process, the medium of the writing process should be noted because the medium will alter what and how the case study is written. The medium of the report or narrative can reshape how we as researchers come to describe and understand the case.

As a case in point, writing the case study by hand or by typing will likely have concrete effects on the report or narrative, as well as on the researcher's awareness of the write-up. We know that writing by hand can lead to more detailed planning when compared to screen-based composing (Haas, 1989). Taking notes by hand rather than typing increases recall and conceptual comprehension (Mueller & Oppenheimer, 2014; Shibata & Omura, 2020). Similarly, writing by hand can increase recall of the words written (Mangen et al., 2015), which could suggest for case study researchers that writing by hand may have cognitive benefits for reflecting their research *as they write*. To be clear, typing with word processing software is not something that should be avoided.

Rather, the *modality of writing* has an impact on writing and should be integrated into the planning and process of the case study narrative. Most of us likely compose on screens by default. Denaturalizing the medium of writing coerces us to write in unexpected ways. It may force our thinking into alternative perspectives on the research, which is especially vital

150 *Writing and visualizing the digital case*

when describing the multiple realities of case studies. A few practical ways of doing this could include:

- When stuck with writer's block, changing the medium from screen to paper or vice-versa. Many anecdotes from writers also suggest that using voice-to-text may help overcome writer's block.
- Outlining in a different modality than when drafting full paragraphs. In my experiences, I type out "lousy" rough drafts and then create an outline with a pen and paper. I then type the outline to concretize it.
- Using handwritten notecards. As I type out my narrative, I use handwritten notecards to mentally note words, phrases, sentences, or paragraphs that aren't working well but belong in another section of the narrative.
- For Gantt charts and other planning documents, installing a physical whiteboard or chalkboard may help to "get off the screen" and overcome the limits of what can be seen at one time.

In terms of digital innovations, researchers may use digital technology and networking to write in the following ways:

- Starting blogs to write for more public audiences and gauge colleagues' interest during the writing process. Several researchers I have interviewed use blogging as a site for testing out new ideas.
- Sharing short snippets on social media to gauge audience reception.
- Creating and sharing videos of findings to present information beyond traditional alphabetic text.

With respect to emergent technologies, such as artificial intelligence (AI) writing technologies, case study research will likely not benefit greatly because case studies require particularity and specificity. However, these technologies could be used as a way of coping with writer's block or to determine if a machine knows of related syntax.

Literature reviews

Case study theorists have developed a wide repertoire for writing literature reviews, some of it contradictory simply due to the wide range of disciplinary differences and purposes of writing a case study. This includes:

- Conducting a preliminary literature review during the design phase, including research questions and literature review, is complementary (Yin, 2009, p. 180).
- Literature reviews, and other traditional research reporting, may be "ill-fitted" for case studies because there may not be a hypothesis.

- Seeking out alternative formats and templates may be useful in these types of cases (Stake, 1995, p. 128).
- Acknowledging that, and how, a literature review will change as the research moves from earlier stages (i.e., dissertation or thesis) to a more broadly disseminated published work (i.e., book or article) (Duff, 2008, p. 190).
- The literature review might be viewed as part of the problem the researcher is investigating, providing context and understanding to the problem (Merriam, 1998, p. 228).
- There is a dialogic relationship between theory and practice, which can be demonstrated in the back-and-forth between survey of literature and development of theoretical propositions and clarification/focus of study (Rule & John, 2015, p. 8).
- Conducting a literature review, as an exercise, appears to help revise research questions (Bartlett & Vavrus, 2017, p. 32).
- In more quantitative social science, the literature review might also help connect the case study to a model and analytic narrative (e.g., Levi & Weingast, 2022).

From these studies and my own experiences of observing faculty writing papers, the literature review often serves to make the work *legible* and *viable* to disciplinary or community audiences. Writing a literature review unfortunately follows no set form or established template but it does typically set the scope of the inquiry.

The best scaffolding I've encountered for writing literature reviews involves that of a scholarly conversation. There is an often-cited passage that uses the metaphor of a parlor to describe such conversation:

> Imagine that you enter a parlor. You come late. When you arrive, others have long preceded you, and they are engaged in a heated discussion, a discussion too heated for them to pause and tell you exactly what it is about. In fact, the discussion had already begun long before any of them got there, so that no one present is qualified to retrace for you all the steps that had gone before. You listen for a while, until you decide that you have caught the tenor of the argument; then you put in your oar. Someone answers; you answer [them]; another comes to your defense; another aligns [themselves] against you, to either the embarrassment or gratification of your opponent, depending upon the quality of your ally's assistance. However, the discussion is interminable. The hour grows late, you must depart. And you do depart, with the discussion still vigorously in progress.
> (Burke, 1941, pp. 110–111)

In the author's original formulation, this "unending conversation" was about deliberation, but it can be readily applied to literature reviews of case studies. Literature reviews are the parlor in this extended metaphor. They are conversations that predate the case study and larger set(s) of inquiry. Researchers need to identify the conversation, including identifying, reading, and synthesizing scholarly articles as well as joining relevant organizations, such as attending scholarly conferences, finding online research groups, and communities. The literature review situates the researcher within the conversation, allowing them to articulate how their work joins in the conversation, reorient and extend the current conversation, and describe how their work could shape the conversation at some future point. In the metaphor, it might be tempting to say something along the lines of: "Find out what people aren't talking about." This might acknowledge the often-cited idea of identifying a "gap" in existing literature. While gaps in the conversation are an effective place to start, learning about what gaps are relevant and important is more useful. In the conversation metaphor, we might instead ask, "What aren't people talking about and why will introducing that element help to move along the conversation?" Moving along the conversation is salient specifically for case study research because a case, whether typical or edge, can prompt new conversation starters and challenge existing ones.

With the speed, scale, and acceleration of information exchange on social media and other networked technologies, following, learning, and contributing to the conversation is much more difficult. Due to the rise of preprints, electronic publishing, and media-rich publication opportunities, the volume of publications and the rate of publication have dramatically increased. This may inhibit our abilities to identify a conversation when attempting to write a literature review. In my own experiences with writing this book, in fact, I continually had to monitor new publications. I often revisited written chapters to add in citations where necessary and rethought sections based on emerging scholarship.

The volume and rate of publication, when trying to write literature reviews in our digitally mediated and saturated world, has resulted in what is called *research debt*, or the necessary knowledge needed to contribute to a research conversation. Research debt has been likened to climbing a mountain:

> Achieving a research-level understanding of most topics is like climbing a mountain. Aspiring researchers must struggle to understand vast bodies of work that came before them, to learn techniques, and to gain intuition. Upon reaching the top, the new researcher begins doing novel work, throwing new stones onto the top of the mountain and making it a little taller for whoever comes next.
> (Olah & Carter, 2017, par 1)

Wading through research debt requires reading, reflecting, and synthesizing what came before. With respect to case study research, this debt not only applies to existing literature but also to a learning debt when *reading* case studies because case narratives are typically lengthy, granular, and unique. An underrated and underdiscussed aspect of writing the literature review in our digital age is reading through the sheer number of in-depth case studies. Long-form reading is on the decline both in terms of academic reading (Baron & Mangen, 2021) and the general public (Carr, 2010). This decline is attributed to digital reading technologies and social media distraction. I recommend sitting down with case studies and "getting to know them." If the core of a case study is its narrative (Flyvbjerg, 2006), then we need to read them. We probably need to read these studies not necessarily away from screens—which would be ironic given the very point of this book—but in a space where we can focus. Many studies show a value—in terms of recall, focus, and comprehension—in reading on paper and not on a screen, advantages that appear to be increasing from 2000 to 2017 (Hillesund et al., 2022). Personally, I have found making the time for reading—whether on paper or away from internet connectivity where I can focus without distraction—my colleagues' case studies to be the best scaffolding for thinking and writing.

Part IV: Revision, cycling, and "passes"

Digital technologies have impacted the revision process of writing case study research by enabling collaborative editing, automated writing (the use of AI), and disrupting what we consider to be *drafting*. The idea of a draft, as a discrete artifact, may no longer exist with word processing programs that exist across device, platform, and collaborator. Printing out drafts is no longer a typical practice as it once was (Dave & Russell, 2010).

Phasing out drafts, as discrete artifacts, does not imply that revision does not exist. Rather, it's important to examine how revision is shaped by our networked electronic writing technologies. Electronic writing technologies often result in more local revision but are less likely to result in global revision (Dave & Russell, 2010). While the causes are highly variable and entangled, it's likely a mixture of being unable to see the full document and a willingness to perceive individual sentences as mutable. Word processors tend to give early-drafts an aesthetically pleasing appearance, thus potentially discouraging writers from making larger organizational or conceptual changes because a digital document appears more "finished" as compared to a hand-written document.

Two alternative ways of approaching revision, beyond the notion of drafting, may be helpful for researchers: document cycling and "passes." Document cycling is a term used to describe the heterogeneous practices of revising documents in an ongoing fashion within timeframes, typically amongst collaborators in scientific, technical, and professional contexts (e.g., Ochs & Jacoby, 1997; Østerlund & Boland, 2009; Read, 2019, 2020; Read & Papka, 2016). Document cycling typically includes the study of organizational report writing. These reports tend to be internally produced for external purposes and audiences (Read & Papka, 2016). Of note for case study researchers is that document cycling occurs over the course of time.

Document cycling is useful for collaboration and individual researchers. Document cycling allows teams of case study researchers to iteratively revise documents rather than rely on discrete drafts. For rapidly developing digital research, document cycling enables co-authors to write their narratives as information is identified and respond to their fellow co-authors. In my experiences and observations, a key to successful document cycling is making the entire team is aware of the process as this builds relationships (e.g., Hart-Davidson et al., 2007; Swarts, 2010). For example, graduate students new to a team project or new researchers are often unaware of the extensive iteration and revision necessary for publication. Mentors need to ensure these collaborators are aware of document cycling to set expectations, thereby enculturating team members to expect long timelines for producing narratives and reports. Making the document cycling explicit emphasizes the important role of writing to researchers who do not identify as writers or understand the central role of writing for case studies.

Individually, document cycling provides a framework for engaging in revision not in terms of drafts but as a continual process. In part, then, the writing may more firmly be integrated into the rest of the research process, including design, collection, and analysis, or recycling of writing (c.f., Swarts, 2010). One clear example of recycling is the movement of memos throughout the case study. Memos could be used as collected evidence, such as observations. They can be edited to become analytical memos, revised many times to subsequently become paragraphs or even sections in the final case narrative or report.

One apt metaphor useful to adopt for revision is that of "passes." Because we typically use some sort of software to write, editing and revisions are easy to make. Rather than drafts, adopting the stance of a "pass" over the document may (1) more accurately describe our revision processes, and (2) reduce the need for a new draft when revising. A pass could be granular or large-scale, such as at the sentence-level or reorganizing the entire document.

Part V: Writing up the methods section, the "heart" of the case study

Writing the methods section of a case study can be confounding. Even in experimental laboratory settings, it's not clear exactly what to include or exclude. How much detail do readers need to perform an experiment? This kind of question is even trickier with case studies, wherein the context is part of the phenomena. Determining *what* to include in case study methods sections, when writing our findings and reports, is a complicated query because case studies are integrated, holistic bounded systems. Case study researchers are intimately familiar with their cases, and digital researchers likely have a host of data that will not make it into final manuscripts and publications. Appropriate context should be provided so that readers can "understand the processes that were followed and how the conclusions were reached" (Crowe et al., 2011, p. 7). I have found asking the following questions to be a useful guiding ethic:

- How does including or excluding this data help to answer my research questions?
- Does the inclusion or exclusion of this analysis help audiences to learn about the case study without too much repetition or overwhelming readers?
- What information is necessary to understand the process of data collection, analysis, and interpretation?
- What are the limitations in the methods used and have they been addressed?
- What are ethical considerations that need discussion in the methods section, such as informed consent, confidentiality, conflicts of interest, and personal investments in the case study?

Smagorinsky's "The method section as conceptual epicenter in social science research reports" (2008) is an excellent, in-depth approach for writing methods sections. The method section is a space for transparency and trust (Smagorinsky, 2008, p. 408). The methods section, too, is a fulcrum of the case itself.

> The Method section, then, has evolved to the point where, in order for results to be credible, the methods of collection, reduction, and analysis need to be highly explicit. Further, the methods need to be clearly aligned with the framing theory and the rendering of the results.
> (Smagorinsky, 2008, p. 392)

The methods section is the connective or interstitial tissue of the empirical work, where the rationale for the analysis is explained.[5] Well written methods sections allow for transparency about this process, although not necessarily to reproduce the case study. The lack of reproducibility in a case study methods section is both practical and epistemic: case studies are often not about replication but rather what is to be learned from the case study. The methods section could still be useful for building and extending new projects and future research. The methods section is for readers to understand the steps taken. As a result, suggesting potential limitations or biases of the methods could be placed in this section. The limitations of the design might be left for later sections but doing so in the methods section helps readers understand the context and constraints under which the research was conducted.

Positionality statements

Whether part of the methods section or an appendix, positionality statements have become increasingly important to write for many researchers, with case studies being no exception. In short, positionality statements are statements that describe the position or perspective of the researcher, often about the researcher's identity, background, and personal experiences which can affect their research process, methodology, and interpretation of data (e.g., Bourke, 2014; Clark & Vealé, 2018; Darwin Holmes, 2020; Grimaldi et al., 2015; Martin et al., 2022; Secules et al., 2021). Writing positionality statements promotes introspection and self-analysis. Positionality statements are, however, a *minimum* for engaging in the reflexive nature of research (Martin et al., 2022).

Positionality statements are nothing new in case study research and it is important to reveal the "social identity and values" of the researcher, notably when making controversial or value judgments (Bassey, 1999 p. 90). Positionality "acknowledges and recognizes that researchers are part of the social world they are researching and that this world has already been interpreted by existing social actors" (Darwin Holmes, 2020, p. 3). Being transparent about positionality allows researchers to provide readers with a better understanding of how their subjectivity may have influenced their construction of the case. Doing so may increase—though it does not guarantee—the credibility and trustworthiness of the research and allow readers to more critically evaluate the study's results.

Positionality statements do not, however, guarantee transparency or effectiveness for case studies unless they connect the positionality to the case in concrete terms that go beyond stating the categories of the researcher's social belongings. Concretizing positionality statements, therefore, need to (1) account for the epistemic nature of identity, and (2) be of practical use. The first involves acknowledging the instability of identity categories and social belongings:

> Researcher positionality must be understood in "intersectional terms" as a result of multiple social belongings (gender, age, "race"/ethnicity, sexual identity, biography, and so on) that may impede or allow for certain relationships and insights. However, it is crucial to go beyond a categorical understanding of researcher's positionality that is relational, unstable, and contextually situated within the interaction between the researchers, the researched and the social and political situation within which the interaction occurs.
>
> (Grimaldi et al., 2015, p. 140)

This perspective augments the relational and constructive nature of case studies. The entities within a case study are unstable and contextualized; researchers make them stable through their designs as well as data collection and analysis. The case study therefore depends on the researcher in addition to the study itself.

Second, positionality statements need to explicitly engage choices about the design, collection, and analysis. They cannot simply be biographical statements. For example, writing out principles of selection in the methods section assumes there are excluded factors. Explaining exclusion factors with a rationale is critical to understanding the position of the researcher(s) and could be discussed in a positionality statement. The challenging element in this regard is that researchers may be unaware of their own biases. Engaging in pre-peer review with co-authors or colleagues, via document cycling, is one such option for increasing the efficacy of the position statements as well as addressing the criticism that such statements are impossible to address because of one's own implicit biases.[6] A practical strategy here is to suggest alternatives for the choices made during the design, collection, and analysis of the case study. Such reflection on choices made may be particularly useful for digital case studies in which evidence and contexts rapidly change. Reflecting on how the study could be shaped differently than when the project began could be a powerful way to situate one's positionality.

In terms of *digital* networked case studies, a positionality statement could be used to acknowledge (1) the researcher's access and exposure to the internet and personal uses of the social media, (2) technical skills and competencies, (3) collaborations and relationships, and (4) algorithms and automation. First, a researcher could describe their familiarity, or lack thereof, with specific technologies, the online communities they are studying, and their previous experiences with digital media. This information can help readers understand the researcher's perspective and how it may have influenced their research methodology and analysis. Doing so may reveal the biases of the algorithms and automatic content filtering that have shaped the perceptions of digital researchers, including before and after the design and implementation of the study. In other words, positionality statements may be even *more* necessary for digital researchers who are exposed to certain types of content while conducting their inquiry. The writing of the positionality itself presents an opportunity to address *random* or *systematic* problems with collection and analysis.

Second, positionality statements could underscore the researcher's technical skills and competencies, as these may have influenced their ability to navigate digital environments, collect and analyze data, and interpret findings. Doing so provides transparency about expertise and potential limitations or advantages of the researcher's technological and platform knowledge. One element of digital research that may belong in a positionality statement is how website or software terms and conditions shaped the study. For example, the work I did on Facebook communities in 2013 is simply no longer possible due to the regulatory oversight of web-scraping that emerged after the Cambridge Analytica scandal. When discussing how I executed this past work, I need to account for past privilege in the collection methods and offer suggestions for alternatives now that regulations have changed. A positionality statement that addresses this "moment in time" could thus focus on issues of power and privilege related to the cultural moment.

Third, it is necessary to acknowledge digital collaborations or relationships with other researchers, community members, or stakeholders that contributed to the research process, including how these relationships influenced the study's design, data collection, and data analysis. Some collaborations provide data and resources otherwise not accessible to other researchers; I myself have benefited from being given access to internet forums that are private. Further, doing self-study of my relationships with participants has revealed unanticipated positionalities. When I have interviewed participants who are at my institutions or in my own field, for example, the interviews tend to be longer, more jovial, and more detailed than when I interview strangers or people outside my field.

Finally, I believe substantial introspection and investigation should be given to the role of automation and algorithms when producing case studies. Whether or not automation and algorithms should play a role in digital research is likely a moot point; they *inevitably* play a role in a world rife with surveillance capitalism (Zuboff, 2019). Researchers might consider, then, how they accessed the data they collected and whether they were *suggested* that data based on their own algorithmically sorted content. Researchers should consider whether the algorithms and content to which they are exposed are the same algorithms or content of their participants and research inquiries.

Part VI: Visualizing the case

Visuals complement any case study writing: "Charts, diagrams, illustrations, and overviews are much easier to digest" (Swanborn, 2010, p. 136). If the data makes it possible, nearly every case study theorist mentions some form of visualization. Visuals break up walls of text. They increase readability from a technical standpoint, often allowing for findings to be condensed, so long as appropriate attribution, captions, and/or descriptions are provided for accessibility. From an emotional and aesthetic perspective, visuals often increase the *pleasure* of reading about a case.

The emotions involved in connecting audiences to content via visuals (e.g., Lim et al., 2008; Norman, 2005) are critically important as an element in case study research. Visualizations have always had emotional valences to them (Kostelnick, 2016), although in the 2010s and 2020s, with the intense engagement with visualized dashboards of the COVID19 pandemic (Sorapure, 2023), audiences are more familiar with them when they are encountered. Digital technologies afford case study researchers the opportunities for audiences to engage in dashboards and interactive visualization such that the audience may be more emotionally invested in the case study narrative.

From a methodological perspective, visuals not only help readers grasp stories and complex narratives quickly but also may present findings and observations in ways that do not rely on the linearity of texts. Visuals may help to understand contradictions within a case. In my own experiences, participants have given contradictory answers depending on when they were interviewed. Case studies may be able to resolve these contradictions—researchers should certainly try to address them—but sometimes contradictions are *the very findings of case study*.

Producing images, screenshots, videos, and animations allow these contradictions to be communicated about digital case studies. Images and screenshots can display when users express contradictions. Researchers could produce videos and animations to describe a process difficult to write in only text. All four types of visuals—images, screenshots, videos, and animations—may provide explicit and concrete ways to tell the story of the case or report on findings.

As a complement, these multimedia images, flowcharts/diagrams, timelines, and maps can communicate the technical elements of case study efficiently. Flowcharts and diagrams can explain processes, relationships, or hierarchies within a case study, such as the ways that an interview is planned, recorded, conducted, transcribed, atomized, and analyzed. For digital research, these visuals can trace the development of the case study as it was studied across platforms and, if applicable, circulated to other platforms. Tables can summarize findings, providing readers with direct information of what the researcher collected, including quantities, time/dates, and descriptions. Timelines illustrate the sequence of events or the development of a particular issue over time, thereby providing a chronological progression of a case study, even if the findings are not temporal in nature. Maps visualize the location/space of the case study or can produce spatial representations of data.

Conclusion: Dissemination and the afterlife of case studies

A fitting end to this chapter involves addressing how one's writing and reporting is disseminated and circulated. Much of the case study literature discusses dissemination in terms of the venue published, typically either in an academic journal or as a book. With the dramatic rise in social media, many academics have turned to using social media to promote their research. Such promotion typically increases the impact of the research in terms of metrics and citations, with durable findings replicated across disciplines (e.g., Luc et al., 2021; Özkent, 2022; Tonia et al., 2016; Wang et al., 2015). However, a caveat here: the direct effect of promoting one's research has high degrees of variability. As I have argued elsewhere (Gallagher, 2020), the "afterlife" of writing—dissemination and circulation—is a crucial consideration of the writing process because it may influence how the writing is produced initially. While many dissemination and circulation practices are idiosyncratic and specific to the research output, there are some general strategies that may be useful to deploy for digital case study research, five of which I discuss here.

First, case study researchers might consider *writing follow-ups or updates*, such as with a blog post or even posting an artifact to an online repository. Follow-ups keep the research updated and relevant. Specific to digital case studies, there may be new developments that could change the case or even undermine judgments made during the publication process. Follow-ups could be an ethical act to demonstrate to participants that the researcher remains invested in the project and concomitant community associations. Follow-ups have several advantages.

- Follow-ups address developments in the case study after publication. Digital technologies, platforms, and social dynamics change frequently. Writing updates allows researchers to address these changes and discuss their implications for the original case study.
- Follow-ups enable revisiting assumptions and judgments made prior to the publication process.
- Writing and circulating updates may increase the visibility and impact of the original case study research.

Second, sharing case studies on social media will likely increase the visibility of the case study. Platforms such as Twitter, LinkedIn, and ResearchGate can be used to share links to publications and engage with researchers in the research field or domain(s). Third, managing the shared research is a necessary component of the case study dissemination, including building a scholarly or research "brand" across platforms and sharing in consistent ways. Both ways can help inculcate a sense of community (e.g., Gentle, 2012; Pigg, 2015). Fourth, remediating[7] the published research into newer forms of media may keep the work relevant and keep the attention of fellow researchers. Adapting the research output to social media platforms, podcasts, videos, or other digital media, researchers could increase the visibility and accessibility of their work. For example, a podcast series discussing a research project may attract listeners who are in related fields but are not familiar with the topic (or vice-versa). Remediations can, too, create opportunities for collaboration and networking. Video presentations on YouTube, by embodying the researcher, may introduce the researcher to the audience as much as the result or study itself.

Lastly, the public engagement of digital media and exposure can have drawbacks and benefits. While dissemination on social media and other interactive media can increase the visibility and impact of the research, it exposes the research to added scrutiny. Researchers should be prepared to engage, attend, and manage discussions and debates about their research. Researchers, especially those who identify as, or are legibly, women online are likely to experience harassment. Sparby (2022) has discussed engaging in feminist self-care when performing research in and on digital spaces there are potentially dangerous, such as 4Chan. Sparby's (2022) suggestions include taking care of one's mental and physical health, taking breaks, developing a flexible timeline, understanding self-care as anti-capitalist and anti-institutional, and creating and belonging to a community (p. 54). I recommend adopting this stance, and these tips can be extended to sharing one's research online. Other drawbacks to sharing research include unwanted attention, such as attracting unwanted political attention. For example, researchers may be "astroturfed." Astroturfing is when fake accounts create the appearance of grassroots support for, or opposition to, a particular event or idea.

The benefits of engaging the public include potentially increasing the impact of the case study beyond limited research (academic or industry) circles. Non-academics may weigh in, making observations that could open perspectives not previously considered. This could increase trust between experts and non-experts as well as researchers and the public at large. Such possibilities, I believe, could help make case studies more relevant and applicable across a wider range of domains.

Notes

1 See Smith (1994, pp. 79–81).
2 With respect to the scholarly scaffolding of scholarly work, Bacaller (2021) suggests that scholars have four routes: (1) omit references, (2) add audio effects while reading the references, (3) reading references at the conclusion of chapters, or (4) including references as an optional text-based (e.g., PDF) copy.
3 Writing-to-learn has a rich, detailed pedagogical history that is too long to summarize in this book. For further reading, I recommend Bazerman (2009), Emig (1977), Forsman (1985), and Herrington (1981). While many of these theories are geared toward students and faculty, in my view they are especially useful for the messiness of case study researchers by using writing as a way to learn *about* case studies during the collection, analyses, and writing phases.
4 It may feel to us digital researchers that our work requires multitasking, especially when we are moving between analyses, such as memos and results, and the writing of the case. In my past experiences, the iteration of case study collection and analyses has made me accept the need to welcome multitasking into my writing. But multitasking has been found to be a myth: we are generally only cognitively capable of performing one task at a time. What is labeled "multitasking" is really task switching that can negatively affect performance (e.g., Lu et al., 2017; Rosen, 2008; Wang & Tchernev, 2012).

5 "As a reader, I want to know the principles by which an author has either eliminated data or selected something representative. Simply announcing that something is representative of the larger corpus is not convincing" (Smagorinsky, 2008, p. 397).
6 "[P]ositionality statements are incapable of serving their intended purpose because as a matter of necessity, the statements are constrained by the very positionality they seek to express" (Savolainen et al., 2023).
7 See Bolter and Grusin (2000) for an extended discussion of remediation.

References

Auken, S. (2021). Genres inside genres. A short theory of embedded genre. *Discourse and Writing/Rédactologie*, 31, 163–178.

Bacaller, S. (2021). Academic integrity and audiobooks: Exploring the transposition of referencing materials. *Logos*, 32(2), 34–42. https://doi.org/10.1163/18784712-03104016.

Baron, N. S., & Mangen, A. (2021). Doing the reading: The decline of long longform reading in higher education. *Poetics Today*, 42(2), 253–279. https://doi.org/10.1215/03335372-8883248.

Bartlett, L., & Vavrus, F. (2017). *Rethinking case study research: A comparative approach*. Routledge.

Bassey, M. (1999). *Case study research in educational settings*. Open University Press.

Bazerman, C. (2009). Genre and cognitive development: Beyond writing to learn. In C. Bazerman, A. Bonini, & D. Figueiredo (Eds.), *Genre in a Changing World* (pp. 279–294). Parlor Press, WAC Clearinghouse.

Bolter, J. D., & Grusin, R. (2000). *Remediation: Understanding new media*. MIT Press.

Bourke, B. (2014). Positionality: Reflecting on the research process. *The Qualitative Report*, 19, 1–19. https://doi.org/10.46743/2160-3715/2014.1026.

Burke, K. (1941). *The philosophy of literary form*. University of California Press.

Carr, N. (2010). *The shallows: What the internet is doing to our brains*. WW Norton & Company.

Clark, K. R., & Vealé, B. L. (2018). Strategies to enhance data collection and analysis in qualitative research. *Radiologic Technology*, 89(5), 482CT–485CT.

Colbjørnsen, T. (2015). The accidental avant-garde: Audiobook technologies and publishing strategies from cassette tapes to online streaming services. *Northern Lights: Film & Media Studies Yearbook*, 13(1), 83–103. https://doi.org/10.1386/nl.13.1.83_1.

Crowe, S., Cresswell, K., Robertson, A., Huby, G., Avery, A., & Sheikh, A. (2011). The case study approach. *BMC Medical Research Methodology*, 11(100), 1–9. https://doi.org/10.1177/108056999305600409.

Darwin Holmes, A. G. (2020). Researcher positionality—A consideration of its influence and place in qualitative research—A new researcher guide. *Shanlax International Journal of Education*, 8(4), 1–10. https://doi.org/10.34293/education.v8i4.3232.

Dave, A. M., & Russell, D. R. (2010). Drafting and revision using word processing by undergraduate student writers: Changing conceptions and practices. *Research in the Teaching of English*, 44(4), 406–434.

Duff, P. (2008). *Case study research in applied linguistics*. Lawrence Erlbaum Associates.

Ede, L., & Lunsford, A. (1984). Audience addressed/audience invoked: The role of audience in composition theory and pedagogy. *College Composition and Communication*, 35(2), 155–171. https://doi.org/10.2307/358093.

Emig, J. (1977). Writing as a mode of learning. *College Composition and Communication*, 28(2), 122–128.

Flyvbjerg, B. (2006). Five misunderstandings about case-study research. *Qualitative Inquiry*, 12(2), 219–245. https://doi.org/10.1177/1077800405284363.

Forsman, S. (1985). Writing to learn means learning to think. In A. R. Gere (Ed.), *Roots in the sawdust: Writing to learn across the disciplines* (pp. 162–174). National Council of Teachers.

Gallagher, J. R. (2018). Considering the comments: Theorizing online audiences as emergent processes. *Computers and Composition*, 48, 34–48.

Gallagher, J. R. (2020). *Update culture and the afterlife of digital writing*. Utah State University Press.

Gentle, A. (2012). *Conversation and community: The social web for documentation*. XML Press.

Grimaldi, E., Serpieri, R., & Spanò, E. (2015). Positionality, symbolic violence and reflexivity: Researching the educational strategies of marginalised groups. In K. Bhopal & R. Deuchar (Eds.), *Researching marginalized groups* (pp. 134–148). Routledge.

Haas, C. (1989). How the writing medium shapes the writing process: Effects of word processing on planning. *Research in the Teaching of English*, 23(2), 181–207.

Hart-Davidson, W., Bernhardt, G., McLeod, M., Rife, M., & Grabill, J. T. (2007). Coming to content management: Inventing infrastructure for organizational knowledge work. *Technical Communication Quarterly*, 17(1), 10–34. https://doi.org/10.1080/10572250701588608.

Herrington, A. J. (1981). Writing to learn: Writing across the disciplines. *College English*, 43(4), 379–387. https://doi.org/10.2307/377126.

Hillesund, T., Schilhab, T., & Mangen, A. (2022). Text materialities, affordances, and the embodied turn in the study of reading. *Frontiers in Psychology*, 13, 1–9. https://doi.org/10.3389/fpsyg.2022.827058.

Jocher, K. (1928). The case method in social research. *Social Forces*, 7(2), 203–211. https://doi.org/10.2307/2570141.

Kostelnick, C. (2016). The re-emergence of emotional appeals in interactive data visualization. *Technical Communication*, 63(2), 116–135.

Levi, M., & Weingast, B. R. (2022). Analytic narratives, case studies, and development. In J. Widner, M. Woolcock, & D. Ortega Nieto (Eds.), *The case for case studies: Methods and applications in international development*. www.ssrn.com/abstract=2835704.

Lim, Y., Donaldson, J., Jung, H., Kunz, B., Royer, D., Ramalingam, S., Thirumaran, S., & Stolterman, E. (2008). Emotional experience and interaction design. In C. Peter & R. Beale (Eds.), *Affect and emotion in human-computer interaction* (Vol. 4868, pp. 116–129). Springer Berlin Heidelberg. https://doi.org/10.1007/978-3-540-85099-1_10.

Lu, J. G., Akinola, M., & Mason, M. F. (2017). "Switching on" creativity: Task switching can increase creativity by reducing cognitive fixation. *Organizational Behavior and Human Decision Processes*, 139, 63–75. https://doi.org/10.1016/j.obhdp.2017.01.005.

Luc, J. G. Y., Archer, M. A., Arora, R. C., Bender, E. M., Blitz, A., Cooke, D. T., Hlci, T. N., Kidane, B., Ouzounian, M., Varghese, T. K., & Antonoff, M. B. (2021). Does tweeting improve citations? One-year results from the TSSMN prospective randomized trial. *The Annals of Thoracic Surgery*, 111(1), 296–300. https://doi.org/10.1016/j.athoracsur.2020.04.065.

Lunsford, A. A., & Ede, L. (1996). Representing audience: "Successful" discourse and disciplinary critique. *College Composition and Communication*, 47(2), 167–179.

Mangen, A., Anda, L. G., Oxborough, G. H., & Brønnick, K. (2015). Handwriting versus keyboard writing: Effect on word recall. *Journal of Writing Research*, 7(2), 227–247. https://doi.org/10.17239/jowr-2015.07.02.1.

Martin, J. P., Desing, R., & Borrego, M. (2022). Positionality statements are just the tip of the iceberg: Moving towards a reflexive process. *Journal of Women and Minorities in Science and Engineering*, 28(4), v–vii. https://doi.org/10.1615/JWomenMinorScienEng.2022044277.

Merriam, S. B. (1998). *Qualitative research and case study applications in education*. Jossey-Bass.

Mueller, P. A., & Oppenheimer, D. M. (2014). The pen is mightier than the keyboard: Advantages of longhand over laptop note taking. *Psychological Science*, 25(6), 1159–1168. https://doi.org/10.1177/0956797614524581.

Nair, L. B., Gibbert, M., & Hoorani, B. H. (2023). *Combining case study designs for theory building*. Cambridge University Press.

Norman, D. A. (2005). *Emotional design: Why we love (or hate) everyday things*. Basic Books.

Ochs, E., & Jacoby, S. (1997). Down to the wire: The cultural clock of physicists and the discourse of consensus. *Language in Society*, 26(4), 479–505. https://doi.org/10.1017/S0047404500021023.

Olah, C., & Carter, S. (2017). Research debt. *Distill*. https://doi.org/10.23915/distill.00005.

Østerlund, C., & Boland, R. J. (2009). Document cycles: Knowledge flows in heterogeneous healthcare information system environments. *2009 42nd Hawaii International Conference on System Sciences*, 1–11. https://doi.org/10.1109/HICSS.2009.166.

Özkent, Y. (2022). Social media usage to share information in communication journals: An analysis of social media activity and article citations. *PLOS ONE*, 17(2), e0263725. https://doi.org/10.1371/journal.pone.0263725.

Pigg, S. (2015). Coordinating constant invention: Social media's role in distributed work. *Technical Communication Quarterly*, 23(2), 69–87. https://doi.org/10.1080/10572252.2013.796545.

Read, S. (2019). The infrastructural function: A relational theory of infrastructure for writing studies. *Journal of Business and Technical Communication*, 33(3), 233–267. https://doi.org/10.1177/1050651919834980.

Read, S. (2020). How to build a supercomputer: US research infrastructure and the documents that mitigate the uncertainties of big science. *Written Communication*, 37(4), 536–571. https://doi.org/10.1177/0741088320939541.

Read, S., & Papka, M. E. (2016). Improving models of document cycling: Accounting for the less visible writing activities of an annual reporting process at a supercomputing facility. *2016 IEEE International Professional Communication Conference (IPCC)*, 1–10. https://doi.org/10.1109/IPCC.2016.7740504.

Rosen, C. (2008). The myth of multitasking. *The New Atlantis*, 20, 105–110.

Rule, P., & John, V. M. (2015). A necessary dialogue: Theory in case study research. *International Journal of Qualitative Methods*, 14(4), 160940691561157. https://doi.org/10.1177/1609406915611575.
Savolainen, J., Casey, P. J., McBrayer, J. P., & Schwerdtle, P. N. (2023). Positionality and its problems: Questioning the value of reflexivity statements in research. *Perspectives on Psychological Science*, 174569162211449. https://doi.org/10.1177/17456916221144988.
Secules, S., McCall, C., Mejia, J. A., Beebe, C., Masters, A. S. L., Sánchez-Peña, M., & Svyantek, M. (2021). Positionality practices and dimensions of impact on equity research: A collaborative inquiry and call to the community. *Journal of Engineering Education*, 110(1), 19–43. https://doi.org/10.1002/jee.20377.
Shibata, H., & Omura, K. (2020). *Why digital displays cannot replace paper: The cognitive science of media for reading and writing*. Springer. https://doi.org/10.1007/978-981-15-9476-2.
Smagorinsky, P. (2008). The method section as conceptual epicenter in social science research reports. *Written Communication*, 25(3), 389–411. https://doi.org/10.1177/0741088308317815.
Smith, F. (1994). *Writing and the writer* (2nd ed.). Lawrence Erlbaum Associates.
Sorapure, M. (2023). User perceptions of actionability in data dashboards. *Journal of Business and Technical Communication*, 1–28. https://doi.org/10.1177/10506519231161611.
Sparby, E. M. (2022). Toward a feminist ethic of self-care and protection when researching digital aggression. In V. Del Hierro & C. VanKooten (Eds.), *Methods and methodologies for research in digital writing and rhetoric centering positionality in computers and writing scholarship* (Vol. 2, pp. 45–64). The WAC Clearinghouse; University Press of Colorado. https://doi.org/10.37514/PRA-B.2022.1664.2.11.
Stake, R. E. (1995). *The art of case study research*. Sage Publications.
Stoecker, R. (1991). Evaluating and rethinking the case study. *Sociological Review*, 39(1), 88–112. https://doi.org/10.1111/j.1467-954X.1991.tb02970.x.
Swales, J. M. (1990). *Genre analysis: English in academic and research settings*. Cambridge University Press.
Swanborn, P. (2010). *Case study research: What, why, and how?* Sage Publications. https://doi.org/10.1136/eb-2017-102845.
Swarts, J. (2010). Recycled writing: Assembling actor networks from reusable content. *Journal of Business and Technical Communication*, 24(2), 127–163. https://doi.org/10.1177/1050651909353307.
Tonia, T., Van Oyen, H., Berger, A., Schindler, C., & Künzli, N. (2016). If I tweet will you cite? The effect of social media exposure of articles on downloads and citations. *International Journal of Public Health*, 61(4), 513–520. https://doi.org/10.1007/s00038-016-0831-y.
Wang, X., Liu, C., Mao, W., & Fang, Z. (2015). The open access advantage considering citation, article usage and social media attention. *Scientometrics*, 103(2), 555–564. https://doi.org/10.1007/s11192-015-1547-0.
Wang, Z., & Tchernev, J. M. (2012). The "myth" of media multitasking: Reciprocal dynamics of media multitasking, personal needs, and gratifications. *Journal of Communication*, 62(3), 493–513. https://doi.org/10.1111/j.1460-2466.2012.01641.x.
Yin, R. K. (2009). *Case study research: Design and methods*. Sage Publications.
Zuboff, S. (2019). *The age of surveillance capitalism*. Public Affairs.

Conclusion
Case study work in an era of artificial intelligence

As with any argument about digital methods and methodology, this book is a product of its time. I composed the bulk of this book during the COVID19 pandemic and its aftermath, i.e., the spring of 2020 to the spring of 2023. Over the course of this time, I watched and experienced the rapid wide-scale adoption of video communication, which will have long-lasting effects on interviewing techniques, protocols, and approaches. Simultaneously, the hype and histrionics around artificial intelligence (AI), such as automated writing technologies, reached a fever pitch in the spring of 2023. It is with the hurried adoption of these technologies as a backdrop that I conclude this book with three brief sections. First, I reiterate why case study research is critical in our digital age. Second, I make two remarks about "loose threads" for digital case study theory. Third, I discuss future trajectories of digital case study research.

Granularity: The importance of case studies in the digital age

If the 2000s were an era of interactive information, and "Web 2.0" and the 2010s were an era of big data, then the 2020s are an era of AI (narrow AI, not artificial general intelligence). This ideology of automation and scale has an inability to account for contradiction and complexity. Deep learning algorithms *must* come up with an answer; in many ways, these algorithms aren't identifying or finding answers but *creating* them. Machine learning, predicated on the idea of executing tasks, produces answers. What happens when there are multiple answers, some of which are overlooked by algorithmic procedures? More troubling, what happens when answers contradict one another?

Case study research *epistemologically* answers these questions by describing and documenting granularities and complexities, something that big data and AI both miss. Case study research is in many ways a counter to experimental, statistical laboratory work in that it provides valuable insights obscured by aggregated predictive trends. As we enter an era of predictive and generative AI, studying the multiple realities of human experiences becomes even more important. AI tools often risk

DOI: 10.4324/9781003402169-8

overlooking these intricate, multidimensional factors that are often unpredictable and ambiguous. Case study research acts as a counterbalance to AI by emphasizing the importance of in-depth contextualized inquiries. What AI tools may understand as statistical noise, case study researchers may see as critical elements in their stories.

Loose threads: The concept of a "study" and macro case studies

With the emergence of AI, big data, and digital ideologies, there are three loose threads that need further exploration but are outside the scope of this book. First, the concept of a *study* might need to change in response to AI, big data, platform capitalism, and networked economics. The first and second chapters of this book discussed the "case" in case study but this book has largely left the concept of a "study" unexplored. How might case study researchers reconceptualize a case in which multiple aspects of the study are driven by automated analytics?

Second, with the emergence of AI and large-scale computing, more theory and practical approaches could be useful for producing "macro" case studies. While many disciplines have tackled governmental and political case studies at a large scale, these cases are likely to evolve with AI that uses petabytes of training data. One methodological way to develop macro case studies is to *deploy* and *use* AI within a case study.

Future of digital case study research

The integration of AI into our existing tools, and increasing level of automation in collection and analysis, necessitates an evolution of case study methodologies. Future digital case study research, in my view, will likely involve a reciprocal relationship between AI-driven analysis and human interpretation. AI can be used to process vast amounts of data, identify patterns, and generate insights, while human researchers can provide the necessary context, interpretation, and critical analysis of these findings.

Transdisciplinary collaboration will be needed to study AI, either as an inquiry itself or as a methodology to assist further inquiry. Digital case study researchers will need to collaborate with experts from other disciplines, such as computer science, data science, and social sciences, and with those in business and industry. In fact, any sort of case study framework requires transdisciplinarity. The framework I've sketched out here has been an attempt to look beyond case studies embedded in individual domains. The path forward in our rapid, information-soaked world is to focus on telling the stories of our case studies with specificity in transdisciplinary ways.

Index

Note: Page locators in **bold** refer to tables and page locators in *italic* refer to figures.

access 6, 73, 88, 158
addressing/invoking 145
agential cuts 29–30, 38
agential realism (AR) 28–30
algorithms 82, 158, 166; bias and 12–13; content creation and 72; corrupt data and corporate 89; iterative design and accounting for 45–46, 59
analysis for digital cases 93–120; analytical techniques 106–115; atomization 94–95; attention 96; automation 103–104; distribution and circulation in relation to production of data 98–99; efficient processes 103; facets between collection and formal analysis 94–99; networks 96–97; Pareto principle and power users 97–98; pre-processing data 104–106, **105**; qualitative techniques 107–111; quantitative techniques 111–115; structures 95; task definition and specification 101–102; tools and technologies 102; as a type of ethics 115–116; vocality 98; workflows 99–104
application programming interface (API) scraping 87
artificial intelligence (AI) 13–14, 166–167; and future of digital case study research 167; writing technologies (AIWT) 127, 129, 132
atomization 94–95

attention 96; incentives 96; research participants seeking to gain 124, 127
audience considerations 144–146
audiobooks 147
automation 103–104, 158, 166, 167

backstage and frontstage processes 72–73, *73*
Bain, R. 69
Barad, K. 28, 29
Bartlett, L. 15, **16**, 22, 23, 33n3, 38, 40, 41, 68, 106, 134, 137, 144, 151
Bassey, M. **16**, 22, 39, 67, 106, 156
Baxter, P. 20–21
Bennett, A. 15, **18**, 106
bias 12–13, 115, 157
big data 13–14, 24, 166, 167
Black, M.L. 55–56
Blatter, J. **16**, 20, 106
blogging 147, 150
Bogost, I. 52, 56–57
boundary creation and challenges of holism 39–43
bounded systems, case studies as 3–4, 15, 20, 21, 22, 24, 29 *see also* iterative bounding
Bratton, B. 60, 61n2
Briggs, C. 79
Bromley, D. B. 15, **16**, 20, 22, 121–122
Buckland, M. 86
Burke, K. 151

captology 53
Carter, S. 152

Index   169

case studies 10, 14–22, **16–19**, 32n1, 33n2, 33n3; advantages for research of digital phenomena 2–4; as bounded systems 3–4, 15, 20, 21, 22, 24, 29; contradictions within 15, 26, 77, 159, 166; demarcations between analysis and context 15, 20, 24; dissemination and afterlife 159–161; epistemically open-ended 15, 20, 21; flexibility 3, 4, 32, 121; importance in digital age 166–167; irreducibility of 14; macro 167; as a maligned form of research 21–22; multiple sources of data 15, 20–21; reframing center of 24–27; size 5; triangulation 20; yielding complex results 21
case studies, digital 1–7, 10; avoiding overstatement and overload 49–51, **50**; case study approach 2–4; digital intensity 5–7
case, terminology 11, 22–24
casuistry 132, 133
categorical imperative 125
Chasins, S. E. 87
ChatGPT 127, 128, 129, 132
Chun, W. 13
circulation 5, 10, 71–72; of case studies 159–161; of data in relation to production of data 98–99
collaborations 158, 160, 167; document cycling and 153, 154
Colton, J. 125, 131
comments, online 95, 103; ethical issues 48, 124; *The New York Times* 2, 97, 124; power users 2, 97
comparative case study approach (CCS) 41
complexity 3, 4, 21; granular 13, 14, 24, 166–167
computational models 59, 115
computer code 55–56
consent process 126, 138
consequentialism 125, 128–130, 136; drawbacks 129–130; strengths 129
consistency in ethical decision-making 126, 127
content, concept 101–102
content creators 52, 72, 96, 97
content moderators 12, 97, 128
contradictions within a case 15, 26, 77, 159, 166
Cornett-Whittier, C. **18**

corrupt data 89
cycling 71, 77, 153–154

data collection practices, practical methods 74–90, **83**; corrupt data and corporate algorithms 89; digital observations and fieldwork 74–77, **75**; documentation 85–86; fieldnotes 77–79; interview modality 82–84, **83**; interviews 79–81, **81**; questionnaires and surveys 84–85; web-scraping 86–89, **86**; when to stop collecting data 89–90
data collection practices, theoretical stances 66–73; data collection as creation of entities 67–68, 68–69; family resemblance 70; front- and backstage processes 72–73, *73*; iterative collection phase and circulation and distribution 70–72; self-critique 68
data, "getting to know" 94–99; atomization 94–95; attention 96; distribution and circulation in relation to production of data 98–99; networks 96–97; Pareto principle and power users 97–98; structures 95; vocality 98
data, pre-processing 104–106, **105**
databases 57–59, 75
DeLanda, M. 25
deliberate drifting 76, 77
denaturalization 54
deontology 125–128, 130, 136; drawbacks 127–128; strengths 126–127
design, iterative 37–65; algorithms 59; boundary creation and challenges of holism 39–43; computational models 59; computer code 55–56; databases 57–59; digital considerations 51–65; infrastructure 59–61; interfaces 52–55; iterative bounding in a digital era 43–47; overstatement and overload 49–51, **50**; software/applications 56–57; spheres of influence 47–48, *47*; users 51–52; websites 55–56
DeVoss, D. N. 49
digital case studies 1–7, 10; case study approach 2–4; digital intensity 5–7
digital entities 30–31
digital ephemera 75–77
digital observations and fieldwork 74–77, **75**

Index

digital, terminology 11–14
disciplines 32
discoverability 96
discursive interface analysis (DIA) 108
dissemination and afterlife of case studies 159–161
distributed denial of service (DDoS) attacks 87
distribution of data 5, 10, 71–72; in relation to production of data 98–99; social media and 26, 38, 71, 72, 96, 99
document cycling 153–154
documentation 85–86; produced from web-scraping 86–89, **86**
drafting 153
Duff, P. 15, **17**, 20, 29, 67, 70, 137, 144, 146, 151
Duffy, J. 131, 134
Dufour, S. **18**
Dush, L. 102, 116n1
Dyson, A. H. 4, 14, 15, **17**, 20, 22, 38, 39, 67, 106

eBook formats 146
Ede, L. 145
efficient processes 103
embodiment, describing 110–111
emojis 109, 116n7; coding 109, **110**
emotion, measuring 114–115
emotivism 122–123
empty state pages (ESPs) 76
entities 11, 24–27, 32, 41; data collection as creation of 67–68, 68–69; digital 30–31; practical implications 28–30
ephemera, digital 75–77
ethics 121–142; analysis as a type of 106, 115–116; and cases worth having 140; consequentialism 125, 128–130; deontology 125–128, 130; emotivism and 122–123; ethical influences and boundaries 47, *47*, 48; ethical paradigms 124–136; ethical researchers 139–140; Facebook social contagion study 123; habits and practices 136–139; *The New York Times* comments study 124; participant identities and 124, 127, 136–137; postmodern ethics 125, 130–133; virtue ethics 125, 133–136, 137, 140
eudaimonia 134, 140

face-to-face interviews 82, **83**
Facebook 57, 58, 76, 158; centralized network 96–97; social contagion study 123
family resemblances 68–69; and digital collection 70
Feagin, J. R. **17**
fieldnotes 74, 75, 77–79
fieldwork and digital observations 74–77, **75**
flexibility of case studies 3, 4, 32, 121
Flyvbjerg, B. 3, 14, 15, 21, 22, 39, 134, 153
Fogg, B. J. 31, 53
follow-ups and updates, writing 160
Fortin, D. **18**
forums, research 146–147
frequency 5, 49, **50**
friction 53, 54
frontstage and backstage processes 72–73, *73*
future of digital case study research 167

Gallagher, J. R. 3, 21, 39, 42, 53, 59, 76, 87, 97, 103, 124, 137, 139, 145, 160
Galloway, A.R. 6, 52
generative thematizing, quantitative techniques for 111–115; machine learning 115; named entity recognition 113–114, 115; sentiment analysis 114–115; topic modeling 111–113, 115
Genishi, C. 4, 14, 15, **17**, 20, 22, 38, 39, 67, 106
genre expectations 146
George, A. **18**, 106
Gerring, J. 2, 3, 4, 6, 15, **18**, 20, 21, 22, 24, 38, 39, 106
GIFs 109, 110, 111
glitching evidence 138–139
Goffman, E. 72, 74, 84
granular complexity 13, 14, 24, 166–167
Grimaldi, E. 156
grounded theory 104, 107, 115

habits and practices, ethical 136–139
Hamel, J. **18**
Harvey, D. 6, 38
Haverland, M. **16**, 20, 106
"hermeneutics of suspicion" 133
holism, challenges of 39–43
holistic representations, cases as 15, 20, 25–26
Holmes, S. 53, 76, 124, 125, 128, 131

Index

influence, spheres of 47–48, *47*
informed consent 126, 138
infrastructure 59–61; replicating historical precedence and biases 12–13
institutional review board (IRB) applications 137–138
interface analysis 107–108
interfaces 52–55; denaturalizing 54; documenting 54; as mediated moments of discontinuity 53
interviews 79–81, **81**; modality 82–84, **83**; note taking in 82–84
iterative bounding 38–39; digital considerations 51–61; in a digital era 43–47
Ittersum, D. Van 100

Jack, S. 20–21
jargon 84, 85
Jocher, K. 3, 15, 143

Kant, I. 125
Kendall, L. 43, 47
Kilvington, D. 72
Kramer, A. D. 123
Kripke, S. 113–114
Krosnick, J. A. 84, 85

Latent Dirichlet Allocation (LDA) 56, 112
legitimation and representation 70
literature reviews 150–153
Lockridge, T. 100
Lunsford, A. 145

machine learning 13–14, 24, 115, 166
macro case studies 167
Markham, A. 78
Marres, N. 87
measurement, differences in 27
Mejias, U. A. 13
memes 37–38, 71
memos 147, 154
mentorship 94
Merriam, S. B. 3, 4, 15, **19**, 20, 22, 106, 144, 151
messaging interviews 82–84, **83**
messiness of research 3, 42
metacommunication events, interviews as 79–80
methods section, writing up 154–158
Microsoft Word 57
mockup wireframing 76–77

modularization of activities 101
monovocality 98
Mozilla 55–56
multiple realities 4, 15, 20–21, 48, 68, 82

named entity recognition (NER) 113–114, 115
narrative 14, 21; writing up *see* writing up digital case study narratives
networks 96–97
The New York Times 2, 97, 124

observations, digital, and fieldwork 74–77, **75**
Olah, C. 152
Olinger, A. R. 82, 111
online comments 95, 103; ethical issues 48, 124; *The New York Times* 2, 97, 124; power users 2, 97
open-source code databases 75
OpenAI 127, 132
Orum, A. M. **17**, 22
overload and overstatement 49–51, **50**

Pareto principle 97–98
"passes" 154
PDFs 102
persuasive technologies 53
Peters, B. 11
planning documents 149, 150
planning, time and 148–153
podcasts 160
polyvocality 98
positionality statements 156–158
postmodern ethics 125, 130–133; drawbacks 133; strengths 131–132
power users 2, 97–98
prediction, ideology of 13
Presser, S. 84, 85
privacy, protecting user 124, 127, 136–137
procedural rhetoric 56–57
publishing industry, literary 12–13

qualitative techniques 106, 107–111; coding emojis 109, **110**; describing embodiment 110–111; integration of data types 109–110; interface analysis 107–108
quantitative techniques 106, 111–115; generative machine learning 115; named entity recognition 113–114, 115; sentiment analysis 114–115; topic modeling 111–113, 115

questionnaires and surveys 84–85; order of questions 85

racism, historical 12–13
Raley, R. 54
reading, long-form 153
real-time embodied (RTE) data collection 82
real-world context 66–67
record-keeping 49, **50**
Reddit 1, 30, 96–97
relational boundaries 43, 46–47, 48, 54
remediation 52, 102, 160
representation and legitimation 70
research debt 152–153
revision processes 153–154
rhetorical velocity 49
Riddick, S.A. 27, 76, 77
Ridolfo, J. 49

rigid designator 113–114
Sandvig, C. 130
sansdisciplinarity 31–32
satisficing 85
scale 5, 49, **50**
searchability 49, **50**
semi-structured interviews 80, 81, **81**
semiotics, analyzing multimodal 109, **110**
sentiment analysis (SA) 114–115
Shaw, L. 123
size of a case study 5
Sjoberg, G. **17**
Skinner, B. F. 27
slang 84, 85
Smagorinsky, P. 155
So, R. J. 12–13
social media: content creators 72; content moderators 12; and deciding of spatial boundaries 44; disseminating research on 159–160, 161; distribution and circulation of data 26, 38, 71, 72, 96, 99; front- and backstage processes 72–73, *73*; historical bias on platforms 12–13; interfaces 53; real-time posts impacting on case studies 27; user participation 30, 31
software/applications 42, 56–57
Sparby, E. M. 161
spatial boundaries 43, 44–45, 48, 54
speed 5–6, 49, **50**
spheres of influence 47–48, *47*

Spinuzzi, C. 15, 21, 22, 39, 42, 100–101
The Stack 60–61, 61n1
Stake, R. E. 4, 14, 15, **19**, 20, 22, 23, 24, 25, 38, 39, 85, 94, 100, 106, 121, 134, 137, 143, 144, 148, 151
Stanfill, M. 108
Stengers, I. 26, 27
stickers 109, 110
structured interviews 80–81, **81**
structures, data 95
study, concept of a 167
subjectivity 29–30, 143, 156
surveys and questionnaires 84–85; order of questions 85
Swanborn, P. 15, **19**, 22, 33n2, 39, 143, 158

task definition and specification 101–102
telephone interviews 82, **83**
temporal bounding 24, 43, 45–46, 48, 54, 56, 57
terminology: "case" 11, 22–24; "case study" 10, 14–22, **16–19**; "digital" 11–14
terms and conditions, website and software 157–158
Teston, C. 107
Thacker, E. 6
Thomer, A. K. 57–58
TikTok 132
time and planning 148–153
time-space compression 6, 38
tools and technologies 102
topic modeling (TM) 111–113, 115
transcription 103, 110–111
transdisciplinary approach 2, 167
triangulation 20

Unicode 109, **110**, 116n7
units of analysis 11, 23–24, 30; tensions between cases and 22–23
unstructured interviews 80, 81, **81**
users 51–52; power 2, 97–98
utilitarianism 128

Vallor, S. 135
Vavrus, F. 15, **16**, 22–23, 33n3, 38, 40, 41, 68, 106, 134, 137, 144, 151
venues. research 146–147
video interviews 82, **83**, 84

videos 27, 30, 54, 74–75, 99; livestreaming 74, 75, 77; presentation of research 147, 150, 159, 160
Virilio, P. 6
virtue ethics 125, 133–136, 140; drawbacks 135–136; strengths 135, 137
virtues, ethical researcher 139–140
visualizing case studies 158–159
visualizing-to-learn (VTL) 148
vocality 98

web scraping 86–89, **86**, 104, 106, 158
websites 3, 55–56; accessing architecture 88; front- and backstage processes 72–73, *73*
Weltevrede, E. 87
Wertsch, J. 22, 31, 32
Whitehead, A. N. 24–25, 26
Wickett, K. M. 57–58
Wittgenstein, L. 15, 68–69
women, harassment online 161
Woolgar, S. 51, 52
workflows for digital case study analysis 99–104; automation 103–104; efficient processes 103; needed tools and technologies 102; task definition and specification 101–102
wrangling 104–106, **105**
writer's block 147, 150
writing-to-learn (WTL) 147–148
writing up digital case study narratives 15, 143–165; audience considerations 144–146; dissemination and afterlife 159–161; distractions 149; document cycling 153–154; follow-ups and updates 160; forum determination and digital opportunities 146–147; genre expectations 146; literature reviews 150–153; methods section 154–158; modality of writing 149–150; "passes" 154; positionality statements 156–158; revision processes 153–154; time and planning 148–153; visualizing the case 158–159; visualizing-to-learn 148; writing-to-learn 147–148
Wynn, J. 11

Yin, R. K. 3, 4, 14, 15, **19**, 20, 21, 22, 23, 24, 25, 33n3, 38, 39, 41, 51, 66, 67, 94, 100, 121, 134, 137, 144, 150

Zagzebski, L. 134

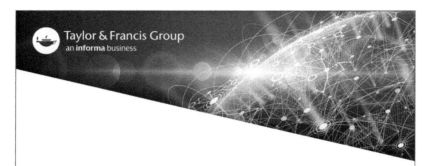

Milton Keynes UK
Ingram Content Group UK Ltd.
UKHW050641210624
444299UK00003B/8